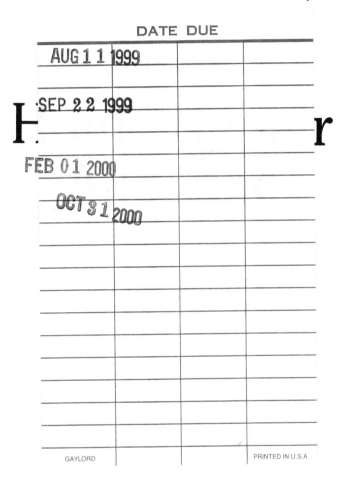

DATE DUE

AUG 1 1 1999		
SEP 2 2 1999		
FEB 01 2000		
OCT 3 1 2000		
GAYLORD		PRINTED IN U.S.A.

The New York Times

Home Repair Almanac

A season-by-season guide for maintaining your home

WRITTEN & ILLUSTRATED BY

EDWARD R. LIPINSKI

Copyright© 1999 The New York Times

Published by Lebhar-Friedman Books
Lebhar-Friedman Books is a company of Lebhar-Friedman Inc.
Visit our Internet site at www.lf.books.com

Printed in the United States of America

Lipinski, Edward R., 1943-
      The New York Times home repair almanac : a season-by-season
   guide for maintaining your home / Edward R. Lipinski.
            p.   cm.
      Includes index.
      ISBN 0-86730-759-5 (pbk.)
         1. Dwellings—Maintenance and repair—Amateurs' manuals.
   TH4817.3.L56   1999
   643' .7—dc21
                                                    99-10048
                                                      CIP

Home Repair Almanac

🌹 SPRING 🌹

☀ SUMMER ☀

TABLE OF CONTENTS

FALL

WINTER

The New York Times Home Repair Almanac
is organized around the seasons as a guide for home maintenance and repair. The reason for adopting this format is that
some home maintenance tasks are difficult or impossible to
do when the weather is bad. It is, for example, almost impossible — and unsafe — to attempt roof repair in winter when
high winds and snowy conditions prevail. That job is best left
to the spring or early fall when the weather is mild and the
roof is dry. This does not mean that the homeowner should
be idle in the cold-weather months. On the contrary, a number of cold-weather indoor jobs can be tackled to keep the
home shipshape.

The prudent homeowner always should consider the climate changes brought on by the seasons when he is prepar-
ing a yearly maintenance plan. The seasonal-almanac plan
has one problem: It really doesn't match the calendar. Our
calendar begins with January. At this time we are already
halfway through winter. Thus a truly seasonal plan will begin
either in December when winter starts or in the middle of
March with the onset of spring.

Read through the book to get an overview of the seasonal
maintenance schedule and then use a pencil to organize it
throughout the calendar.

Needless to say, the calendar schedule is simply a planning guide, not a rigid agenda. It should be flexible to accommodate rest, relaxation, and social activities; after all, owning
a home should not be all work and drudgery.

Safety First

A home maintenance schedule will help keep your entire house in good working order throughout the year, and it will help to keep minor problems from turning into major headaches. Most homeowners want to do as much as possible without having to resort to hiring a professional contractor. In that way they can control the quality of the finished job while saving money.

Most, but not all, of the tasks outlined in this book are within the skill range of the average do-it-yourselfer, but some jobs, like installing lightning rods or termite inspection, should be done only by a professional contractor; often local building codes specify that a job be performed by a licensed professional. Those jobs may require special tools and training, or they may involve handling hazardous materials. Whenever possible, the author has tried to point out those jobs that a do-it-yourselfer should not tackle.

However, other jobs are not particularly difficult in themselves but can be potentially dangerous to the unskilled worker. Consider making roof repairs, for example. Most roof repairs are relatively easy to do, but the work must be done on top of the house. Here there is the risk of a fall that can result in a serious injury.

With each task discussed in the book, the author has tried to forewarn the reader of any potential risks; but skills, tools, materials, and working conditions vary widely. The reader must take the time to understand each job and then decide if he or she has the skills and tools necessary to do it properly and safely.

Always obey all building codes, follow manufacturers' operating instructions, wear the proper safety gear, read all labels carefully, and observe warning labels. Personal safety always must be the primary consideration. When in doubt about any procedure, consult with professional inspectors or builders before continuing. It is better to spend the money for professional services than risk personal injury. Neither the author nor the publishers can assume responsibility or liability for those injuries that result from ignoring those cautions.

Safety with Tools

Most do-it-yourselfers assume that hand-held tools are easy to use, and consequently they often disregard even basic safety precautions. The U.S. Consumer Product Safety Commission

SAFETY
GOGGLES

reports that each year almost 100,000 people are treated for injuries resulting from hand-held tools. Such injuries could have been prevented with simple safety guidelines.

Eye injuries are the most traumatic of those accidents, and the majority of workshop eye injures could have been prevented with safety goggles. Safety experts advise donning goggles even before reaching for any tool.

But goggles shouldn't be the only item in the personal safety wardrobe. Gloves also can add to the safety margin. Heavy-duty leather gloves can protect your hands from flying metal or stone chips when you are using a hammer and chisel. They are a must when handling sheet metal. Without gloves the sharp edges of the metal easily can cut into the skin and cause a serious injury. In addition, gloves can be helpful in securing a good grip on tools with smooth metal handles.

Rubber gloves are essential for protecting the hands from solvents, particularly paint remover. In addition to the gloves, a full-length rubber or plastic apron can help shield your body from chemical spills.

A respirator is another indispensable item in the workshop. Most people don't think of a block of wood and a piece of sandpaper as hand tools, but they are. Sanding produces airborne particles that can lead to allergies and respiratory ailments. Remember that the simple dust mask does not protect against the fumes from solvents and spray paints. For those airborne agents you need a respirator with the appropriate filter and a flexible cushion that will conform to facial contours. The res-

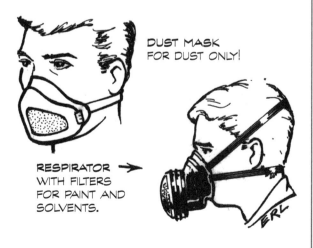

DUST MASK
FOR DUST ONLY!

RESPIRATOR ➜
WITH FILTERS
FOR PAINT AND
SOLVENTS.

pirator should be approved by an authority like OSHA or the National Institute for Occupational Safety and Health (NIOSH).

Finally, for ear protection, either ear plugs or muffs are important safety items to don when you are working with power tools. Even tools that have sound-absorbing housings to muffle the noise of the motor drive can produce high-pitched sounds as they cut into hard materials. Proper ear protection can help prevent hearing loss.

Sometimes a hard hat can be an important safety item, particularly when you are working in the attic. Many attics have nails protruding down through the roof. A hard hat can help protect your head from those sharp nails if you misjudge the height of the ceiling as you straighten up.

The average homeowner owns just one hammer, usually a carpenter's claw hammer, which he uses for a variety of tasks. That is wrong. The claw hammer should be used only for driving and pulling nails.

More than two dozen styles of hammers are available. They come in different shapes, weights, profiles, and metallurgies. Each is designed for a specific purpose. Injuries can and do result from using the wrong hammer on a job. Ballpeen hammers — also called machinist's hammers — not claw hammers, should be used with chisels and for metal work. A lightweight tack hammer should be used to drive tacks and small nails. Use a club or hand-held sledge hammer for driving masonry drills and chisels.

Never use a hammer that has a loose head or a broken handle. Always strike with the hammer face, not the cheek. When using a hammer and chisel, choose a hammer that has a face that is larger than the chisel head. The larger face will offer surer contact with the chisel and make the hammer less likely to glance off the striking surface. Match the weight of the hammer to the task at hand. A heavy hammer usually will maul delicate work — and your fingers; conversely, using a lightweight hammer on a heavy job can cause muscle fatigue, which invites injuries.

Before using a chisel, check the cutting edge carefully. A dull chisel can cause more injury than a sharp one. Chisels with mushroomed heads and cracked or chipped shafts should be discarded. Match the chisel to the job; never use a hot chisel for cutting metal or masonry.

Like hammers, screwdrivers come in many shapes and sizes. The homeowner should have a variety of screwdrivers in his tool kit. Short, stubby screwdrivers help you get into tight spots, and long-handled screwdrivers help you get into hard-to-reach places. Generally, screwdrivers with thick handles offer a better mechanical advantage than screwdrivers with thin handles and make it less fatiguing to drive screws.

Never use a screwdriver as a chisel, pry-bar, punch, or scraper, and never hit a screwdriver with a hammer. Do not try to apply excessive torque to the blade by twisting the shank with pliers or a wrench. When working on a small piece, hold the work in a vise or clamp, not in your hand. If the screwdriver slips on a hand-held piece, the result could be a nasty cut.

Make sure that screwdriver tips are in good condition, not chopped or worn from constant use. When purchasing a screwdriver, choose a model with a wide flange where the blade enters the handle. That acts as a guard and prevents the hand from slipping whenever a downward thrust is applied.

Pliers are designed to grip objects and to form and bend metal and wire. They are not wrenches and should not be used to apply torque to nuts, screws,

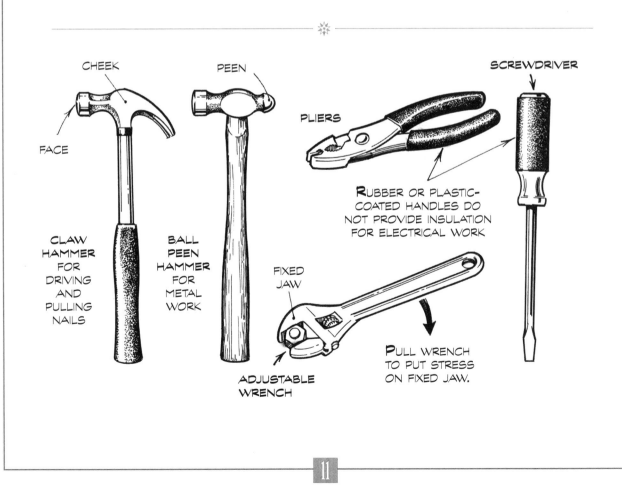

CHEEK   PEEN   SCREWDRIVER

FACE   PLIERS

RUBBER OR PLASTIC-COATED HANDLES DO NOT PROVIDE INSULATION FOR ELECTRICAL WORK

CLAW HAMMER FOR DRIVING AND PULLING NAILS

BALL PEEN HAMMER FOR METAL WORK

FIXED JAW

PULL WRENCH TO PUT STRESS ON FIXED JAW.

ADJUSTABLE WRENCH

or pipes. Choose pliers that have the proper grip for your hands. The grip span is the distance between the handles when they are open. Usually, it is about 2 to 3 inches. If your hand is small, you may find that a large span causes you to use your fingertips to close the tool. That could result in excessive muscular fatigue and possible injury.

When using pliers, hold them at a 90-degree angle to the work and use a steady, even pressure; avoid rocking motions. When the jaws or handles of the pliers become worn, chipped, or broken, it is best to discard and replace them. Fixing pliers or any tool by welding is not recommended.

Wrenches are tools especially designed to apply torque. They do have their limits, however. Never try to increase torque by adding a makeshift extension to the handle or by hitting the handle with a hammer. Use adjustable wrenches for limited torque applications and open-end or box wrenches for jobs that require greater force. When using an adjustable wrench, make sure that the stress is on the fixed jaw, not on the adjustable one.

To avoid having the wrench slip off the work, make sure that it is the proper size for the piece. Never use inch wrenches for metric work. The jaws of a wrench should be smooth and parallel,

the handle free from cracks and chips. When using a wrench, stand firmly on both feet and apply force with your arms and shoulders. Avoid leaning into or away from the work.

A vise is useful for holding work. Secure the vise to the workbench with bolts, not wood screws. Never use an extension on the vise handle. Clean and lubricate the drive screw frequently.

When buying tools, choose ones with good balance and handles that afford a firm grip. Soft, plastic grips are preferable to bare metal because they are nonslip and more comfortable to hold. Tools that are comfortable to use will be safer. Keep in mind, however, that the plastic or rubber grips are designed for comfort and do not insulate any tool for electrical work.

Power tools cut, shape, drill, and plane faster than ordinary hand tools. Naturally, they can cause serious injuries if not handled correctly. Be sure you are thoroughly familiar with the way the tool operates and handles before using it. Read the owner's manual before you use the tool. If necessary, test it out on scrap stock before working on a serious project.

When using any power tool, make certain that you stand balanced on solid ground, that the power cord is clear of the tool, and that no obstructions are in the path of the tool. Do not put the tool down to rest until the motor comes to a complete stop. Never make adjustments on the tool until the power cord is disconnected. If any tool malfunctions while you are working, stop and repair it before continuing.

Always make sure that the work piece is secure with clamps or in a vise before attempting to work on it. Always wear the proper safety gear and focus all your attention on the tool and the work piece. Stop working if anything distracts you.

On some jobs the cord from the tool may not be long enough to reach the nearest outlet, and you may need an extension cord. Never use an ordinary light-duty household extension cord for that purpose. Those cords cannot handle the power requirements for the tool. Instead, choose a heavy-duty cord with an amperage rating that matches that of the tool. Since you are working with electricity, be sure to work on a dry surface; do not work out of doors in damp weather.

For some jobs you may not have the proper tool and may decide to rent one. Look for an established rental store that is neat and well-organized — an indication that its tools will be properly cared for and in good working order. Ask the dealer to demonstrate any tool that you are not familiar with. It's always a good idea to test a tool before leaving the store. In that way you can be sure that it is working properly and that you do, in fact, understand how it operates. A qualified dealer will make sure that you are comfortable with the tool and that you have everything you need to operate it.

When you are finished with any job, clean up the work area and all tools before putting them away. Replace or sharpen dull blades.

⩔

Working with Electricity

The electrical system in the average home does not need preventive maintenance although it is a good idea to check the circuits in your home to make sure they are properly grounded. The do-it-yourselfer needs to work in the system only when a malfunction occurs or when he wants to make a modification, e.g., installing a GFCI or an exhaust fan. At that point it may be necessary to tap into existing circuits.

Working around electricity can be dangerous. The do-it-yourself should be familiar with the circuits involved and with the safe practices necessary for working with them. In addition it is wise to consult the electrical codes to make sure that he or she is indeed permitted to make the appropriate modifications. The following sections will give the reader some idea of the electrical system in the average home and proper safety procedures for working with electricity.

Electrical Safety

Electrical problems and malfunctions are more than a nuisance; they can be lethal. That's why most homes have system safeguards to prevent fires and personal shocks. To be effective, however, they must be in good working order.

Most homes today have a three-wire hookup that brings incoming power into the main-service panel in the house. The service panel serves two functions: It distributes the power to separate circuits throughout the house, and it shuts off the power to any circuit if the current exceeds a specified amount. The later function is controlled by circuit breakers or fuses that are designed to trip or burn out ("blow") if a current overload occurs. Circuit breakers and fuses are one safeguard in your electrical system.

You should know where your service panel is located and how to reset a tripped breaker or replace a blown fuse. Remember, always replace a blown fuse with one of the same amperage.

An electrical circuit has at least two wires. The hot wire carries the electricity from the service panel to the load device — for example, a power tool or an appliance. It has color-coded insulation, usually black or red — actually it can be any color except white, gray, or green. The neutral wire carries the current back to the service panel where that wire is grounded. The neutral wire is color coded with white or gray insulation.

Modern electrical circuits have a third, equipment-grounding wire, which adds an extra measure of protection to the system. Appliances, tools, and lamps deteriorate with age, and their connections and insulation often leak electricity. That leak can cause the housing of the unit to become hot. The equipment grounding wire provides a safe path channeling the leaks back to the service panel. It may be either a bare copper wire or one with green insulation.

In 1960 the National Electrical Code (NEC) required the ground wire to be installed in all new homes. If you have an older house, you may not have that equipment ground. You can check for it by glancing at the outlets and receptacles in your house. Grounded outlets have two parallel slots to accept a plug and a half round hole under the slots to accept a grounding prong.

However, even the presence of the three-prong receptacles is no guarantee that the outlet is grounded properly. It is possible, for example, that there is no connection between the receptacle and the ground. You can check the outlet for proper ground with a circuit analyzer. That small gadget can be purchased in most home centers or electronic supply stores for around $5. Just plug it into any wall outlet. The lights on the device will indicate faults in the circuit. If you have expensive electronic equipment, then you might want to invest in a hazardous ground tester that also

indicates the presence of possible faulty ground connections. A. W. Sperry Instruments Inc. manufactures one model, which sells for about $20.

What should you do if you don't have any equipment ground circuits? Ideally, you should replace the old receptacles with new grounding receptacles, making sure that they are grounded properly. That is especially important on those circuits that service major appliances. Never attempt to modify a three-prong plug by sawing off the ground prong.

You can use a three-prong adapter for small appliances and power tools. Plugging the adapter into the outlet does not provide ground protection unless the adapter's ground lug is connected to the center face-plate screw. Even that may not be enough if there is

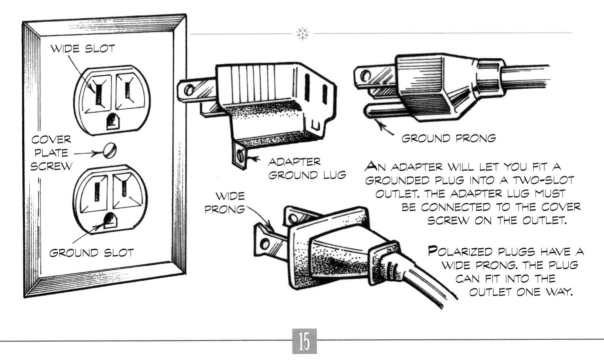

WIDE SLOT

COVER PLATE SCREW

GROUND SLOT

ADAPTER GROUND LUG

WIDE PRONG

GROUND PRONG

AN ADAPTER WILL LET YOU FIT A GROUNDED PLUG INTO A TWO-SLOT OUTLET. THE ADAPTER LUG MUST BE CONNECTED TO THE COVER SCREW ON THE OUTLET.

POLARIZED PLUGS HAVE A WIDE PRONG. THE PLUG CAN FIT INTO THE OUTLET ONE WAY.

THE GROUND-FAULT CIRCUIT INTERRUPTER

THE GFCI HAS A SMALL INTERNAL TRANSFORMER THAT SENSES CURRENT LEAKS AND REACTS TO INTERRUPT THE CIRCUIT. "TEST" AND "RESET" BUTTONS ALLOW YOU TO CHECK FOR MALFUNCTIONS.

no internal ground connection to the mounting yoke on the receptacle. So make a final check by plugging the circuit analyzer into the adapter.

Even with the equipment ground it's possible to get a shock from an appliance if you're around metal faucets. Faucets are ideal grounds that allow electricity to bypass the neutral path and go through your body directly into the ground. Thus, shutting off a water faucet while trimming your whiskers with a faulty electric razor could be fatal.

Engineers developed the GFCI (ground-fault circuit interrupter) receptacle to provide protection in such areas as kitchens, bathrooms, pool areas, and garages. The GFCI has a small internal transformer that instantly senses current leaks and reacts to interrupt the circuit within one-fortieth of a second. The GFCI has a "test" and a "reset" button that allow you to check the receptacle for malfunctions. To make the test, plug an appliance such as a hair dryer into the GFCI and turn it on. Now push the "test" button. The hair dryer should go off. Press the "reset" button, and the dryer should come back on. Make that test once a week and replace the GFCI if it fails.

Another safety feature in modern electrical circuits is the polarized plug and receptacle. Many appliances have plugs with one enlarged prong. The plug can be inserted only one way in the outlet. That ensures the circuit's hot wire will connect properly with the appliance. Of course, the appliance will run no matter which way the plug is inserted, but many appliances are insulated only on the hot side. Reversing the plug causes power to flow through less-insulated connections, creating a potential shock situation. Some manufacturers double-insulate their tools so that the plugs don't have to be polarized. But many appliances don't have that feature. If your house doesn't have polarized receptacles, replace them with polarized ones. And never attempt to modify a polarized plug by filing down the big prong; you could be creating a lethal appliance.

Fuses and Circuit Breakers

If you insert a plug into a socket, there's enough power to run an appliance. Most homeowners take electricity for granted because the power is available, convenient, and safe. But should the light or the appliance fail, then the frustrated homeowner wonders what went wrong. Sometimes the failure can be traced to the power company when, for example, a power cable goes down or a generator malfunctions. More often, however, the problem is within the home.

Overloaded circuits are the cause of most home power failures, which happens when an appliance draws too much current and causes a fuse to blow or a circuit breaker to trip. It may seem difficult to imagine that a small household appliance could overtax the power system; after all, the home is hooked up to the resources of the power company.

The problem, however, lies in the home. Each house has a network of wires that carry electricity from the service panel — the point where electricity enters the house — to outlets throughout the structure. The wires are designed to carry a fixed amount of current, generally 15 or 20 amps. A number of appliances plugged into the same circuit can draw more current than the wires can carry. The overloaded wires heat up, and they could cause a fire.

Sometimes the problem may occur within an appliance. That can happen when two worn wires, the hot and neutral wires, contact each other, creating a new path. The new path is called a short circuit, and it allows a large surge of current to overload the wires.

Fortunately, safeguards, in the form of fuses or circuit breakers, are built into the system. Fuses and breakers are designed to sense power overloads and interrupt the flow of electricity.

Fuses have an internal metal link that melts to cut off the power. A blown

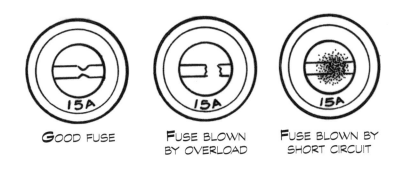

GOOD FUSE   FUSE BLOWN   FUSE BLOWN BY
                    BY OVERLOAD   SHORT CIRCUIT

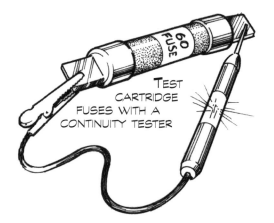

TEST CARTRIDGE FUSES WITH A CONTINUITY TESTER

fuse must be replaced with a new one with the same amperage rating. Some people, frustrated by buying and replacing blown fuses, attempt to install a new fuse with a higher rating. Now the circuit designed to carry 15 amperes is "protected" by a 20-ampere fuse. The new fuse will take longer to blow, but in the meantime the wires within the walls will heat up. Obviously, it is an unsafe practice.

Service panels with fuse protection have plug fuses. They may also have cartridge fuses. The cartridge fuses have higher amperage ratings and are used to protect circuits that supply large appliances. Other cartridge fuses may protect the main power circuit.

Plug fuses, also called Edison base fuses, screw into a socket in the panel. A small window in the face allows you to inspect the condition of the fusible metal link and pinpoint the malfunction. An overloaded circuit will melt the link but leave the window clear. The

sudden power surge of a short circuit will cause the link to vaporize and discolor the window.

Cartridge fuses are plastic or fiber cylinders with a metal cap at either end. The cap may be either a plain ferrule or a flat knifeblade. The fusible metal link is in the center of the fuse body. Unfortunately, there is no way to tell if the fuse has blown simply by looking at it. You can, however, test it with a continuity tester. Remove the fuse from the panel and then touch the test probes to the fuse ends. If the tester lights, the fuse is good.

Before removing any fuse, turn off the main power. Have a flashlight handy when you do this. Some fuse boxes have a lever switch that controls the power. Other fuse boxes have pullout blocks — boxes that hold cartridge fuses — that can be removed to shut off power. To remove the pullout block, grab it by the metal handle and pull it straight from the panel.

To remove a plug fuse, grasp it by the rim and turn it counterclockwise. To be on the safe side, use only one hand, keep the other hand in your pocket. In that way you avoid making a ground contact. Make sure that you stand on a dry surface. As an extra safety precaution you can keep a board on the floor by the panel. A 16-inch length of 2 x 6 is ideal. Standing on it will provide additional insulation when you replace fuses.

Do not attempt to remove cartridge fuses with your fingers. Instead, use a nonconductive fuse puller, available at hardware and electrical supply stores. Grip the body of the fuse with the puller and yank it from the spring clips.

In comparison to fuses, circuit breakers are much easier to work with. You don't have to replace them because they do not burn out. Inside the breaker a bimetallic element heats up and bends when an overload occurs. That trips the switch and opens the contacts which allow electricity to flow. Some breakers have a small window, which exposes a red flag when the switch is tripped. To reset a circuit breaker, flip

the switch to the "off" or "reset" position and then push it to "on." With some breaker models it's only necessary to push the tripped switch to the "on" position.

Of course, replacing a fuse or resetting a circuit breaker may restore power, but it will not correct the overload problem. So, before attempting to restore power, unplug all lamps and appliances from the circuit. If the circuit fails immediately after power is restored, the problem may be in the circuitry itself. In that case it's best to leave the power off and consult a professional electrician to troubleshoot.

Assuming that the breaker doesn't trip, you can start plugging the appliance back into the circuit. Examine

TURN OFF THE MAIN POWER BY REMOVING THE PULLOUT BLOCK.

PLUG FUSES

USE ONLY ONE HAND TO REMOVE A FUSE OR RESET A CIRCUIT BREAKER. STANDING ON A BOARD WILL PROVIDE INSULATION FROM THE GROUND.

each one carefully for defects, such as worn cords or loose plugs. Repair or replace the faulty pieces.

Making Electrical Tests

Most of us tend to take electricity for granted. When we flick a switch, we expect the power to be there. We expect that power to be safe and constant. That is not always the case. Often the power fluctuates with surges or drops in voltage. Your house wiring also can have problems that can be a threat to your personal safety. That's why it's important to know how to test the circuits in your home.

Making electrical tests sounds complicated and expensive, but it's not. You can buy a few simple testers that are easy to use for less than $20.

Start with a circuit analyzer, which is a small gadget, not much bigger than the common three-prong adapter. It can be purchased at most home centers or electronic supply stores and usually sells for less than $5. Using a circuit analyzer is simplicity itself; just plug it into any wall outlet. Three lights on the instrument will light in different patterns to reveal if any problems exist in that circuit. For example, the analyzer will tell you if the circuit is improperly grounded or if the hot and ground wires are reversed. Either of these conditions can give you a nasty shock. Many of today's appliances need to be plugged into a grounded circuit. We often assume that plugging a three-pronged plug into a socket automatically

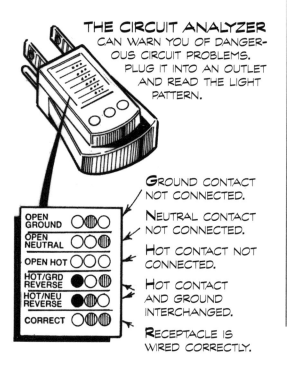

THE CIRCUIT ANALYZER CAN WARN YOU OF DANGEROUS CIRCUIT PROBLEMS. PLUG IT INTO AN OUTLET AND READ THE LIGHT PATTERN.

OPEN GROUND		GROUND CONTACT NOT CONNECTED.
OPEN NEUTRAL		NEUTRAL CONTACT NOT CONNECTED.
OPEN HOT		HOT CONTACT NOT CONNECTED.
HOT/GRD REVERSE		HOT CONTACT AND GROUND INTERCHANGED.
HOT/NEU REVERSE		
CORRECT		RECEPTACLE IS WIRED CORRECTLY.

THE CIRCUIT TESTER

USE IT TO MAKE SURE THAT THE POWER IS ACTUALLY OFF IN A CIRCUIT.

grounds the appliance. That is not always the case because the outlet may not have a ground connection. A circuit analyzer will show this. You should check all the outlets in your house, particularly those in the kitchen and the bathroom.

You'll also want to buy a circuit tester; it should be in every do-it-yourselfer's toolbox. The circuit tester is basically a neon bulb with two test leads that is used to indicate the presence of electricity. If, for example, you want to replace a wall switch, the first step is to shut off the power to the circuit. That is basic to all electrical work; never work on an electrical circuit until you are certain that the power is off in that circuit.

You flip the circuit breaker, but how do you know that the power is off in that circuit? It is possible that the breaker is mislabeled or faulty, or maybe the switch has an alternate power source. In that case the switch would be dangerous to handle. The circuit tester will tell you if it is cold or hot.

To use the circuit tester, grasp the leads by the plastic collars — do not hold the metal tips — and make three tests. First, touch one lead to the screw terminal holding the black, or hot, wire and touch the other lead to the metal junction box or the green ground screw. For the second test, touch one lead to

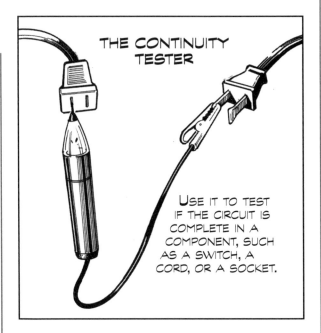

THE CONTINUITY TESTER

USE IT TO TEST IF THE CIRCUIT IS COMPLETE IN A COMPONENT, SUCH AS A SWITCH, A CORD, OR A SOCKET.

the white, or neutral, wire screw terminal and the other to the ground. For the final test, connect one lead to the black-wire screw terminal and the other lead to the white-wire screw terminal. If the neon bulb lights during any of those tests, the circuit is hot, and it's not safe to proceed with the repair.

Another piece of testing equipment that can help save time and money is the continuity tester. It tells whether or not a circuit is complete — whether a switch or wire has broken internal parts. The continuity tester works differently than either the circuit analyzer or the circuit tester in that it has its own power supply. The power in the circuit must be off when you use the tool.

The tester has a metal probe on one end and a wire with an alligator clip on the other. Before testing any electrical component with the continuity tester, it's a good idea to test the tester. Touch the alligator clip to the metal probe. The light should glow. If it doesn't, then either the battery or the bulb in the test is bad and needs to be replaced.

Once your tester is working properly, you can use it to test switches, wires, and fuses. You can use it to isolate malfunctioning components systematically and end trial-and-error replacement.

If you want to test a single-pole wall switch, for example, attach the alligator clip to one screw terminal and touch the metal probe to the other terminal. If the switch is on, the tester bulb should light. If not, then the switch has an internal fault. You also can test three-way and four-way wall switches, pilot-light switches, and timer switches with the continuity tester. Dimmer switches cannot be tested for continuity.

Cartridge fuses sometimes pose a problem for homeowners because they show no external signs of malfunction. How can you tell if the fuse is blown? With a continuity tester touch the alligator clip to one fuse contact and the metal probe to the other. If the light glows, the fuse is good.

The circuit tester also can be used to check newly installed wiring. Use it before you turn on power for the first time. It will tell you if any shorts must be repaired before the circuit is activated.

Another handy device to have is a plug-in voltage tester with a digital read-out, also a very simple device to use. Simply plug it into a wall outlet and read the numbers on the digital monitor. It will tell you if you're getting a full 110 or 120 volts at that outlet. That may seem like useless information. After all, if the electric lamps light and the refrigerator runs, isn't that enough? In the days before microcomputer chips that was enough, but many of today's appliances — computers, microwaves, and VCRs, to name a few — have sophisticated electronic circuits that can be damaged by severe power fluctuations. By monitoring the quality of your electrical power, you can evaluate if you need additional protection devices, such as power-line conditioners or battery backups, for your expensive electronics.

The Basic Tool Kit

If you own your own home, you must have tools to maintain it properly. Most homeowners buy their tools over the years as they are needed, but you always have to start somewhere,

THE BASIC TOOL KIT

especially if you are a new homeowner.

It's best to start with an elementary tool kit that will handle simple repairs and common fix-it problems. When purchasing tools, always buy the best that you can afford. Good tools are more durable than cheap ones, and with proper care they will last a lifetime.

The basic tool kit should include: a carpenter's hammer; a nail set; an eight-point crosscut saw; two screwdrivers, a common tip and Phillips head; pliers; an adjustable wrench; a utility knife; a steel tape measure; a level; a file; a toilet plunger; a circuit tester for checking electrical circuits for power; and a drill with an assortment of bits. In addition,

you also should have an assortment of nails, common and finishing; wire brads; screws; sandpaper in coarse, medium, and fine grits; a bottle of white glue; and a can of lightweight machine oil.

If you live in an apartment or have limited storage space for your tools, you can substitute a toolbox saw for the crosscut saw. It is easy to store in a closet or toolbox because it is only 15 inches long. Toolbox saws cut fast, but they make a coarse cut that must be smoothed with a file and sandpaper.

While it is handy to have at least two screwdrivers, you can get by with a combination screwdriver, which is

---

SOME BASIC TOOLS

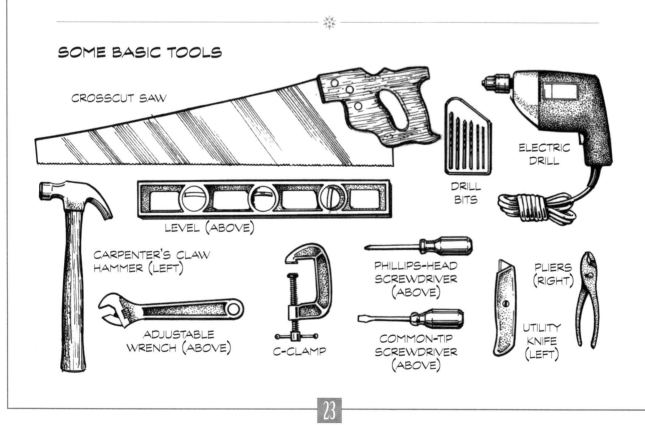

CROSSCUT SAW

ELECTRIC DRILL

DRILL BITS

LEVEL (ABOVE)

CARPENTER'S CLAW HAMMER (LEFT)

ADJUSTABLE WRENCH (ABOVE)

C-CLAMP

PHILLIPS-HEAD SCREWDRIVER (ABOVE)

COMMON-TIP SCREWDRIVER (ABOVE)

PLIERS (RIGHT)

UTILITY KNIFE (LEFT)

THE BASIC TOOL KIT

available at home centers and hardware stores. The handle and shaft of the tool resemble that of a regular screwdriver, but it has changeable heads that plug into a hex hole in the shaft tip. Thus, one tool can become either a common-tip or a Phillips-head screwdriver by changing the head.

Some home centers offer combination screwdriver sets that include a variety of interchangeable sockets for nuts and bolts as well as the screwdriver tips. Those sets are more expensive than the simple combination screwdriver, but they offer a versatile tool assortment in a compact container.

After assembling the basic tool kit, your next purchase should be a quality vise. If you have a workbench, buy a vise that bolts onto the surface. Clamp-on vises are also available. They have screw clamps so that you can attach the vise temporarily to any table surface and then remove it when the work is finished.

When you have the money, add more tools to your kit. Buy a hacksaw and ballpeen hammer, a wood plane, two or more 4-inch C-clamps, a combination square, wire cutters, a propane torch with a soldering tip and flame-spreading tip, a sharpening stone, a putty knife, and a 1/4- and 3/4-inch wood chisel. If your plumbing or heating system has threaded pipe, you also

should add two 10-inch pipe wrenches.

Later on you can add other tools: a back saw and miter box, a wire brush, tin snips, a staple gun, channel pliers, and a soldering iron.

Your first power tool purchase should be an electric drill. It is the unquestioned king of the power tools. Besides drilling holes in a variety of materials, it can be used for grinding, sanding, polishing, and mixing paint. Of course, you will need a variety of attachments for those different functions, but they can be purchased over time. If possible, buy a variable speed drill. You'll find it particularly useful for driving screws; and if the drill also has a reverse switch, you can remove screws as well.

Other useful hand power tools include a circular power saw, a saber saw, an orbital sander, and possibly a chain saw. Which tool you purchase first depends largely upon the type of projects you undertake. If you plan to tackle a construction project such as building a deck, a fence, or interior walls, then buy a circular power saw. You can use it to cut construction lumber to size quickly.

On the other hand, if you need to make intricate cuts in light wood, metal, or plastic, then a saber saw is a better choice. The orbital sander is essential if you are finishing furniture or woodwork. Admittedly, most homeowners never will see the need for a chain saw. It can be very useful, however, if you own a fireplace or wood stove and have to lay in a supply of firewood each year.

While this tool list seems complete, it is not all-inclusive. If, for example, you plan on doing any painting, then you will have to purchase at least one wide and one narrow brush, a paint roller and tray, and a wide taping knife. If you do electrical repairs, then you also may want to invest in a multimeter.

⬦

Measuring and Marking

Careful and accurate measuring can save you time and money on any household job — whether it be installing shelves, replacing a pane of glass, or buying window shades. To measure anything accurately, you need the right tools. Basic measuring and layout tools, such as rulers, tapes, and squares, are simple and easy to use and should be in every homeowner's toolbox.

Start with a basic shop or bench ruler. Rulers are available in lengths ranging from 6 to 48 inches. A 12-inch length is probably the most convenient. You can buy rulers made of wood or plastic, but a steel ruler is thinner, making it easier to mark the work, more durable, and usable as a straightedge with a utility knife. The most obvious place to buy a shop ruler is in a hardware store or home center. Frequently, however, artist's supply stores carry a larger selection of rulers. They vary in length, thickness, and flexibility, and some have rubber or cork backing strips to keep them from sliding around.

For jobs more than a foot long you'll need an extending ruler. The classic carpenter's ruler is the folding wood rule, also called the zigzag rule. Carpenters prefer that ruler to the steel tape because it remains rigid when extended and it can be used to measure wide openings, such as stairwells. For internal measurements, such as the interior width of a drawer or cabinet, the folding ruler has a brass slide rule built into the end section.

Most people find that it's a bother to open and close a folding ruler so they opt for a "push-pull" steel tape. That is a flexible, spring-loaded steel ruler that rolls into a small case when not in use. Tapes come in 3/8-, 1/2-, 3/4-, and 1-inch widths from 8- to 30-feet long. Generally, a 20-foot tape is the most practical length for the average do-it-yourselfer. The 3/8- and 1/2-inch widths are more compact and easy to carry conveniently in your pocket, but the tapes do not stay rigid when extended any distance. The wider blades remain rigid without support but are often bulky; some models have a belt clip. Buy a tape with a blade lock and power return.

A good tape measure has a sliding hook at the end of the blade. That hook grips the end of the work and holds the blade as you extend it for measuring. When you are making internal measurements, the hook slides into the blade and does not affect the accuracy of the measurement. With internal measurements it's important to add the case length measurement, which is indicated on the case, to the blade reading. It may seem that a tailor's tape measure would make a good substitute for a steel tape, but it stretches after frequent use and can result in inaccurate measurements.

In addition to measuring length and width, you frequently will have to draw lines for right-angle cuts and check joints and surfaces for squareness. Squares are the tools used for obtaining true right angles. The try square traditionally has been the cabinet maker's tool-of-choice for laying out right angles. It consists of two parts: the blade and the handle. Both parts are riveted together in a fixed position. The handle is thicker than the blade and is placed against the edge of the work. The blade extends across the face of the work at a right angle to the edge.

The combination square is more versatile than the try square and is therefore a better choice for the basic toolbox. It consists of two parts: a blade that is a 12-inch steel ruler and a head that can slide in a groove along the blade. The head has two faces. One face is perpendicular to the blade and is used to draw right angles. The opposite face is at a 45-degree angle to the blade and can be used to lay out miter cuts for picture frames or moldings.

The combination square also can be used as a marking gauge to draw lines parallel to the edge of a board. That is useful if you want to rip — cut along the grain — the board to make it narrower. To mark a parallel line, place the 90-degree face of the head against the edge of the board. Adjust the blade to the desired projection away from the edge and lock it in place by turning the lock nut on the head. Place a pencil at the end of the blade and hold it there as you pull the square down the length of the board. As the square slides down the edge of the board, the pencil held at the end of the blade will draw the line.

MEASURING AND MARKING

The carpenter's, or framing, square is another useful tool to have in your toolbox. The carpenter's square consists of two arms, the tongue and the blade, marked with numerical graduations in inches and fractions of an inch. Since the square is cut from a single piece of steel, it is of uniform thickness and therefore will lie flat on the surface of a panel. That allows you to lay out large patterns in the center of counter tops, plywood, or wallboard. The framing square also can be useful if you want to cut a picture aperture in matte board.

Sometimes you'll want to draw an angle that is greater or less than 90 degrees. The T bevel — also know as a sliding bevel — is ideal for that. The T bevel consists of a handle and an adjustable blade. To set an angle on the T bevel, place the handle at the base of a protractor. Slide the blade around so that it intersects through the desired angle gradation on the protractor scale. Lock the blade in place by turning the lock nut in the handle. The angle now is set, and you can easily transfer to your workpiece.

When doing any maintenance or construction job, remember the craftsman's adage: "Measure twice and cut once." ⊕

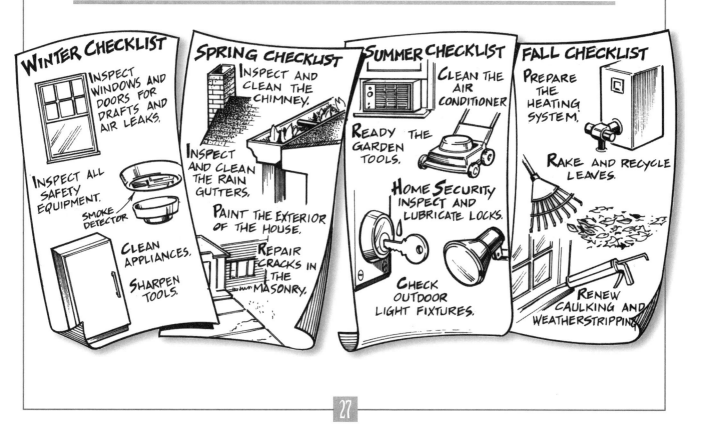

WINTER CHECKLIST
INSPECT WINDOWS AND DOORS FOR DRAFTS AND AIR LEAKS.
INSPECT ALL SAFETY EQUIPMENT.
SMOKE DETECTOR
CLEAN APPLIANCES.
SHARPEN TOOLS.

SPRING CHECKLIST
INSPECT AND CLEAN THE CHIMNEY.
INSPECT AND CLEAN THE RAIN GUTTERS.
PAINT THE EXTERIOR OF THE HOUSE.
REPAIR CRACKS IN THE MASONRY.

SUMMER CHECKLIST
CLEAN THE AIR CONDITIONER
READY THE GARDEN TOOLS.
HOME SECURITY INSPECT AND LUBRICATE LOCKS.
CHECK OUTDOOR LIGHT FIXTURES.

FALL CHECKLIST
PREPARE THE HEATING SYSTEM.
RAKE AND RECYCLE LEAVES.
RENEW CAULKING AND WEATHERSTRIPPING.

SPRING INSPECTION

WINTER is officially over. The short, cold days are behind us, replaced by longer, balmy days. Now is a good time to inspect your home for damage caused by the fluctuating temperatures and ice of the winter months. You'll probably find that many parts of your house are in good condition and require only minor maintenance. Attending to those tasks now will help prevent costly repairs later and allow you to enjoy a trouble-free summer.

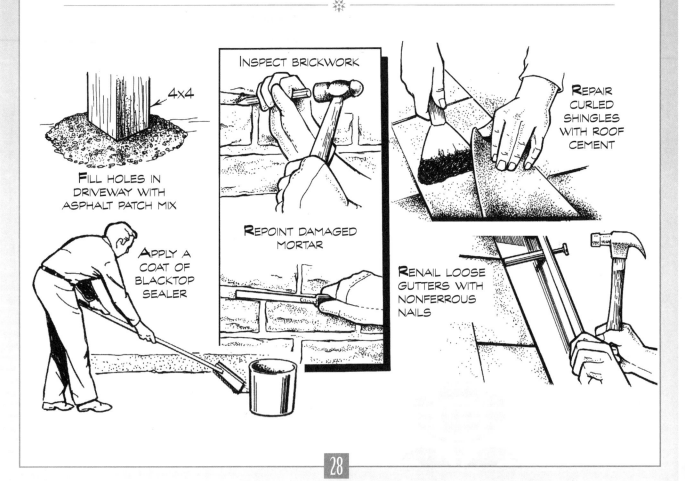

FILL HOLES IN DRIVEWAY WITH ASPHALT PATCH MIX

APPLY A COAT OF BLACKTOP SEALER

INSPECT BRICKWORK

REPOINT DAMAGED MORTAR

REPAIR CURLED SHINGLES WITH ROOF CEMENT

RENAIL LOOSE GUTTERS WITH NONFERROUS NAILS

 Start with the roof; but before climbing up there, **inspect your ladder for flaws and damage.** Look for loose rungs and splits in the side rails. Make sure that all metal hardware is tight and replace any pieces that are rusted or corroded. After you've attended to the ladder you can use it to climb up and inspect the roof. Do not attempt to work on the roof in wet or windy weather. Wear softsoled shoes, and make sure your ladder is secure.

 Look for damaged or missing shingles. Inspect the chimney for loose bricks or cracked mortar. Finally look carefully at the flashing (the strips of metal between the bricks and shingles or in the valleys between the dormer and roof) for cracks or buckling.

 After inspecting the roof, look at the gutters and downspouts around the perimeter of the roof. First check the gutter hangers; renail loose ones with nonferrous nails.

Next inspect the gutters for accumulations of dead leaves, seed pods, and "gutter muck." After cleaning the gutters inspect them for holes and damage. Repair these with a metal patch and asphalt roofing cement. If your gutters do not have aluminum-mesh leaf guards, now is the time to install them. Next look at the downspouts and clean out any sediment.

While you are up inspecting and repairing the gutters, **look under the eaves at the soffits.** These often deteriorate from rot because moisture frequently collects in them. Examine them carefully and make any needed repairs.

Trees close to the house are a major source of gutter debris. Now is a good time to prune these trees.

Inspect the windows and screens. Remove crumbling glazing compound with a chisel then apply a bead of new glazing compound.

 Inspect the screens for holes. Remove accumulated dust and dirt in the window tracks and around the sill with a brush and vacuum. Inspect the sill for cracks.

 Next inspect the concrete and brickwork around your home.

Blacktop driveways can also suffer from the ravages of winter. Fill holes and depressions with asphalt driveway patch mix (available at home centers).

Even if a thorough inspection reveals that your home is in good repair, **the exterior may be dirty.** It's not necessary to repaint provided the underlying finish is still good. What your house could use is a thorough washing. You can do this in a day if you rent a power washer.

Spring is the time when termites swarm. These are subterranean insects and homeowners cannot always detect their presence until it is too late. Call in a professional pest control expert for a complete termite inspection.

Shingle Roof Repair

- PUTTY KNIFE
- TIN SNIPS
- ROOFING CEMENT
- HAMMER
- ROOFING NAILS
- ALUMINUM FLASHING
- WOOD CHISEL (ONLY FOR WOODEN SHINGLE REPAIRS)
- HACKSAW BLADE

The part of the house that receives the most punishment from the elements is the roof. It is assaulted by rain and snow, baked by the hot sun and buffeted by severe winds. Sooner or later, even the best roof will show signs or wear and tear. Unfortunately, the roof is also the part of the house

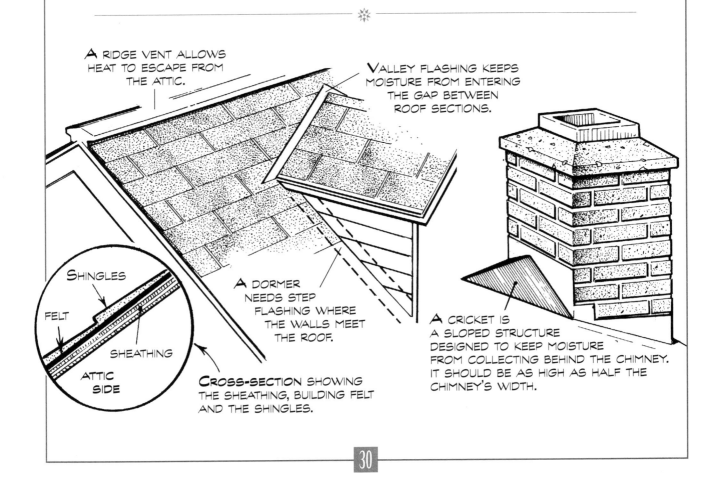

A RIDGE VENT ALLOWS HEAT TO ESCAPE FROM THE ATTIC.

VALLEY FLASHING KEEPS MOISTURE FROM ENTERING THE GAP BETWEEN ROOF SECTIONS.

SHINGLES

FELT

SHEATHING

ATTIC SIDE

A DORMER NEEDS STEP FLASHING WHERE THE WALLS MEET THE ROOF.

CROSS-SECTION SHOWING THE SHEATHING, BUILDING FELT AND THE SHINGLES.

A CRICKET IS A SLOPED STRUCTURE DESIGNED TO KEEP MOISTURE FROM COLLECTING BEHIND THE CHIMNEY. IT SHOULD BE AS HIGH AS HALF THE CHIMNEY'S WIDTH.

that receives the least care because it is relatively inaccessible.

Still, it is essential to inspect the roof at least once a year for signs of damaged or missing shingles. Climbing onto a high roof can be dangerous, especially if it has a steep pitch. Wait for a calm, dry day for the inspection. Wear rubber-soled shoes; do not attempt to climb on a wet roof. Make sure that you understand and follow, all ladder safety rules When moving about on the roof, watch for loose or torn shingles, moss, wet leaves, or other debris. If you are unsure of yourself on a high roof, call a professional to complete the job.

Repairing asphalt shingle roofs

Inspect the roof covering first. If you have asphalt shingles, they may be cracked or have missing corners. These are not serious problems; they can be repaired with roofing cement, which is available at home centers.

FIXING DAMAGED SHINGLES: To repair a cracked shingle, gently raise it and apply cement under the crack. Press the shingle onto the cement layer; then smooth more cement over the crack. If you find a shingle with a torn corner, do not attempt to repair it with a new corner piece. Instead, raise the shingle and cover the exposed area with roofing cement. Press down a piece of aluminum flashing — available in rolls in hardware stores — and nail it

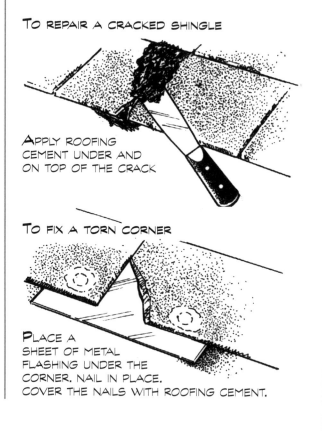

FIXING DAMAGED SHINGLES

TO REPAIR A CRACKED SHINGLE

APPLY ROOFING CEMENT UNDER AND ON TOP OF THE CRACK

TO FIX A TORN CORNER

PLACE A SHEET OF METAL FLASHING UNDER THE CORNER. NAIL IN PLACE. COVER THE NAILS WITH ROOFING CEMENT.

in place. Cover the nail heads with more roofing cement.

Admittedly, repairs with roofing cement are somewhat unsightly, but they are effective in stopping leaks, and few people will see the remedy from below. Perfectionists, however, may prefer to remove the damaged shingle and replace it with a new one.

Cold weather can make asphalt shingles stiff and brittle. Flexing or bending can break them. If possible, wait for a warm, sunny day, when the shingle will be soft and pliable, to make roof repairs.

Some shingles may be curled up away from the roof. Apply a generous dab of roofing cement under the shingle; then press it into the cement. It may be necessary to weight it down until the cement sets.

REPLACING A SHINGLE: Shingles that are torn severely or missing must be replaced. Before you can position the replacement, you'll have to remove the torn shingle and also the roofing nails that secure it. The nails will be concealed under good shingles overlapping the damaged one. Gently bend them back and pull the nails with a pry bar. Do not attempt to do so on a cold day, or the good shingle may break.

Another way to remove a damaged shingle is by slipping a hacksaw blade under it and sawing through the hold-down nails. Wrap one end in tape to protect your hand, or use a mini-hacksaw. Slide the new shingle in place and secure it with roofing nails. Finish the job by dabbing roofing cement under the new shingle and the ones above it.

REPLACING A SHINGLE

To REMOVE A DAMAGED SHINGLE, CUT THE HOLDING NAILS WITH A HACKSAW BLADE.

NAIL THE NEW SHINGLE IN PLACE. COVER THE NAILS WITH ROOFING CEMENT.

SHINGLE ROOF REPAIR

Repairing wood shingle roofs

Not all roofs are protected by asphalt shingles. Some have wood shakes or shingles. Wood shingles are smaller and lighter than wood shakes, and commonly are sawed on one or both sides. Common problems with wood shakes and shingles include splits and cracks, buckles, and severe rotting.

Cracks or splits in wood shingles will let water seep through the roof. Fill narrow cracks with roofing cement. Wider cracks — 1/2-inch or more — should be backed with aluminum flashing. Secure the flashing by driving a 3d-aluminum or galvanized nail on either side of the crack. The bottom of the nail head should be flush with the surface of the shingle, not countersunk into it. Cover the crack and nail heads with roofing cement.

When a wood shingle absorbs too much moisture, it can swell and buckle away from the roof. In order to flatten the shingle, you'll have to remove some wood from the buckle. Use a wood chisel to make two splits about 1/8- to 1/4-inch apart. Remove the sliver of wood from between the cracks. Press the shingle down and secure it with two nails. Cover the crack and nail heads with roofing cement.

REPLACING A DAMAGED WOODEN SHINGLE: Replacing a damaged wood shingle requires a bit more skill. First, you'll have to split the old shingle into pieces with a wood chisel. Be careful with the chisel; you don't want to damage the surrounding shingles, or you'll have to replace them also. Pull out the split pieces; then use a hacksaw blade to cut the nails that held the damaged shingle. Trim a new shingle to size; then tap it into place. The fit should be loose, with about 1/8 inch of space on either side to allow for moisture expansion.

REPLACING A WOODEN SHINGLE

REMOVE THE DAMAGED SHINGLE WITH A WOOD CHISEL.

SHINGLE ROOF REPAIR

NAILING A REPLACEMENT WOOD SHINGLE: Nailing a replacement wood shingle in place is not so simple as nailing an asphalt shingle because you cannot bend back the overlapping shingle. Perhaps the easiest way to nail the shingle in place is by driving a nail through the expansion gaps — one nail in each gap — in the overlapping shingles. Put a dab of roofing cement in the gap to cover the nail heads. Do not overdo the cement here, or you'll clog the expansion joint.

A better way to protect the nail head is with a "copper bib." That is a small piece of flexible copper about 4 inches square. Bend the copper until it has a slight concave shape and slip it under the overlapping shingle, concave side up, until it covers the nail head. The slight bend in the metal will create a friction fit that will keep the piece in place. ⊕

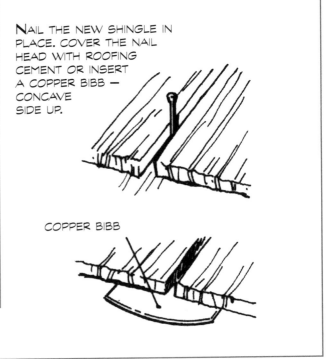

NAIL THE NEW SHINGLE IN PLACE. COVER THE NAIL HEAD WITH ROOFING CEMENT OR INSERT A COPPER BIBB — CONCAVE SIDE UP.

COPPER BIBB

HOUSEHOLD HELPS • SOLVENTS

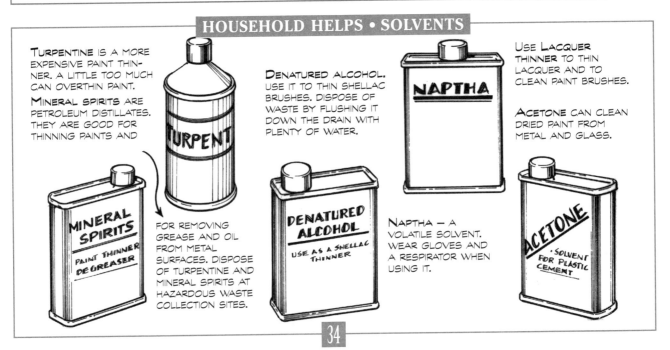

TURPENTINE IS A MORE EXPENSIVE PAINT THINNER. A LITTLE TOO MUCH CAN OVERTHIN PAINT. MINERAL SPIRITS ARE PETROLEUM DISTILLATES. THEY ARE GOOD FOR THINNING PAINTS AND

FOR REMOVING GREASE AND OIL FROM METAL SURFACES. DISPOSE OF TURPENTINE AND MINERAL SPIRITS AT HAZARDOUS WASTE COLLECTION SITES.

MINERAL SPIRITS
PAINT THINNER DEGREASER

TURPENT

DENATURED ALCOHOL. USE IT TO THIN SHELLAC BRUSHES. DISPOSE OF WASTE BY FLUSHING IT DOWN THE DRAIN WITH PLENTY OF WATER.

DENATURED ALCOHOL
USE AS A SHELLAC THINNER

NAPTHA

NAPTHA — A VOLATILE SOLVENT. WEAR GLOVES AND A RESPIRATOR WHEN USING IT.

USE LACQUER THINNER TO THIN LACQUER AND TO CLEAN PAINT BRUSHES.

ACETONE CAN CLEAN DRIED PAINT FROM METAL AND GLASS.

ACETONE
SOLVENT FOR PLASTIC CEMENT

Slate Roof Repair

A roof with slate tiles can last for years without much maintenance, but occasionally individual tiles may deteriorate with age — called flaking or delaminating — or they may be dam-

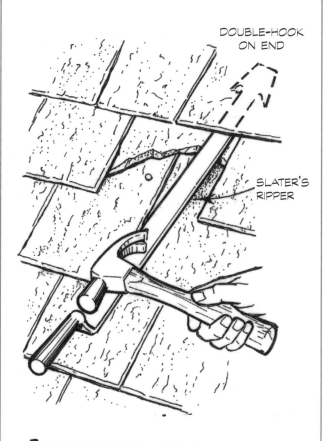

DOUBLE-HOOK ON END

SLATER'S RIPPER

REMOVE THE DAMAGED TILE. CUT THE HOLDING NAILS WITH A SLATER'S RIPPER.

aged by falling debris from a nearby tree. Tiles also can work loose and fall out when buffeted by high winds. Tiles that are not exposed to the sun may grow moss.

Repairing and replacing slate-roofing tiles is not a difficult procedure, but it can be dangerous because slate tiles are slippery and slate roofs are often steep. Walking on a slate roof also can crack or damage the existing, good tiles. For those reasons it is best to leave major repairs to a professional and confine your repair work to those jobs that can be done near the edge of the roof from an extension ladder.

Moss growth on tiles can be eliminated with common weed killer. Use a garden sprayer to apply the weed killer and a stiff-bristled brush with an extension handle to rub off the moss.

REMOVING DAMAGED TILES: Whenever you find damaged tiles, you first must remove them before you can insert a replacement. If the holding nails have rusted away, you may be able to slide the broken tile out without too much trouble. Otherwise, you will have to cut the nails. For that you will need a special tool called a slater's ripper, also called a "shingle nail remover."

The slater's ripper is a flat, metal bar with two sharpened hooks on one end and a handle on the other. Slip the ripper under the damaged tile and move it about to the left and right until one of the hooks catches a nail. Pull down on the handle to cut the nail. If you need more force to slice through the nail, rap the top of the handle with a hammer.

You also can use a hacksaw blade to cut holding nails. Wrap one end of the blade with heavy-duty tape — that will serve as a handle — and slip the other end under the tile. When the saw comes in contact with a nail, move the blade up and down to cut it. Remember that

HOLDING REPLACEMENT TILES

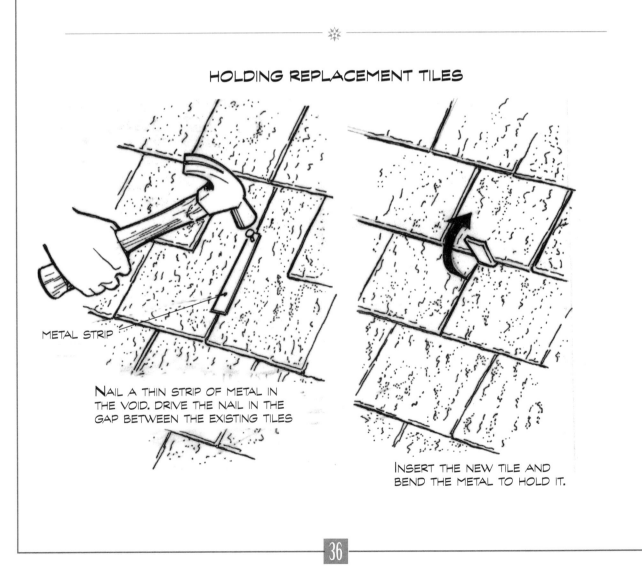

METAL STRIP

NAIL A THIN STRIP OF METAL IN THE VOID. DRIVE THE NAIL IN THE GAP BETWEEN THE EXISTING TILES

INSERT THE NEW TILE AND BEND THE METAL TO HOLD IT.

SLATE ROOF REPAIR

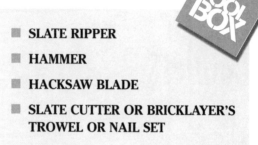

each tile is held in place with two nails, and you must cut both nails to free the tile.

Take a piece of the broken tile with you when you purchase a replacement. You can use it to match color and thickness, but you probably will not find a slate tile with the same length and width. In that case you will have to cut one to size.

You can rent a slate cutter. That makes tile cutting easy but may not be worth the rental expense if you have only one or two tiles to cut. You also can use a bricklayer's trowel to resize tiles. Place the tile on a flat worktable with the amount to be removed projecting beyond the edge of the table. Use the edge of the trowel to chop off the projecting piece.

Another method for cutting tiles is with a nail set. Use it to punch a series of small holes along a scored cutting line. You then can break the tile along the perforated line by pressing it against the edge of a table.

- ■ **SLATE RIPPER**
- ■ **HAMMER**
- ■ **HACKSAW BLADE**
- ■ **SLATE CUTTER OR BRICKLAYER'S TROWEL OR NAIL SET**
- ■ **TIN SNIPS**

HOLDING REPLACEMENT TILES: The traditional way to hold the replacement tile in place is with a thin strip of metal, preferably of copper or zinc. Cut a piece 1 inch wide and about 8 inches long. Place the metal strip in position where the new tile will sit, and secure it by driving a nail into the roof. The nail must go in the gap between the slate tiles already on the roof. Slide the new tile in place. The end of the metal strip will project beyond its bottom edge. Bend the strip up to form a hook and hold the tile in place. ⊕

Ladders

If you own a home, you should own a ladder. It's almost impossible to maintain a house properly without one. Most people know what a ladder is used for, but they don't always know how to use one properly. The U.S. Consumer Products Safety Commission estimates that every year about 65,000 people are hospitalized be cause of ladder accidents.

TYPES OF LADDERS: Different types of ladders are available, but homeowners need be concerned only with the two most common ones: the step ladder and the extension ladder. Both types are available in wood, aluminum, and fiberglass.

The main advantage in buying a wooden ladder is that it is cheaper than an aluminum or fiberglass one. Many users are more confident when climbing a wooden ladder because wood flexes less than metal under loads. Wooden ladders have two drawbacks. First, they are heavy — wooden extension ladders are difficult to carry and to maneuver in place. Second, they deteriorate when left unprotected.

Excessive moisture can penetrate the wood, causing rot and decay. Even a little decay can compromise a ladder's structural integrity and make it unsafe.

Hanging the ladder in a dry place will keep moisture from collecting on the wood. You also can protect it by applying a coat of clear finish to the

DO NOT STAND ON THE TOP SHELF OR THE PAIL SHELF.

WHEN SETTING UP A STEP LADDER MAKE SURE IT IS FULLY OPENED.

PERIODICALLY CHECK THE BRACE NUTS. TIGHTEN THEM IF THEY ARE LOOSE.

wood. Never paint a wooden ladder; the paint will cover splits, cracks or defects that could make the ladder unsafe.

Aluminum ladders are less expensive than fiberglass ones and lighter than the wooden models. The main drawback is that they conduct electricity and can be dangerous to use around electrical wires.

Fiberglass ladders are lightweight, weather resistant, and nonconductive, although a wet or dirty fiberglass ladder can conduct electricity. They are more expensive than either aluminum or wooden ladders. They are also available in orange or yellow. Some consumers wonder if there is any significance to the colors. The answer is no; the manufacturer chooses the color for aesthetic rather than structural reasons.

DUTY RATING & LADDER LENGTH:
Besides price and material, you should consider two other factors when choosing a ladder. The first is the duty rating. It indicates the load capacity the ladder will bear. Type IA can hold 300 pounds, Type I holds 250 pounds, Type II 225 pounds, and Type III 200 pounds. Those ratings indicate the total weight the ladder can hold; that includes the weight of the person on the ladder and also the weight of any tools or materials he may carry. Exceeding the duty rating can jeopardize the safety of the user.

The second factor to consider is the length of the ladder. Obviously you need a ladder long enough to reach your home's highest ceiling or roof peak. Ladder length can be deceiving, because you really can't use the entire length. It's unsafe, for example, to stand on the top step of the stepladder, so a 6-foot stepladder gives you only 5 feet of usable height. Similarly, the top 3 rungs, approximately 3 feet in length of an extension ladder, should be used only for handholds, not for standing.

Stepladders are available in lengths from 2 feet to 14 feet, but the most useful one for homeowners is the 6-foot model. Extension ladders are manufactured in 4-foot increments from 16 feet to 40 feet. To find the right length for you, measure the distance from the ground to the roof eaves or peak and add 3 feet. Remember that a long extension ladder can be difficult to maneuver, and you may require the aid of a helper to set it up.

When using a ladder, remember that it is most stable when your weight is centered between the stiles — the two upright side rails. Avoid over-reaching; leaning or reaching beyond the ladder can cause it to topple. If something is not within your immediate grasp, climb down and reposition the ladder. Read all instruction and caution labels printed on it. Before using any ladder, inspect it carefully for worn or damaged parts. Do not use any ladder that has bent or cracked stiles or rungs. Make sure that the rungs or steps are free from dirt and grease and wear sensible, slip-resistant footwear. Always face the ladder when climbing or descending it.

TO SET UP AN EXTENSION LADDER POSITION THE BOTTOM AGAINST THE HOUSE. WALK FORWARD AND RAISE THE LADDER.

SETTING UP LADDERS: When setting up a stepladder, make sure that it is fully opened and that the folding stays are locked. Never stand or sit on the top shelf or the folding pail shelf. Do not attempt to climb on the back of a stepladder. If you must erect a stepladder in front of a door, either lock the door or post a warning sign on the other side. Periodically, check the brace nuts on the side of the stepladder. If they are loose, use an adjustable wrench to tighten them.

When setting up an extension ladder, watch for overhead power

POSITION THE EXTENSION LADDER SO THAT THE BOTTOM IS ABOUT ONE-FOURTH OF ITS EXTENDED LENGTH.

lines. To erect the ladder, position the bottom against the house. Then, starting from the top, walk toward the bottom, raising the ladder hand over hand. When the ladder is vertical, pull the bottom out so that the feet are one-quarter of its working length from the house. Next, secure the feet of the ladder to keep them from slipping. If possible, nail a cleat behind the ladder or tie the feet to stakes to keep them secure. Never climb on an unsteady ladder; when in doubt enlist the aid of a helper to hold the ladder in place.

Keep your ladder in top condition by taking proper care of it. Store it by hanging it on a wall with supports positioned every 6 feet. Clean and lubricate all moving parts periodically. ⊕

MAKE SURE THE BOTTOM OF THE LADDER IS PROPERLY BRACED TO KEEP IT FROM SLIPPING.

Gutters

Spring is a good time for inspecting and cleaning the rain gutters. They probably have accumulations of leaves and dirt that can block the flow of rainwater. The weight of the debris and rainwater can cause the gutters to sag and pull away from the house. Once the gutters are cleaned out, you can inspect them for damage and make any necessary repairs.

If you have a low roof, you can work from a stepladder. Remember, however, never to stand on the top step. If your roof has a gentle slope, you may be able to climb on the roof to clean the gutters. Leaning a ladder directly against the gutters can bend or damage them. One way to avoid that is to use a ladder stay.

USING A LADDER STAY: A stay is a bracket that mounts on the ladder and allows it to rest against the wall under the gutters. Ladder stays are available at most home centers. If you don't have one, you can lay a board across the top of the gutter. The board should be wide enough to extend beyond the gutter edge — about 6 inches — and just long enough to support both ladder stiles.

There are two drawbacks to using the gutter board. First, the board will cover the section of gutter directly in front of you, so you'll only be able to clean those areas within reach on either side of the ladder. Remember to keep

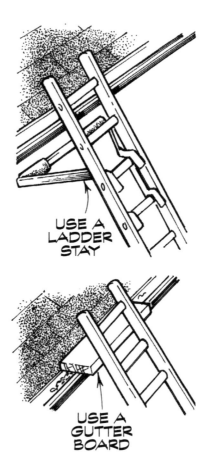

USE A
LADDER
STAY

USE A
GUTTER
BOARD

your weight centered between the ladder stiles and avoid overreaching. Second, setting the board in place is a two-step procedure. You'll have to position the ladder under the gutters to place the board; then reposition the ladder to work on the gutters.

CLEANING GUTTERS: You need only a few tools to clean the gutters: a hose with a spray nozzle, a bucket, a whisk broom, a putty knife, and a small trowel. Clip the bucket handle to a ladder rung with an S-hook. Use the putty knife

- **HOSE WITH SPRAY NOZZLE**

- **BUCKET**

- **WHISK BROOM**

- **GARDENER'S TROWEL**

- **PUTTY KNIFE**

- **PAINT BRUSH (FOR REPAIRS)**

- **CAULKING GUN WITH CARTRIDGE OF GUTTER SEALANT**

- **SANDPAPER (FOR REPAIRS)**

- **POP-RIVET TOOL AND RIVETS (FOR REPAIRS)**

- **TIN SNIPS (FOR REPAIRS)**

and trowel to dislodge and remove the leaves, twigs, and dirt. Use the whisk broom to sweep small amounts of dirt into piles for easier pickup. You can also use your hands to scoop out the debris, but be sure to wear heavy duty gloves. Deposit all of the collected material in the bucket. After you have removed the debris, wash the gutters clean with a hose.

Next, examine the downspouts and make sure they are not clogged. If one is clogged, chances are that you'll find wet leaves in an elbow joint. Try to pull the leaves out — you may have to remove the elbow to do this. Do not attempt to force leaves through the downspout; that will push them into the center section and make matters worse.

If the clog is deeper into the downspout, you may be able to clear it with water. Use the hose to shoot a strong stream into the opening. Take care to avoid getting hit by any overspray. Another way to remove an obstruction is by forcing a plumber's snake down the downspout.

REPAIRING GUTTERS: When the gutters and downspouts are clean, inspect them for corrosion and cracks. If you find a damaged section, use a wire brush to remove the rust; then apply a liberal coating of roofing cement over

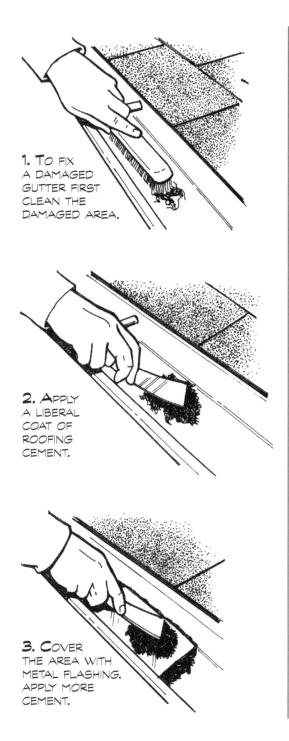

1. TO FIX A DAMAGED GUTTER FIRST CLEAN THE DAMAGED AREA.

2. APPLY A LIBERAL COAT OF ROOFING CEMENT.

3. COVER THE AREA WITH METAL FLASHING. APPLY MORE CEMENT.

the area and at least 6 inches beyond in both directions. Cut a piece of metal flashing large enough to cover the damaged area. Embed the patch in the cement and apply a second coat of roofing cement.

You also can use roofing cement to give the inside of the gutters a protective finish. Thin the roofing cement with mineral spirits; then brush it on all areas where the paint has become worn.

FIXING GUTTER LEAKS: Inspect all gutter seams for possible leaks. It's difficult to tell if a seam leaks when there is no water in the gutter, but the seams often drip dirty water and leave dark streaks on the siding below. If you suspect any seam of being less than watertight, you should seal it before it gets worse.

Sometimes, for minor leaks, you can force sealant into the seam without taking the pieces apart. Use a caulk-sealant specifically formulated for aluminum gutters. It is synthesized to adhere and remain resilient in hot and cold temperatures. Gutter sealant is available in cartridges at well-stocked home centers.

SEALING THE SEAMS: If you cannot push the sealant into the joint, you'll have to open the seam. Gutter seams usually are held in place with pop rivets. Remove the rivets by drilling them out with a bit that is slightly larger than the hole in the center of the rivet. With the rivets removed, you can pull the seams apart and clean them with a putty knife or coarse sandpaper. Remove all traces of the old sealant and make sure the surfaces are smooth.

OPEN A LEAKY SEAM BY DRILLING OUT THE RIVETS. CLEAN THE JOINT AND APPLY A BEAD OF SEALANT.

Apply a new bead of sealant, reassemble the joint, and install new pop rivets.

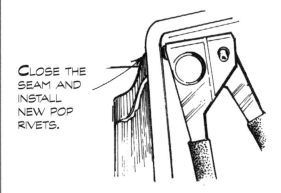

CLOSE THE SEAM AND INSTALL NEW POP RIVETS.

After you've made all the necessary repairs to the gutters, inspect the mounting brackets to ensure that they are secure and the gutters haven't pulled away from the roof. Don't forget to check the brackets that hold the downspouts to the wall. ⊕

HOUSEHOLD HELPS • FILES

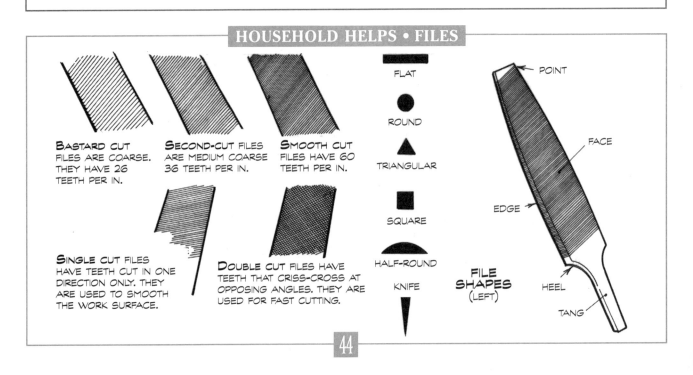

BASTARD CUT FILES ARE COARSE. THEY HAVE 26 TEETH PER IN.

SECOND-CUT FILES ARE MEDIUM COARSE 36 TEETH PER IN.

SMOOTH CUT FILES HAVE 60 TEETH PER IN.

SINGLE CUT FILES HAVE TEETH CUT IN ONE DIRECTION ONLY. THEY ARE USED TO SMOOTH THE WORK SURFACE.

DOUBLE CUT FILES HAVE TEETH THAT CRISS-CROSS AT OPPOSING ANGLES. THEY ARE USED FOR FAST CUTTING.

FLAT
ROUND
TRIANGULAR
SQUARE
HALF-ROUND
KNIFE

POINT
FACE
EDGE
HEEL
TANG

FILE SHAPES (LEFT)

Soffits

Soffits are the narrow strip of ceiling material, either wood or metal, that covers the underside of the roof eaves. That rather innocuous area often is ignored by homeowners until rot or decay develops, which usually is caused by leaks in the roof that drip down and collect in the eaves and on the soffit boards. Homeowners should inspect the soffits every spring because soffit decay is an indication of even greater damage in the roof structure above.

In most cases a visual inspection will tell whether you have problems or not. Look for badly peeling paint, warped boards, brown water stains, and of course, rotted sections. It's not enough simply to paint over the area or even replace the soffits. The soffits

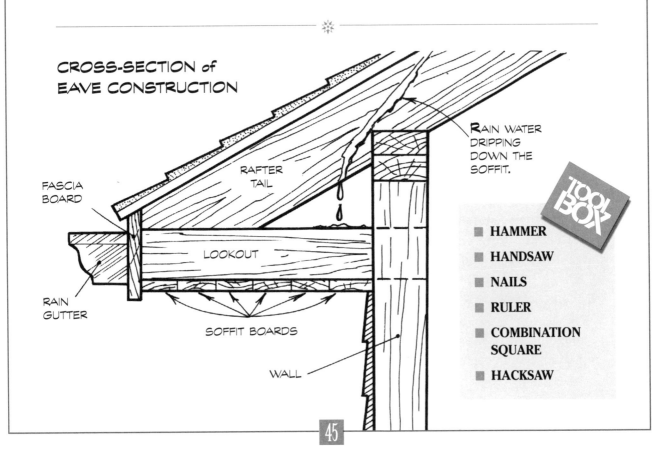

CROSS-SECTION of EAVE CONSTRUCTION

FASCIA BOARD

RAFTER TAIL

RAIN WATER DRIPPING DOWN THE SOFFIT.

LOOKOUT

RAIN GUTTER

SOFFIT BOARDS

WALL

TOOL BOX

- ■ HAMMER
- ■ HANDSAW
- ■ NAILS
- ■ RULER
- ■ COMBINATION SQUARE
- ■ HACKSAW

should be removed, which can be dirty, dusty work, so wear a dust mask and goggles. Now you can examine the projecting rafter boards, called the rafter tail; the fascia boards, the flat boards nailed to the ends of the rafter tails; and the 2 x 4s that run from the rafter tails to the house, called the "lookouts," which provide a nailing surface to hold the soffits in place.

PROBLEMS & HAZARDS: Close inspection and soffit removal entail working up under the eaves. That may not be difficult if your house is only one-story high, but working above can be hazardous on a two-story house. Call a professional to tackle the job if you are unsteady around heights. Also bear in mind that the incoming power lines may be close to the eaves. Be careful working around these lines, and do not touch them.

Another problem with working around the soffits is that they may harbor wasp or hornet nests. If the nest is small, you can spray it with an insecticide and then remove it. A professional exterminator, however, should remove large nests.

REPAIRING DAMAGED RAFTER TAILS, FASCIAS, AND LOOKOUTS: Rotted or damaged boards should be repaired or replaced; but because those problems are caused by leaks in the roof, the first step should be to locate the source of the leak and fix it. It's easier to find the source if you wait for a rainy day. From the attic check the underside of the roof with a flashlight to see where the water is dripping through. Mark the spot so that you can return to it on a dry day and make repairs. Do not attempt to make a roof repair yourself if you are unsteady working at heights or if your roof has a steep pitch. Instead, call a roofing professional.

After all of the roof repairs have been made, you can return to the soffits. If the soffits are in bad shape, the chances are good that other boards also will be rotted. Examine all boards and framing members. Use an awl or screwdriver to probe into decayed areas to determine the extent of the damage. The rafter tails support the edge of the roof, the lookouts support the soffits, and the fascia holds the gutters. All of those pieces must be sound; if not, they should be replaced. Allow time for all moist or wet areas to dry thoroughly before attempting repairs.

Before you can work on the rafter tails or lookouts, you may have to remove the fascia boards. First, remove the gutters. Those may be held in place with gutter spikes, long nails that go through a metal sleeve in the gutter and into the fascia, or with hanger straps

FASCIA
BOARD

RAIN
GUTTER

When replacing the
soffits, add a strip vent.
The vent will allow air to
circulate in the eaves and
eliminate moisture build-up.

that are nailed to the roof under the shingles. Remove the gutters; then pry the fascia boards free. You can use a hacksaw to cut the holding nails if they are rusted badly.

Damaged rafter tails cannot be replaced easily because they are part of the rafters. The rafters extend from the eaves under the roof and up to the peak. The tails, however, can be repaired by nailing a length of 2 x 6 directly to the rafter. That reinforcement piece is called a "partner" board. It should be about twice the length of the rafter tail and extend from the end of the tail into the attic. Use 10d nails or

3-inch screws to secure the partner to the rafter tail.

Lookouts are easier to fix because the entire length of the board is accessible. You can repair them by attaching a partner board, but it is better to remove the lookout and replace it with a new piece. Since most lookouts are made from 2 x 4s, it is necessary only to cut one to the proper length and nail it in place.

Damaged fascia boards should be replaced. Simply cut a new board to the dimensions of the old and nail it to the rafter tails; then remount the gutters. With the fascia boards in place, you can replace the soffit boards.

Soffits on older homes are made of narrow, tongue-and-groove boards nailed to the lookouts. You may find that some of the boards are in good condition, while others are not. You can use the good boards provided that you can find new boards that match. If not, it may be better to replace all the boards.

You also can replace the wooden boards with aluminum soffits. They are more durable but require closer periodic inspections because they do not show signs of leaks, as do the wooden boards. Therefore, rain or water damage can be present in the eave structure before any visible warning signs appear in the soffits. ⊕

Cleaning Windows

Spring is here. It's the season when many homeowners give their homes a thorough "spring cleaning." Perhaps the most tedious and frustrating part of the annual spring-cleaning campaign is window cleaning. The average person attacks a dirty window with a roll of paper towels in one hand and a spray bottle of the leading commercial glass cleaner in the other. The strategy consists of spraying generous amounts of cleaner on the glass and wiping it off with copious quantities of paper toweling.

That method is expensive and inefficient. The paper towels usually absorb the cleaner and leave much of the dirt behind. The result is a window with streaks, dull film, and cloudy patches. There are better methods. They are the methods employed by professional window cleaners who face grimy windows every working day.

Professionals start with the right tools. They prefer to use a squeegee to remove the window solvent. The squeegee should be of high-quality brass or stainless steel. They are available in different lengths, but a 10- to 14-inch blade is the most practical. If the blade is too long, you can shorten it with a hacksaw. You also can purchase an extension pole for the squeegee that will allow you to wash second-floor windows while you are standing on the

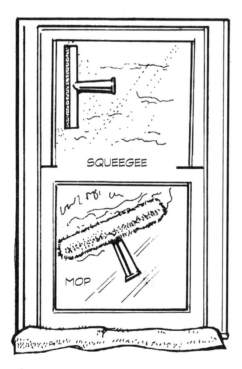

SQUEEGEE

MOP

APPLY THE CLEANING SOLUTION WITH A WINDOW CLEANER'S MOP. REMOVE THE SOLUTION WITH A HIGH-QUALITY SQUEEGEE.

ground. Avoid the temptation to clean the outside of your windows by sitting on the sill. If your windows do not tilt out, clean them by raising and lowering the sashes so that you can reach the surfaces from the inside.

The best time to wash windows is in the early morning, when it's still cool outside. Later in the day the hot sun will cause the window to dry too fast leaving a residue behind. Before attempting to clean the glass, vacuum out the frame and around the sills. Use the brush attachment to remove dust, cobwebs, and as much loose dirt as possible.

TOOL BOX

- ◼ **VACUUM WITH BRUSH ATTACHMENT**
- ◼ **SQUEEGEE**
- ◼ **LAMB'S WOOL WAND**
- ◼ **CLEAN CLOTHS**
- ◼ **NEWSPAPER**
- ◼ **BLACKBOARD ERASER (FOR POLISHING DULL WINDOWS)**
- ◼ **STEEL WOOL (FOR ALUMINUM FRAMES)**
- ◼ **PASTE WAX (FOR ALUMINUM FRAMES)**
- ◼ **SCRUB BRUSH AND GARDEN HOSE (FOR SCREENS)**

AMMONIA

PROFESSIONAL WINDOW CLEANERS USE CLEAN, WARM WATER TO WASH WINDOWS. FOR VERY DIRTY WINDOWS ADD 1/4 CUP OF AMMONIA TO THE WATER.

Professional window cleaners use clear, warm water to wash windows. For very dirty windows, you can add 1/4 cup of clear ammonia or white vinegar to the water. Do not use both, since vinegar and ammonia neutralize each other. You can use a sponge to apply the solution, but a lambs wool wand — also called a "window cleaner's mop" — is more effective. That is simply a sleeve made of lamb's wool or cotton, which is available at janitorial supply stores and some home centers, that fits over the squeegee. It loosens and removes grime. A sponge often traps

PROTECT THE SILL
AND FLOOR WITH
TOWELS.

the dirt, which scratches the glass.

Before applying any cleaning solution, fold a bath towel into a narrow roll and place it on the floor near the wall. This will catch any drips that might stain the floor or carpet. If you have a wooden window sill, you might want to protect it with a folded towel also.

Dip the wand in the solution and apply it to the window. Wait a few seconds for the solution to dissolve and suspend the dirt. Take the squeegee and wipe the blade with a damp cloth. That will lubricate the blade so it will slide easily across the glass. Now, starting at an upper corner, draw the blade across the window. Wipe the blade again to remove the accumulated solution and grime. Wipe the blade after each pass. Make another pass, overlapping the first, and with successive passes work your way down the window. Use a clean cloth to wipe away any excess water that may have collected at the bottom of the window frame.

For problem spots, such as those caused by hard-water deposits, use white vinegar. Apply it with a nonabrasive nylon pad and scrub gently.

The squeegee will not fit in smaller windows. You can, of course, purchase a smaller squeegee, but it's probably not worth it if you only have a few small panes. Here it's best to apply the cleaning solution to the glass and wipe it off with newspaper. Curiously, newspaper cleans glass better than paper towels, and it's cheaper too.

After your windows are washed, they should sparkle. Sometimes the glass in older windows can be dull even after washing. Believe it or not, you can polish those windows with a blackboard eraser. Simply rub it across the surface to bring a shine to the glass. Make sure that the eraser and the glass are clean before trying this.

Don't forget to clean the window sills. Aluminum sills can be cleaned with liquid abrasive or fine steel wool. After cleaning apply a coat of paste wax. A painted sill usually can be cleaned with a damp cloth. Wooden sills are best cleaned with a wood cleaner or a spray-on furniture cleaner. Do not use water-based cleaners on wooden sills because they cause the wood to swell.

CLEANING SCREENS: If you are cleaning the outside of your windows, you also should clean your screens. Dirty screens can obscure your view as much as a dirty window. They also cut down on airflow and block cooling breezes from entering your home. The best way to clean screens is to remove them from the window and place them on a flat surface, such as a picnic table or an old worktable. Cover the table first with an old rug or bed sheet. Scrub them with a soft-bristle scrub brush and detergent solution. Rinse the screen by spraying it with a garden hose.

Another way to clean metal screens is with foaming bathroom cleaner. Spray the cleaner on and let it set for a few seconds and wash it off. Foaming bathroom cleaner should not be used on nylon screens because it could damage them. Shake the excess water from the screen and let it sun dry. ⊕

To clean screens lay them on a table, scrub them with a soft-bristle scrub brush and detergent solution. Rinse by spraying with a garden hose.

HOUSEHOLD HELPS • SCREWDRIVERS

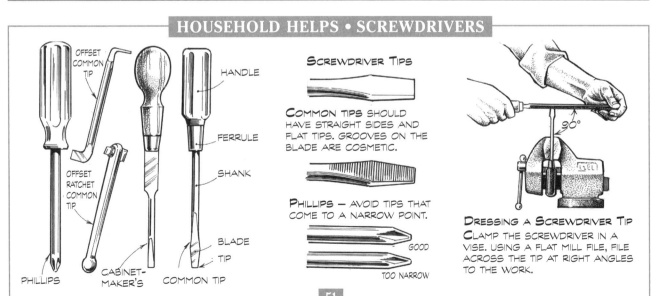

OFFSET COMMON TIP

HANDLE

OFFSET RATCHET COMMON TIP

FERRULE

SHANK

BLADE

TIP

PHILLIPS

CABINET-MAKER'S

COMMON TIP

SCREWDRIVER TIPS

COMMON TIPS SHOULD HAVE STRAIGHT SIDES AND FLAT TIPS. GROOVES ON THE BLADE ARE COSMETIC.

PHILLIPS — AVOID TIPS THAT COME TO A NARROW POINT.

GOOD

TOO NARROW

90°

DRESSING A SCREWDRIVER TIP
CLAMP THE SCREWDRIVER IN A VISE. USING A FLAT MILL FILE, FILE ACROSS THE TIP AT RIGHT ANGLES TO THE WORK.

Minor Window Repairs

Four types of windows are designed for residential homes: sliding windows that slide from side to side; casement windows that swing open on hinges; awning windows that swing out from the bottom (multipaned jalousie windows are a variation of awning windows); and double-hung windows. Most homes have double-hung windows.

Double-hung windows have two sashes that move up and down in channels in the window frame. Balancing mechanisms in the window assist in raising and lowering the sashes and prevent them from sliding downward when released. In older windows the balancing mechanism consists of a counterweight attached to the sash. The weights are concealed in cavities, called the side jambs, on either side of the window. Raising the window lowers the weight and vice versa.

Some double-hung windows may have tubular-type spring balance or a spring-tape balance mechanism to control the sash movement. The tubular balance has a spiral spring encased in a long, metal tube. The tube is attached to the bottom of the sash and the window frame. Tension maintained in the spiral spring counterbalances the weight of the sash. The spring-tape balance has a flexible steel tape, similar to a steel tape measure, encased in a metal box. The box is set in the window frame, and the end of the tape is attached to the sash. As the sash is raised the tape winds into the box and holds the sash in place.

Newer double-hung windows may be made of wood, metal, or wood clad in vinyl or metal. Those units are virtually maintenance-free although sometimes the sash can stick in place or be difficult to move. When that happens, the culprit usually is dirt or grit

TOOL BOX

- **HAMMER**
- **NAIL SET**
- **PLIERS**
- **UTILITY KNIFE**
- **STIFF PUTTY KNIFE**
- **WOOD CHISEL**

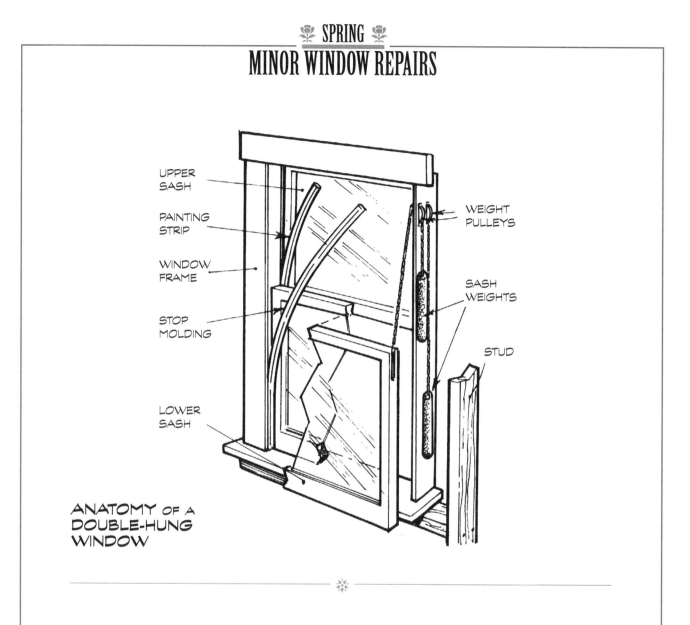

UPPER SASH

PAINTING STRIP

WINDOW FRAME

STOP MOLDING

LOWER SASH

WEIGHT PULLEYS

SASH WEIGHTS

STUD

ANATOMY OF A DOUBLE-HUNG WINDOW

---

deposits in the window channel. Cleaning the channel and applying a lubricant, such as silicone or paraffin, should correct the difficulty.

In some cases the problem may be more serious. Windows in newer houses may stick if too much insulation was packed between the window jamb and the jack stud. That extra insulation can compress the window frame against the sash, making it difficult to open or close

the window. Sometimes the window itself may be slightly out of square if it was stored improperly at the factory. The window also can become distorted if the house settles. The shifting foundation will twist the house framing and cause the window to warp.

To isolate the problem, remove the molding around the window to expose the jamb and framing. If the jamb has been overfilled with insulation, remove the excess by digging it out with a screwdriver. Check the window with a framing square and make sure that it is true and plumb. If not, you may be able to straighten it by wedging blocks between the studs and window. If the window is badly warped, you may have to replace it.

FIXING STICKY WINDOWS: Older windows often stick after they've been painted. The paint forms a seal around the sash and frame and literally glues the parts in place. To free the sashes, use a utility knife to cut the paint film

FORCE A PUTTY KNIFE IN THE SEAM BETWEEN THE MOLDING AND THE SASH.

around the edges of the stop molding adjacent to the sash.

Next, force a wide, stiff-bladed putty knife in the seam between the molding and sash. That will dislodge any paint that may have seeped into the gap. It may help to use a hammer and gently tap the knife handle so that the blade will penetrate to the window channel. Work around the entire perimeter of the window, being careful not to mar the window surface. The procedure should free the sash so that you can move it.

Sand or scrape the surface of the window sash to remove the dried paint ridge. Seal any bare wood with primer and repaint the sash. As the paint is drying, periodically move the sash to prevent a new paint seal from forming.

For stubborn cases you'll have to remove the stop molding around the frame. Use the stiff putty knife to pry the molding away from the window frame. The stop molding on older windows is apt to be dry and inflexible, so lift carefully at the nail locations to avoid breaking it. After you've removed the stop molding, the lower sash will be easy to lift out.

REPAIRING WINDOWS WITH SASH WEIGHTS: If the window has a sash weight, you'll have to detach the chains or ropes before you can set the window aside. Tie a knot in the cord or slip a

SLIP A NAIL IN ONE OF THE LINKS TO KEEP THE SASH WEIGHT FROM DROPPING.

WHEN DETACHING A TUBULAR-SPRING BALANCE, HOLD THE TUBE IN PLACE AS YOU REMOVE THE HOLD-DOWN SCREW.

nail in one of the chain links to keep it from falling back into the jamb cavity.

REPAIRING WINDOWS WITH SPRINGS: Windows with a spring-tape balance can be detached by unscrewing the tape from the sash. Hold the tape as you remove the screws; then let it coil back into the metal box — a ring at the end will allow you pull the tape out later. Tubular-type spring-balance mechanisms are a little trickier to detach because the spiral spring is apt to be under tension. Removing the retaining screw will release the tension and cause the spring to snap around, so maintain a grip on the metal tube and allow the spring to unwind gently.

To free the upper sash, you'll have to remove the parting strip that separates the two sashes. ⊕

Replacing a Broken Window

Replacing a broken window pane is not a difficult task, but it does require care to avoid injury.

STEP 1: Start by removing the broken glass. Wear heavy gloves to protect your hands and put on safety glasses for your eyes. Position a cardboard box nearby to receive the broken pieces as you remove them. Do not attempt to pick out small slivers or shards of glass with your fingers. Instead, use pliers or pieces of masking tape.

STEP 2: Remove the hardened glazing compound. You can do that two ways. The first method uses heat; the second requires chiseling out the old compound. Professional glaziers use a spe-

- **PLIERS**
- **GLASS CUTTER**
- **STRAIGHT EDGE**
- **BRUSH AND KEROSENE**
- **BRUSH AND LINSEED OIL**
- **PUTTY KNIFE**
- **GLAZING COMPOUND**
- **GLAZIER'S POINTS**
- **WOOD CHISEL**

cial heating iron to soften and remove the hardened compound, but you also can use a heat gun. Do not use a propane torch. Direct the heat at the compound till it softens; then pry it out

REPLACING A BROKEN WINDOW

with a stiff putty knife. Using a heat gun is much safer than using a torch. The risk of fire is minimal, but it's still a good idea to keep a pail of water or a small fire extinguisher nearby as a safety precaution.

STEP 3: To chisel out the old compound, use a sharp wood chisel and work carefully to avoid damaging the wood. That method can be difficult and tedious if the compound is old and rock-hard. Sometimes it helps to use a utility knife to score the compound where it meets the wood frame. If you use the knife, place a metal straight edge on the wood to protect it should the knife slip.

Once the old compound is removed, pry out any glazier's points or nails and scrape out any remaining debris from the frame. Now, scrape the rabbet — the recess in the frame that holds the glass — to the bare wood using a sharp chisel held vertically. You also can use a

wood scraper for that. Take care not to damage the wood. Next, sand lightly using a small sanding block. The block will keep the sandpaper flat and prevent it from rounding the edges of the wood frame.

STEP 4: Coat the exposed wood with linseed oil or apply a coat of exterior primer. Do not neglect that step because it prevents the wood from absorbing the oil from the new glazing compound. That would cause the compound to dry prematurely and crack. While the linseed oil is penetrating the wood, measure the opening in the frame. Note the width and height and subtract 1/8 inch from each dimension to allow for clearance.

CHOOSING & CUTTING GLASS PANES: Most hardware stores sell replacement glass and will cut it to your specifications. Be sure to tell the dealer that your measurement includes the clearance allowance. Window glass comes in two thicknesses: single strength — 3/32 inch — and double strength — 1/8 inch. Use single strength for smaller panes; double strength should be used in large windows, over 200 square inches, or in storm windows. Some building codes require that tempered (heat-strengthened) glass be installed in hazardous locations: for example, patio doors, some overhead windows, and windows below 18 inches. That type of glass cannot be cut and must be ordered to size from the manufacturer.

For windows in high-traffic areas of locations that make them susceptible to breakage, consider installing break-resistant acrylic panels. Be aware, however, that while plastic panes resist breakage, they scratch more readily than glass and some types may yellow with age.

It's possible that you may already have a glass pane that is usable but needs to be cut to size. To cut it you'll need a glass cutter and a straight edge — a framing square is ideal. Be sure to wear heavy-duty work gloves and eye protection.

Strictly speaking, you do not cut glass; instead you break it along a scored line. To do that, measure the pane and mark the cut with a fine-line felt-tipped marker. Place the straight edge along the line. Dip the glass cutter

in kerosene, then holding it straight up between the index finger and middle finger draw it along the line. Use an even, but not hard, pressure. Make one pass; do not try to rescore. Rescoring usually results in a bad break.

Place the pane, scored side up, over a piece of thin, flat wood — a yardstick is ideal — with the scored line positioned on the edge. Press down on both sides of the glass. It will break cleanly at the line. If any small pieces of glass cling to the edge (this usually happens with a bad score), you can "nibble" them off with a pair of pliers. Grab the piece with the pliers and twist it up and down; it should snap off.

STEP 5: Return to the window frame. Apply a 1/8-inch bead of glazing compound around the rabbet. That will cushion the glass and give it a better seal by smoothing out any irregularities in the wood. Be sure to clean the glass before placing it in the frame.

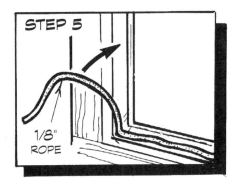

REPLACING A BROKEN WINDOW

STEP 6: The glazing compound creates a watertight seal around the glass, but it doesn't hold the glass in place. Glazier's points do that. There are two types of points. The older style is a small, flat, triangular piece of metal. The other type, of a more recent design, is called a "push point." It has two small tabs that make installation easier. No matter which style point you use, position the points around the edges of the glass at about 6-inch intervals and push them into the wood frame using a stiff putty knife or a screwdriver.

STEPS 7 & 8: With clean hands roll a glob of glazing compound into a rope about 3/8 inch in diameter. Place it around the perimeter of the glass. Press it down so it forms a tight seal and make sure it covers all of the glazier's points. Holding the putty knife at a shallow angle, draw it along the bead that you have just made. That will bevel the compound into a neat edge that slopes away from the glass. Make certain that it is high and wide enough to conceal all of the wood frame.

Sometimes the putty knife drags along the compound, causing it to "crumple" rather than smooth the surface. You can avoid this by first dipping the knife in turpentine. Excess compound can be removed from the glass or frame with a single-edged razor blade. Remove smudges from the glass with a rag dipped in turpentine.

Let the compound dry for about a week and then paint it. Allow the paint to come to about 1/16 inch onto the glass. This will ensure a watertight seal. ⊕

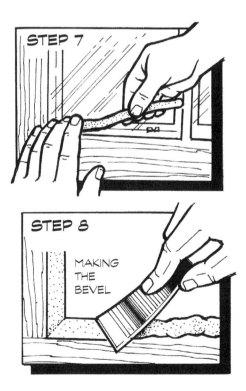

The Exterior Walls

The exterior of the house may be constructed of masonry, brick or stucco, or it may be clad in siding made of wood, vinyl, or metal. No matter what type of material covers the outside of the house, it should be inspected yearly because sooner or later it will need some maintenance and repair. Obviously, it is best to find minor problems before they mushroom into major headaches.

As you walk around your house to inspect the siding, look carefully at those areas most likely to develop problems, such as at the corners near the roof, areas abutting the door or window trim, and those sections that mate with the foundation.

Clapboard Siding

Metaphorically speaking, siding is the skin of a house. It serves two functions: It protects the house from the elements — rain, snow, and cold drafts — and from insects and rodents; and it adds style and beauty to the exterior of the house.

- **SCREWDRIVER**
- **BACKSAW**
- **KEYHOLE SAW**
- **WRECKING BAR**
- **MINI-HACKSAW**
- **HAMMER**
- **NAIL SET**
- **PUTTY KNIFE**

Siding is made of wood, vinyl, or metal. Many manufacturers claim that modern siding materials, vinyl and metal, are maintenance-free. Indeed, they do require less care than wood siding, but those materials still are vulnerable to the ravages of the environment.

At one time wood was the most common material used for clapboard siding on American homes. It was plentiful, easy to work, and provided good insulation. But wood siding requires more maintenance than do other materials. It must be painted or stained to withstand the onslaughts of weather and insects and it is more likely to split than other materials.

The durability of wooden clapboard siding depends largely on the type of wood used. Most siding is made of softwood, such as pine or fir. Older houses have boards cut from massive first-growth trees. That wood has a dense, cellular structure that makes it remarkably rot-resistant. Newer wood cut from second- and third-growth trees is less durable.

When inspecting wooden siding first look for structural defects, such as warps, cracks, or splits in the boards. Those should be repaired before repainting. Boards that are warped away from the house should be straightened because they offer a gap that insects find desirable as nesting sites. Flatten the boards by driving long, galvanized deck screws through the boards into the sheathing or studs behind.

Cracks or splits in the boards are not difficult to repair. Pry open the crack with a screw driver. Be careful not to overdo this or you will split the entire board apart. Then coat both sides with epoxy wood glue and squeeze the board back together.

It may be necessary to wedge a piece of scrap lumber against the bottom edge of the board to keep the crack from opening up before the glue sets.

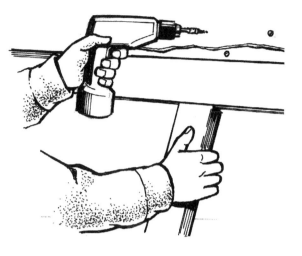

TO REPAIR A SPLIT BOARD, PRY OPEN THE CRACK, COAT BOTH SIDES WITH EPOXY GLUE AND SQUEEZE THE BOARD TOGETHER. USE A WEDGE OR DRIVE SCREWS TO HOLD THE BOARD TOGETHER.

Setting up a wedge is easy enough if the cracked board is close to the ground. For a crack that's higher up, you will have to hold the parts together by driving galvanized deck screws into the board on either side of the crack.

STEP 1: A board that is split badly or has a piece missing should be replaced. It is not necessary, however, to pull out the entire length of siding. Instead, the damaged section can be cut loose and replaced with a new piece. Drive wedges under the board to raise it away from the wall; then use a backsaw to make cuts on either side of the damage.

Before sawing, set a block of scrap wood on the siding below to protect it

STEP 1. USE A BACKSAW TO CUT THE DAMAGED SECTION OUT.

from the saw blade. The backsaw cannot cut completely through the damaged siding because the top edge will be covered by an overlapping board. Switch to a keyhole saw and push the narrow blade under the overlap to finish the cut.

STEP 2 & 3: After making the cuts, you should be able to pull the section out. If it proves stubborn, a few hidden nails may be anchoring it to the wall. Pry the board up with a wrecking bar to expose those nails and cut them with a mini-hacksaw. If you cannot find the nails, use a wood chisel to break up the section and remove it in pieces. Be careful with the chisel so that you don't damage the adjacent boards or the building felt under the siding.

Cut a new piece of clapboard to length and coat the ends with primer. Before pushing the new board into place, examine the building felt on the wall for rips or tears. Patch those with new pieces of felt.

Tap the new board in place and secure it with finishing nails. If you have to nail close to the ends of the board, drill pilot holes first to keep the board from splitting. Countersink the nail heads and fill the holes with wood filler. Caulk the seams on either side of the new board and paint it to match the surrounding wall.

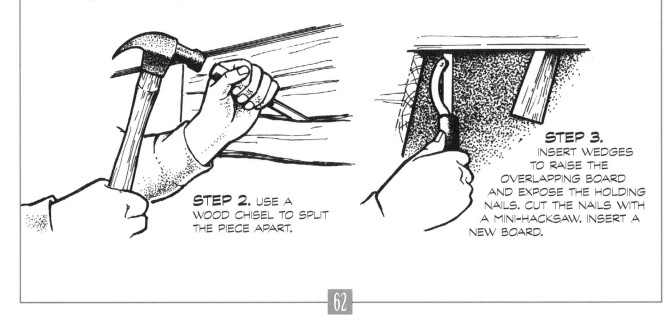

STEP 2. USE A WOOD CHISEL TO SPLIT THE PIECE APART.

STEP 3. INSERT WEDGES TO RAISE THE OVERLAPPING BOARD AND EXPOSE THE HOLDING NAILS. CUT THE NAILS WITH A MINI-HACKSAW. INSERT A NEW BOARD.

Metal and Vinyl Siding

Many older homes have wooden clapboard siding, but the newer ones have siding made of aluminum or vinyl. Vinyl and aluminum require less upkeep than wood does, but they are not entirely maintenance free. They should be cleaned periodically, and damage in the form of dents, splits, and cracks, should be repaired as soon as possible.

Most manufacturers recommend washing the siding twice a year to remove dirt, grime, and mildew. Generally, a forceful spray from a garden hose is enough to wash off light coatings of dust and dirt. Areas with thick accumulations of grime may have to be scrubbed with a brush and cleaning agent. Use a nonabrasive household detergent mixed with water for that purpose.

Connect an extension pole with a brush attachment to your garden hose for scrubbing areas that are out of reach. Those units, available at home centers, have a reservoir that adds detergent to the water and sprays the mixture through the brush attachment. After scrubbing the siding, rinse off the detergent with clear water.

In some places the siding may have dark gray or black patches that resemble soot, and resist cleaning with ordinary detergent. Mildew is the most likely cause of those spots and can be eradicated by washing it with a solution of three parts water to one part chlorine bleach. Wear goggles and rubber gloves when you apply the mixture; it can irritate the skin. After washing the affected area, allow the bleach solution to dry without rinsing.

Aluminum siding is durable, but it can be scratched or dented easily. Remove scratches by sanding the siding with fine-grit sandpaper; then prime the area with a primer formulated for aluminum. Finally, apply an exterior house paint that matches the color of the surrounding siding.

TOOL BOX

- SCRUB BRUSH
- HOSE WITH EXTENSION AND BRUSH ATTACHMENT
- ELECTRIC DRILL WITH BITS
- SCREWDRIVER, WASHERS, AND SHEET-METAL SCREWS
- PLIERS
- SANDPAPER
- AUTOBODY FILLER
- UTILITY KNIFE
- CAULKING GUN WITH COMPOUND
- POP-RIVET TOOL AND RIVETS

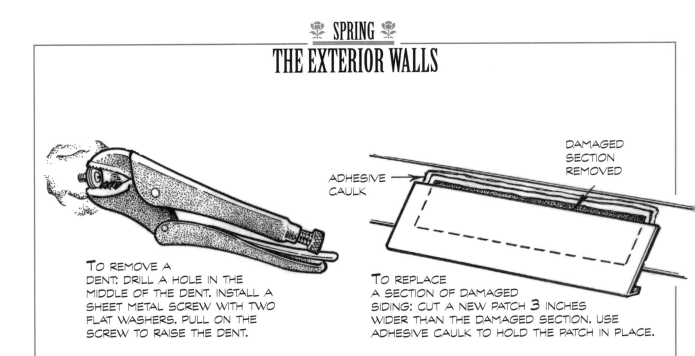

TO REMOVE A DENT: DRILL A HOLE IN THE MIDDLE OF THE DENT. INSTALL A SHEET METAL SCREW WITH TWO FLAT WASHERS. PULL ON THE SCREW TO RAISE THE DENT.

ADHESIVE CAULK

DAMAGED SECTION REMOVED

TO REPLACE A SECTION OF DAMAGED SIDING: CUT A NEW PATCH 3 INCHES WIDER THAN THE DAMAGED SECTION. USE ADHESIVE CAULK TO HOLD THE PATCH IN PLACE.

REMOVING DENTS: Dents have to be pulled out. If the depression is roughly circular, drill a 1/8-inch hole in the center. For irregular-shaped dents, drill a series of holes, about 1 inch apart around the deepest part of the depression. Drive 3/4-inch long sheet metal screws with two flat metal washers under each head into each hole. Grip the washers with a pair of pliers and pull on the screws to raise the dented metal.

Remove the screws; then sand the area. Sanding will remove rough spots and expose the bare metal. Fill the holes and remaining depressions with two-part auto body filler, which is available at auto supply stores. Use the plastic applicator provider in the filler kit to spread the filler compound and smooth it so that it is level with the surrounding area. After the patch hardens, sand it and then prime and paint it to match the surrounding area.

REPLACING DAMAGED SECTIONS: Splits or cracks are best repaired by removing the damaged section and replacing it with a new piece. Start by cutting out the damaged section with a sharp utility knife. Leave an inch-wide strip of siding along the top, where it is attached to the wall. That will provide a gluing base for the new patch. Make vertical cuts about 3 inches on either side of the damaged area and lift it away. Cut the replacement patch, which is 4 inches wider than the width of the damaged piece, from a new piece of siding. Cut off the nailer strip along the top edge.

Apply a bead of adhesive caulking compound around the perimeter of the cutout. Fit the new patch into place, pressing it down to flatten and spread the adhesive. The top edge of the patch should butt against the bottom of the overlapping siding above. The bottom edge should hook under the bottom edge of the damaged siding. In most

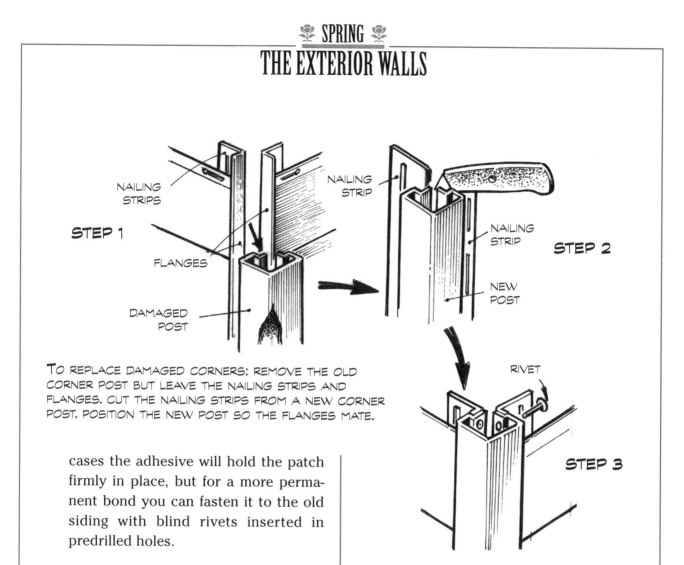

STEP 1

NAILING STRIPS

FLANGES

DAMAGED POST

NAILING STRIP

NAILING STRIP

NEW POST

STEP 2

RIVET

STEP 3

TO REPLACE DAMAGED CORNERS: REMOVE THE OLD CORNER POST BUT LEAVE THE NAILING STRIPS AND FLANGES. CUT THE NAILING STRIPS FROM A NEW CORNER POST. POSITION THE NEW POST SO THE FLANGES MATE.

cases the adhesive will hold the patch firmly in place, but for a more permanent bond you can fasten it to the old siding with blind rivets inserted in predrilled holes.

REPLACING DAMAGED CORNERS: Damaged corner posts also can be replaced, but the procedure requires carefully cutting the main part of the old post away, yet leaving the flanges and nailing strips attached to the house. The flanges will provide a mounting surface for securing the replacement post.

Begin by slicing down the sides of the damaged post with a sharp utility knife. The object is to remove the corner section but leave the nailing strip and the flange that projects at right angles from it. Cut off only the nailing strips, not the flanges, from a new corner post.

Apply a bead of adhesive caulk to the outside of the flanges on the replacement post; then fit it into position so that the flanges on the replacement post mate with those attached to the house. In addition to the adhesive, you will have to install long, blind rivets through both pairs of flanges to keep the new post securely in place. The rivets should be spaced at 18-inch intervals along the flanges.

Stucco

Stucco is a surface coating made of Portland cement, sand, and sometimes a plasticizing agent, such as lime. It is also known as Portland cement plaster. Since stucco can be colored with mortar colorants and textured with a variety of tools, it is an ideal medium for dressing up a drab concrete-block wall. It also can be applied to a wooden surface, provided that building felt and wire mesh are mounted to the substrate beforehand.

Only a few materials are needed for making stucco: a bag of Portland cement and a bag of silica sand, both of which are sold in 100-pound bags and together will cover about 300 square feet; and perhaps some liquid concrete bonding adhesive, sold in quarts and gallons, the label specifying covering capacity. You also can buy liquid mortar colorant if you would like a green, red, buff, rose, or cream-colored wall.

You'll also require a few basic tools for mixing and applying the stucco. For mixing, get a 5-gallon bucket and hand mixer — a tool that looks like a large potato masher. Mixing stucco is hard work, but you can make it less of a chore if you use a 1/2-inch electric drill (do not use a 3/8-inch drill for this chore; the motor may burn out under the heavy load) and a power-mixing attachment. You'll need a cement trowel for applying the stucco, a rubber float for smoothing it, and a gardener's trowel for scooping it from the mixing bucket.

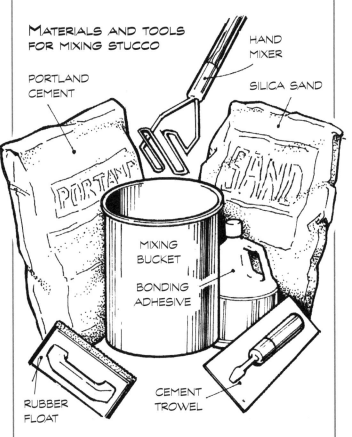

MATERIALS AND TOOLS FOR MIXING STUCCO

PORTLAND CEMENT

HAND MIXER

SILICA SAND

MIXING BUCKET

BONDING ADHESIVE

RUBBER FLOAT

CEMENT TROWEL

In general, stucco will adhere well to new concrete walls because the surface has an open texture that quickly draws the stucco into the minute pores of the concrete. Since the materials are similar, there is also a chemical bond as well as a mechanical one. Surface preparation consists of dampening, but not saturating, the wall with a fine water spray. You must keep the surface damp while you are working. Maintaining the damp surface is not necessary if you use a liquid bonding agent. The adhesive works even when it's dry.

Older surfaces may require more work, particularly if they are painted. First, scrape the wall with a wire brush to remove any loose dirt or paint. Next, spray the wall with a fine water mist. If the water is readily absorbed, it's likely that the stucco will form a good bond with the surface. If droplets form and the water runs down the wall, the surface is probably inadequate for a good bond. In that case it's best to apply a liquid bonding agent before attempting

to stucco the wall. In extreme examples, it may be necessary to have the wall sandblasted to expose a more porous surface. Another alternative is to mount waterproof felt and metal lath on the wall.

Pick a mild day to work and avoid days with high humidity; the excessive moisture in the air can extend the drying time of the stucco. It's also best to avoid hot, sunny days. The heat will cause the stucco to dry prematurely, shrink, and develop hairline cracks. If cracks do develop, they can be filled by brushing a slurry — essentially a mixture of Portland cement and water — into the cracks.

Mixing stucco is not particularly difficult, but it can be messy, so wear old clothes — including heavy-duty work gloves to protect your hands — and spread a drop cloth on the work area before you start. Pour two quarts of water into the bucket and add equal parts of cement and sand. Mix everything together, gradually adding more stucco and sand until the mixture has the consistency of a heavy paste. The stucco will harden quickly, so avoid mixing more than you can apply in an hour.

Use the garden trowel to scoop the stucco from the bucket and deposit it on the cement trowel. Trowel it onto the wall in a 1/4-inch thick layer and use the rubber float to smooth the entire

- STUCCO MIX
- 5-GALLON BUCKET
- HAND MIXER
- CEMENT TROWEL
- RUBBER FLOAT
- GARDENER'S TROWEL
- WIRE BRUSH

THE EXTERIOR WALLS

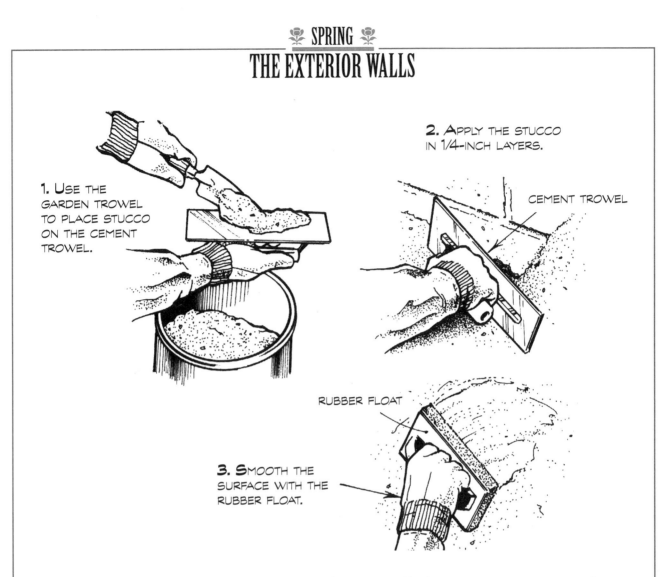

1. Use the garden trowel to place stucco on the cement trowel.

2. Apply the stucco in 1/4-inch layers.

CEMENT TROWEL

RUBBER FLOAT

3. Smooth the surface with the rubber float.

spread. Work in small areas — about 5 feet by 5 feet. That will allow you time to spread and smooth the stucco before it hardens.

Of course, you're not restricted to making a smooth surface. You can experiment with textural effects with improvised tools. You can, for example, grain the surface by dragging a piece of corrugated cardboard through the wet stucco. The cardboard will wear quickly, so have plenty on hand. You also can create a pebbled surface by flicking the stucco mix from a stiff, long-bristled brush. If the texture is too rough, smooth the peaks and bumps by drawing the trowel across the surface. These techniques are not difficult to master, but it's best to practice on a piece of scrap board before attempting to execute them on the finished wall.

Ideally, stucco should not be painted. The color should be added to the mix so that it becomes an integral part of the medium and will not peel or wear off. Even if some of the surface material chips away, the color will remain in the underlying core.

Over the years, however, some stucco walls can become shabby, particularly those with numerous patches. In this case it's necessary to either resurface the wall with a new layer of stucco or paint the surface. Of the two choices, painting may be easier, but it may lead to problems in the future. If the paint starts to peel, you'll have to scrape the loose paint off the wall, which may be difficult on a textured surface, before you can repaint.

If you decide to repaint, choose a top-quality acrylic latex paint. The painted surface will wear well, so repainting will not be necessary for a number of years. Carefully clean the stucco surface to remove all dirt, grease, and loose stucco. Then apply the paint with a long-nap roller or masonry brush.

Repointing Bricks

Bricks have been a popular building material in America since the mid-seventeenth century. The English constructed brick buildings in their Virginia colonies, while the Dutch used brick to build their homes in New York State. Today, brick is still a popular building material.

A brick wall would seem to be an intractable monolith unaffected by time or nature. But that is not the case, and sooner or later all brick structures will show signs of deterioration from age and exposure to the elements. The first signs of decay usually appear in the mortar joints as cracks, gaps, and erosion. Loose mortar joints allow water to permeate and damage the surrounding bricks. Unchecked, water can penetrate to the interior of the building, causing further damage.

The major causes of mortar failure are weathering, ground settling, poor design and construction, and improper exterior maintenance. Of course, no one can control the weather. Rain and snow force some moisture into the mortar. And when the moisture freezes, it expands and breaks apart the mortar.

Ground settling is another condition that we cannot control. The ground expands and contracts with ambient temperature and moisture. The wall will rise and fall with the ground, and eventually cracks develop in the mortar.

Construction techniques also can affect how a mortar joint will weather. It is essential, for example, to shape the profile of the joint, called "pointing," so that it sheds water. The most popular profile is the concave joint, although v-joints, flush joints, and weathered joints are also common. Improper construction materials can cause masonry to deteriorate as well. Mortar that's too hard will contract excessively and develop cracks. Mortar that's too soft will disintegrate in harsh weather.

Finally, it is possible for masonry to deteriorate if it's subjected to excessive amounts of water. That can happen if gutters or downspouts fall into disrepair and dump runoff water onto the masonry. Also, if drains are allowed to clog up, standing water can accumulate around walls and damage the mortar. Those conditions should be corrected before you attempt to repair the masonry damage.

If you have any masonry surfaces around your home, you should inspect them and evaluate their state of repair. Usually, a visual inspection will be enough, but in some areas you may have some doubts concerning the integrity of the mortar. Here you can chip away judiciously at the mortar with a hammer — use a mason's hammer or a ball-peen hammer — and cold chisel. If the mortar crumbles away, the joint should be repaired. The process of removing and replacing damaged mortar is called repointing or tuck-pointing.

After you've evaluated the brickwork, you'll know if the joints must be repointed and the amount of work required. Then you can decide if you want to tackle the job yourself or call in a professional. In general, filling small cracks and replacing missing mortar are

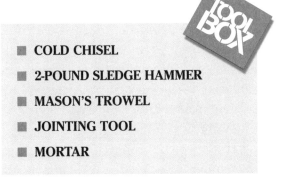

- **COLD CHISEL**
- **2-POUND SLEDGE HAMMER**
- **MASON'S TROWEL**
- **JOINTING TOOL**
- **MORTAR**

within the skills of the average do-it-yourselfer. But extensive repairs and areas with missing or damaged bricks should be left to a contractor. Also, it's not safe to attempt repointing while working from a ladder. So call in a professional to do chimney or second-story repointing or else rent scaffolding.

If you decide to repoint, you'll need a few tools: a cold chisel that should be narrower than the mortar joint; a 2-pound sledge hammer; a mason's trowel, for mixing and holding mortar; a pointing tool, for pushing the mortar into the joint; a jointing tool, for shaping the contour of the joint — if you're creating a concave joint, you can use a convex jointer; a large dowel or even the back of a teaspoon; and a stiff-bristle brush to remove residual mortar. You'll also need the proper safety gear: safety goggles for your eyes, heavy-duty gloves for your hands, work shoes, and if you're working overhead, a hard hat.

Of course, you'll need new mortar. You can make it by mixing type N masonry cement and masonry sand — do not use beach sand. There are different types of masonry cement, designated by the letters M, S, N, and O, indicating the varying proportions of their ingredients. But type N is a good, all-purpose mix. The sand is an aggregate that softens the mortar and allows it to expand and contract with the surrounding bricks.

STEP 1: After you've collected the proper tools and materials, you can begin. Start by chiseling out the deteriorated mortar from between the bricks. Most authorities advocate removing the old mortar to a depth of about two and a half times the width of the joint. Work carefully to remove the old mortar without damaging the surrounding brick.

Chiseling is tedious, but it's possible to make the job easier by renting a power grinder. A power grinder quickly can remove stubborn mortar, but if used carelessly, it can damage the bricks as well. To avoid gouging the bricks, use the grinder only on horizontal joints that are at least a half-inch wide.

STEP 2: After you've chiseled out all the old mortar, wash the joints by spraying them with a garden hose.

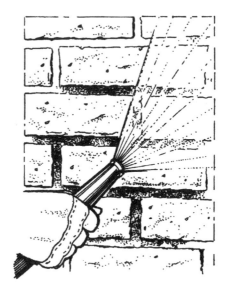

STEP 1. CHISEL OUT THE DETERIORATED MORTAR FROM BETWEEN THE BRICKS. WEAR GLOVES AND EYE PROTECTION.

STEP 2. USE A STIFF BRUSH TO CLEAN THE JOINTS THEN SPRAY WITH A GARDEN HOSE.

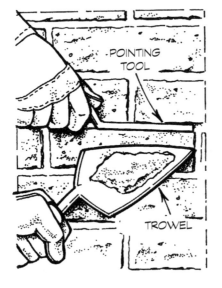

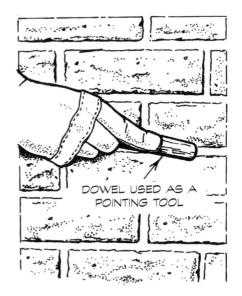

STEP 3. MIX THE MORTAR. POSITION SOME MORTAR ON A TROWEL THEN PUSH IT INTO THE JOINTS WITH A POINTING TOOL.

STEP 4. SHAPE THE JOINT CONTOURS WITH A JOINTING TOOL. SHAPE THE VERTICAL JOINTS FIRST, THEN DO THE HORIZONTAL ONES.

STEP 3: Next, mix the mortar ingredients with the trowel. Mix three parts sand to one part masonry cement and mix only as much as you can work with in about 30 minutes. Dry-mix these ingredients first before adding water. Add water slowly until the mix achieves the consistency of a stiff paste.

Position a ball of mortar on the bottom of the trowel. Use the pointing tool to push it from the trowel into the joint. Allow the mortar to harden slightly.

STEP 4: Shape the contour by running the joint tool along the joint. Shape the vertical joints first and then the horizontal ones. After the mortar has hardened, finish the job by brushing away any excess with the stiff brush. ⊕

Asphalt Driveway

Asphalt, also called blacktop, is basically aggregate — crushed stones or gravel — held together by a petroleum binder. An asphalt driveway may look durable and impervious to the elements, but in fact seasonal temperature fluctuations quickly can cause it to deteriorate into an eyesore. During the summer months, the sun's intense heat dries out the asphalt surface and causes it to oxidize. Soon, a network of hairline cracks develop in the surface.

At first those cracks are only minor imperfections, but left unattended, they can develop into major headaches. Weeds usually force their way through the crevices, widening them. In winter, water entering into the cracks will freeze and expand, opening them even more. The water also can penetrate to the subbase and undermine it. If that occurs, the asphalt surface can cave in and develop into a pothole. A little preventive maintenance can keep your asphalt driveway structurally sound and looking good for many years to come.

Begin by giving the driveway a careful visual inspection. If it's in relatively

- **PUTTY KNIFE**
- **STIFF BRUSH AND CLEANING DETERGENT**
- **ASPHALT PATCH MIX**
- **BALL-PEEN HAMMER**
- **COLD CHISEL**
- **ASPHALT CRACK FILLER**
- **ASPHALT SEALER AND APPLICATOR**

good condition, with only hairline cracks, it can be treated by applying a sealer. Larger cracks, 1/8-inch or wider, should be cleaned and filled with crack filler. Holes and depressions should be cleaned and filled with cold-mix asphalt patch. Sealer, crack filler, and asphalt patch are available at home centers or most large hardware stores.

Before starting the project, check the local weather reports. Blacktop materials set better and form a stronger bond when the temperature is at least 55 degrees, so choose a warm day to work. Postpone the job if rain is in the forecast; rain will wash the sealer away and undo your work.

Next, consider your working clothes. Applying the sealer is messy work, and most sealers have an emulsified asphalt or coal tar base that can be difficult to remove from clothing. It's best then to wear old clothes that you can trash afterward. You also may consider buying disposable coveralls, which are available at auto supply stores. Be sure to wrap your shoes in plastic to protect them.

Surface preparation is an important part of the job. The repair materials will not bond properly to a dirty surface. Start by pulling out all weeds and clumps of grass growing through the cracks. Then use a putty knife or ice scraper to dislodge and remove cakes of mud and grease adhering to the blacktop. Finally, use detergent and a stiff brush to wash the driveway. When you're finished, the surface should be clean and free of dirt, oil, and grease.

PATCHING HOLES: If your driveway has holes or depressions, you can fill them with a cold-mix asphalt patch. Careful preparation is essential to making a strong, solid patch. Dig out any loose debris or aggregate from the hole; then scrape the sides to ensure the edges are firm. If possible use a chisel

to undercut the sides of the hole. That undercutting will help to secure the patch. When the hole is clean and dry, you can fill it. Trowel the patching compound into the hole in 1-inch layers. Pack each layer down by tamping it with a block of 2 x 4. The final layer should be about 1/2 inch above the driveway surface. The patch must be firmly packed down. An effective way to do that is by placing a board on the patch and driving a car over it.

PATCHING HOLES

UNDERCUT THE SIDES OF THE HOLE.

FILL THE HOLE WITH COLD-MIX ASPHALT PATCH.

PACK EACH LAYER DOWN BY TAMPING IT WITH A 4 X 4.

Cold-mix patch works well for small holes, but if your driveway has a number of large holes, consider filling them with hot-mix patch and sealer. The materials needed to apply hot-mix are not available to the do-it-yourselfer; a professional paving contractor must apply them.

FILLING CRACKS: Driveway cracks should be repaired with crack filler, which is available in 1-gallon liquid containers or in cartridges. The cartridges are easy to use. Insert one into a caulking gun and snip off the end of the plastic nozzle. Squeeze the trigger to eject a stream of filler. Cartridges are convenient but are more expensive to use than the liquids.

The crack must be cleaned before you can fill it. Yank out all weeds and vegetation; then remove loose debris with a wire brush or compressed air. Wear a face shield if you use compressed air. Fill deep cracks more than 1/2-inch deep with sand. Carefully tamp the sand down until it is 1/4 inch from the surface. If you're using liquid filler, pour it into the crack until it is level with the surface. Inject cartridge filler into the crack as a continuous bead. Allow it to set for about 10 minutes and then use a putty knife or trowel to smooth and level it with the surface.

After filling the holes and cracks, you'll want to apply a sealer to the blacktop. It's best, however, to wait a few days for the patches to cure properly. The time may vary for each product, so check the manufacturer's instructions before proceeding.

SEALING THE SURFACE: Asphalt sealers usually come in 5-gallon cans, which is enough to cover about 250 square feet. Two types are available: sealers

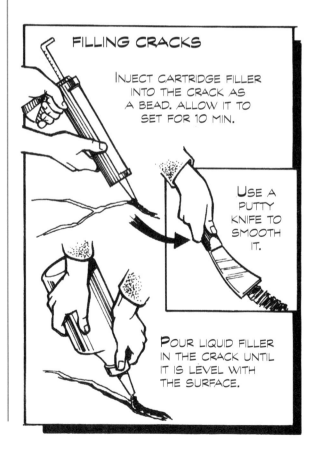

FILLING CRACKS

INJECT CARTRIDGE FILLER INTO THE CRACK AS A BEAD. ALLOW IT TO SET FOR 10 MIN.

USE A PUTTY KNIFE TO SMOOTH IT.

POUR LIQUID FILLER IN THE CRACK UNTIL IT IS LEVEL WITH THE SURFACE.

and sealer/fillers. Ordinary sealers are made with coal-tar emulsions and are fundamentally cosmetic. Sealer/fillers are a better choice because they have tiny fibers mixed in the emulsion and help to seal the hairline cracks that may be present in the asphalt.

In addition to the sealer, you'll need an applicator. Squeegee/brush combinations are available.

The squeegee is good for spreading the sealer, but the brush is better for working it into the surface. Mix the sealer thoroughly before applying it, and then pour a small amount at the garage end of the driveway. Spread the sealer across the width, working it into the surface. Continue the process to the end of the driveway. After you have coated the entire driveway, allow about 48 hours curing time. ⊕

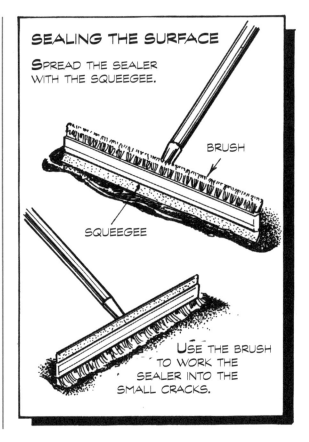

SEALING THE SURFACE

SPREAD THE SEALER WITH THE SQUEEGEE.

BRUSH

SQUEEGEE

USE THE BRUSH TO WORK THE SEALER INTO THE SMALL CRACKS.

Chimneys

Burning wood in the fireplace creates thick deposits of creosote in the flue. Even seasoned hardwood that has a low resin content can contribute to creosote buildup. There are two important reasons for removing these deposits. Creosote and soot deposits are highly flammable and are the leading cause of chimney fires. Also, they are acidic and if not removed, they can attack the mortar and damage the masonry in the chimney.

In medieval times it was not difficult to clean castle or manor house chimneys because the flues were large enough for men to climb into them on ladders. By the 18th century fireplaces and flues were smaller and narrower. Chimney sweeps employed small boys to climb up and sweep out a chimney. The boys often were forced to squeeze into narrow flues and navigate around bends and sharp curves. Sometimes they got stuck and were suffocated by the soot and dust around them. In colonial America, homeowners dropped a live chicken down their chimneys. The frightened bird would squawk and flap its wings dislodging the soot and cre-

Historic America

IN COLONIAL TIMES HOMEOWNERS CLEANED THEIR FLUES BY DROPPING A LIVE CHICKEN DOWN THE CHIMNEY. FOR LARGER FLUES THEY USED A GOOSE.

osote. For larger chimneys the homeowner used a goose.

Now that winter is over, it's a good time to inspect your fireplace and chimney for damage and for soot and creosote deposits. Some homeowners wait until the fall to do that, but if the inspection reveals flue damage, there's not much time to make repairs before the cold weather sets in.

Inspection is not difficult, but it is a dirty job and can be dangerous because it involves climbing on the roof to look at the chimney. Cleaning the chimney is more difficult. If you are unsteady working on your roof or if you have a high, steeply pitched roof, it may be best to leave the job to a professional chimney sweep.

To inspect the flue, first spread a drop cloth in front of the fireplace. Next, carefully open the damper as far as it will go. You'll need a flashlight with a powerful beam to look up into the flue. There's a good chance that dislodged soot or creosote will fall into your face, so wear safety goggles and a respirator for protection.

Inspect the smoke chamber above the damper; then try to look up the flue toward the top of the chimney. If you have a clear view of the entire flue, you can make your inspection without having to climb on the roof. First, look at the condition of the masonry and flue tiles; broken tiles or large cracks should be repaired. Second, look for creosote deposits. Any deposits 1/4-inch thick are a fire hazard. Finally, look for any debris or obstructions that could block the flow of smoke or keep heat from rising.

If you cannot get a good look at the top of the flue from the fireplace, you'll have to climb up and inspect it from the chimney. The safest way to climb up a pitched roof is on a safety ladder. You can make a safety ladder by attaching ridge hooks — available from most home centers or large hardware stores — to one end of a single-ladder section. The hooks grip the roof peak, and the ladder extends down to the eaves. Some roofs, such as hipped roofs, do

ANATOMY OF A FIREPACE & FLUE

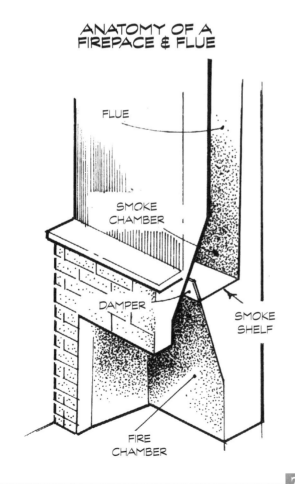

FLUE

SMOKE CHAMBER

DAMPER

SMOKE SHELF

FIRE CHAMBER

not have peaks, so this method will not work. In that case it's probably best to call a professional chimney sweep and not risk injury.

Inspect the flue by shining a light into it. If you find a heavy soot or creosote deposit, it must be swept. A number of makeshift methods can be employed by do-it-yourselfers to clean their chimneys. Some rural homeowners push an old Christmas tree up and down the chimney. Others fill burlap bags with rocks or chains and lower them on ropes in an effort to dislodge deposits. Still others try to scrub the flue by lowering tied bundles of newspapers down. The trouble with such improvised rigs is that they often damage the flue tiles causing bigger problems.

If you're going to tackle the job yourself, it's best to buy brushes designed for chimney sweeping. The brushes are available with round or rectangular shapes and with wire or polypropylene bristles. Round brushes are less expensive than the rectangular ones and will do a good job of general sweeping. Polypropylene bristles are cheaper than the wire bristles, but they're less effective in removing deposits, so it's best to pay a little more for wire brushes.

The brushes are pushed up or down the flue with flexible rods, which are

TOOL BOX

- ■ **FLASHLIGHT**
- ■ **SAFETY LADDER WITH ROOF RIDGE HOOKS**
- ■ **CHIMNEY BRUSHES WITH FLEXIBLE RODS**
- ■ **LONG-HANDLED SCRUB BRUSH**
- ■ **SMALL SHOVEL**
- ■ **PAIL**
- ■ **POLYETHYLENE SHEETING**

screwed into a threaded socket on the end of the brush. Each rod has a socket that allows additional rods to be added, giving you enough length to push the brush up the chimney. The most practical rods are made of fiberglass. They are available in three diameters: thick, .480 inch; medium, .440 inch; and thin, .340 inch. Although most professional chimney sweeps use the thick rods, homeowners will find the less-expensive medium rods just as serviceable.

In addition to the chimney brushes, you'll need a long-handled scrub brush — a professional model is called a pot brush — for scrubbing the fireplace and smoke chamber, a shovel, and a small pail for removing the soot and creosote. A shop-type vacuum cleaner is handy for cleanup. Do not attempt to use a standard household vacuum

CLEANING TOOLS

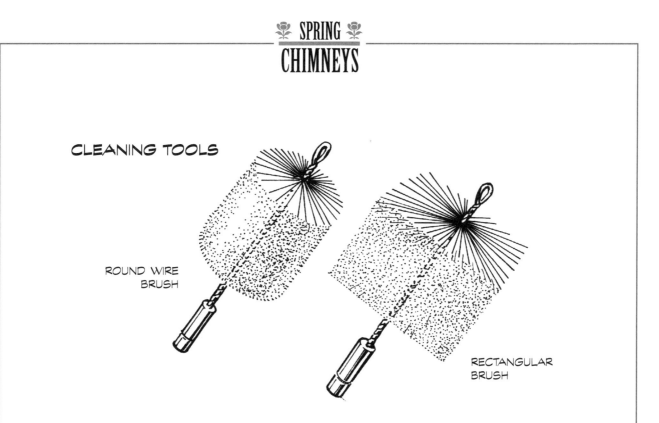

ROUND WIRE
BRUSH

RECTANGULAR
BRUSH

cleaner for the chore. Creosote dust is corrosive and can damage the appliance.

After you've assembled the materials and donned your safety gear, you can start the sweep by laying a drop cloth and sealing the fireplace. To seal the fireplace, tape a large sheet of polyethylene sheeting across the opening. Cut a slit that is large enough for you to manipulate the wire brush and rods in the center of the sheet.

Thread a rod onto the brush and push it past the damper — which obviously should be open — into the flue. Work the brush up and down to dislodge the deposits. Continue to work the brush up the flue by adding more rods. If you run into any obstructions, stop and have a professional inspect the chimney. You may be able to do the

job from the fireplace if you have a short chimney. Otherwise, you'll have to complete the sweep from the roof.

After you've swept the flue, use the scrub brush to clean the smoke chamber and the walls of the fireplace. Shovel all the soot, creosote, and debris into the pail and dispose of it outside. After cleaning the chimney and fireplace, attend to yourself. Creosote is a carcinogen, so put your dirty clothes in the washer and take a shower. ⊕

FLEXIBLE
CONNECTING RODS

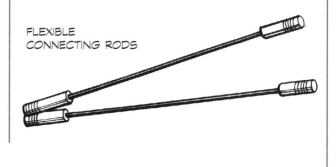

Exterior Cleaning

TOOL BOX

- **CLEANING AGENTS**
- **SCRUB BRUSH**
- **AUTOMOBILE WAND AND BRUSH ATTACHMENT**
- **HOSE**
- **POWER WASHER**

Most homeowners realize the value of interior cleaning but often fail to appreciate how important it is to clean the exterior of the house. It is, after all, the first thing your guests see when they come to visit. More important, however, a good washing will remove the dirt and grit particles that collect during the year. When agitated by the wind and rain, these abrasive particles can quickly mar or damage your siding or masonry. An annual cleaning, therefore, can help prolong the life of those surfaces.

It might seem that washing an entire house is a Herculean task, but actually it's not especially difficult. A number of tools, techniques, and cleaning agents can make the job easier. However, careful planning and preparation are essential if you want to do the job right.

It's best to wait for a warm, dry day. Don't attempt to wash on a windy day, or else you'll be fighting a lot of overspray. Start by protecting the area around the house. Cover small plants, shrubs, and areas of lawn near the house with plastic sheeting. Move lawn furniture and other movable objects away from the house. Use duct tape and plastic sheeting to cover all vents, electrical outlets, and outside light fixtures.

Next, inspect the house carefully: Look for areas with heavy stains (rust, organic or mildew stains, or heavy deposits of grime) or efflorescence (white powdery deposits of crystallized salts) on masonry surfaces. They should be cleaned by hand first, or else the stain may run onto adjacent surfaces when you wash.

In most cases those stains can be removed with soap, water, and a scrub brush. Stubborn stains may require a stronger cleaning agent. Rust, for example, can be removed with a solution of oxalic acid, 1/4 pound of oxalic acid powder per gallon of water. After washing off the stain, neutralize the residue acid by washing the area with a sodium bicarbonate solution, 1/8 cup of sodium bicarbonate per gallon of water. Take the time to repair the rusted metal now or else the stain will reappear.

Use a solution of ammonium sulfamate powder, an herbicide, 1 ounce of powder to a gallon of water, to remove organic stains. Neutralize the area with a sodium bicarbonate solution. Mildew can be removed with a solution of oxygen bleach powder, 1/4 pound and 1/8 cup of dishwashing liquid per gallon of water. Rinse the area with clear water.

You can scrub efflorescence off masonry with a solution of phosphoric acid: 1 part phosphoric acid to 9 parts water. Remember to add the acid to the water and not the water to the acid. Neutralize the area with the sodium bicarbonate solution.

Oxalic or phosphoric acid is available at janitorial or chemical supply centers. Ammonium sulfamate is available at most garden supply centers. Sodium bicarbonate, baking soda, is available at supermarkets. All are strong cleaning agents, so test them in an inconspicuous spot first and avoid using them in concentrated strengths. Remember to wear protective goggles and gloves when you are using them.

Once you've cleaned the trouble spots, you can turn your attention to the rest of the house. If the exterior surfaces are heavily soiled, consider renting a pressure washer to clean the

DO NOT SPRAY DIRECTLY AT WINDOWS.

WEAR SAFETY GOGGLES AND GLOVES.

KEEP THE SPRAY WAND ALMOST PERPENDICULAR TO THE WALL.

PROTECT SHRUBS AND SMALL PLANTS WITH PLASTIC SHEETING.

YOU CAN RENT A GAS-POWERED PRESSURE WASHER. THEY ARE RATED TO DELIVER WATER AT 1000 TO 2,500 PSI.

WASHERS RATED ABOVE 2,500 PSI ARE DESIGNED FOR INDUSTRIAL USE ONLY.

NOZZLES ARE AVAILABLE TO SHAPE THE SPRAY PATTERN.

house. Otherwise you can do the job with an ordinary garden hose and an automobile brush, which is available at auto supply stores. The brush has a threaded coupling that allows you to screw it onto the end of the hose. For reaching overhead sections, you can attach extension poles.

Most brush units have reservoirs for cleaning agents, but first you should try scrubbing the walls with plain water. If that doesn't remove the dirt, add the detergent. Keep in mind that excessive amounts of any cleaning agent can affect the plants and vegetation around your home.

Before starting, make sure that all doors and windows are closed. Turn on the water and start at the top and work down to the bottom of the wall. Work in overlapping sections about 5 feet wide. If you've used a cleaning agent, go over the wall again with clear water to rinse the detergent away. Avoid splashing water on the doors or windows, if possible.

If your house is especially dirty, you can power-wash it with a gas-powered pressure washer. Those units, which are available at most tool rental centers, are rated to deliver water at 1000 to 2,500 pounds per square inch. Washers rated above 2,500 psi are designed for industrial use and should not be used around the home.

The pressure washer generally comes with three different nozzle attachments — 15-, 25-, or 40-degree nozzles — for shaping the width of the spray pattern. The 15-degree nozzle is the most useful because it produces the narrowest and most controlled spray.

Pressure washers also have a reservoir for cleaning agents, but in most cases power spraying with clear water will be enough. For high walls, you can attach an extension wand to the pressure hose. Be careful, however, when you use the extension around electrical lines. Accidental contact with a high-tension line can be fatal.

Pressure washers are not difficult to use, but they can cause damage if not handled properly. Have the rental dealer demonstrate the unit before you take it home. High-pressure water actually can penetrate the skin and cause severe injury; never put your hands near the nozzle or point the spray wand at people or animals. Be sure to wear safety goggles.

When washing lap siding, angle the spray down to keep the water from penetrating under the siding. Do not spray directly at windows. The water pressure could break them. Finally, avoid using a pressure washer on delicate stucco exteriors because the high-pressure water can cause the stucco to disintegrate. ⊕

Termites

In spring the trees begin to bloom and birds and butterflies take wing — a delightful activity that happens above ground. Below ground there is also activity that homeowners are less likely to view with delight. Termites, waking from the inactivity of the long winter, begin to forage for food. From subterranean nests they invade areas where wood contacts the ground, or they build earthen tubes that give them protected access to wood above ground.

Some people believe that termites attack only older, wooden structures, while new homes, brick or stone buildings, and homes with termite barriers remain relatively safe from the marauders. The fact is that new homes — even houses under construction — are susceptible to termite attack. It is true that a building constructed entirely of stone or brick will not be a termite target, but those structures are extremely rare. Even so, termites will enter a home to eat whatever wood is in the house.

Termites can enter the home through expansion joints, plumbing areas, or in hairline cracks in the foundation. They construct "mud tubes,"

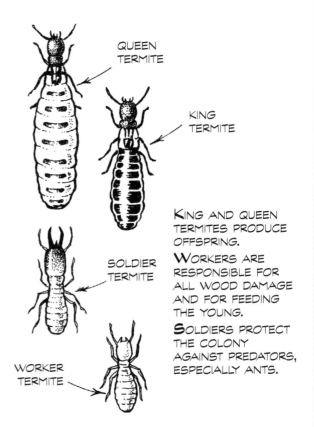

QUEEN
TERMITE

KING
TERMITE

SOLDIER
TERMITE

WORKER
TERMITE

KING AND QUEEN TERMITES PRODUCE OFFSPRING.

WORKERS ARE RESPONSIBLE FOR ALL WOOD DAMAGE AND FOR FEEDING THE YOUNG.

SOLDIERS PROTECT THE COLONY AGAINST PREDATORS, ESPECIALLY ANTS.

essentially termite tunnels, that allow them to travel from the soil up the foundation to the wood trim or frame. Most homes have wooden framing, floors, doors, and furniture that can attract termites. Metal shields or barriers over foundation walls can be an effective barrier against termites — as long as they retain their structural integrity. As a house settles, minute gaps usually open in the foundation and around the shields that allow termite penetration. In some cases termites have built tubes around the shields and entered the house.

Every homeowner should be concerned about termites. It is estimated that these voracious insects damage 1.8 million to 2 million homes each year. Often the homeowner is unaware that there is any termite activity until serious structural damage has occurred. It's difficult to spot termite infestation because the insects do not inhabit the structures of a house; they just forage

there. They live in nests widely spread beneath the soil, sometimes at a considerable distance from the house.

How can you tell if you have termite infestation? Sometimes you can see termites at work boring into your woodwork. You also may be able to see the tunnels and galleries that they create. Most of the time, however, you will not see anything. That's because these pests work within walls, below floors, and above ceilings, attacking structural members that are out of sight and not readily accessible. So it's possible to have termite infestation and not be aware of it. That's why it's a good idea to have your home inspected periodi-

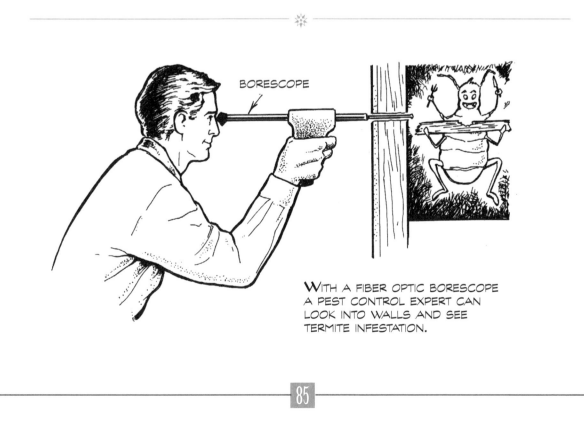

BORESCOPE

With a fiber optic borescope a pest control expert can look into walls and see termite infestation.

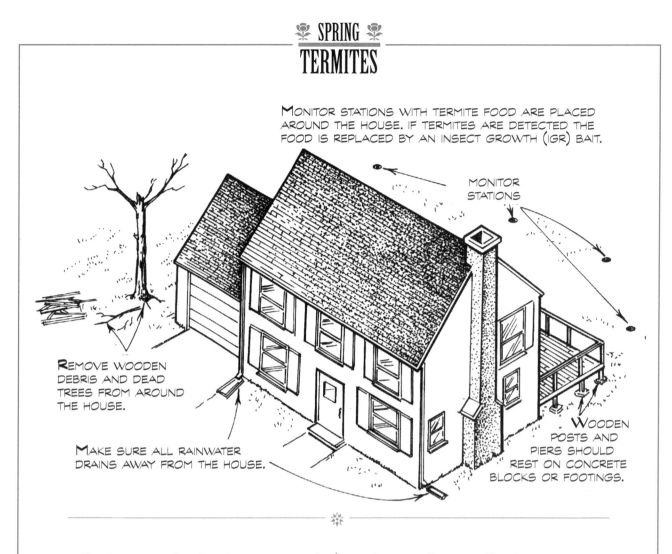

MONITOR STATIONS WITH TERMITE FOOD ARE PLACED AROUND THE HOUSE. IF TERMITES ARE DETECTED THE FOOD IS REPLACED BY AN INSECT GROWTH (IGR) BAIT.

MONITOR STATIONS

REMOVE WOODEN DEBRIS AND DEAD TREES FROM AROUND THE HOUSE.

MAKE SURE ALL RAINWATER DRAINS AWAY FROM THE HOUSE.

WOODEN POSTS AND PIERS SHOULD REST ON CONCRETE BLOCKS OR FOOTINGS.

cally by a professional pest-control operator, or PCO.

Pest-control experts know where to look for termites and have a variety of devices and detectors to determine the extent of infestation. One rather new and effective detector is the fiber optic borescope. With that device a trained technician can insert a small, lighted probe inside walls, beneath flooring, behind panels and other areas that normally are inaccessible for visual inspection and see if infestation is present.

Once infestation is detected, the professional can determine its extent and prescribe an effective treatment. Some homeowners and most environmentalists shudder at the word "treatment." They think it automatically involves using chemical pesticides. It is true that pesticides can be a reliable and effective method for dealing with termites. But they should be used only by professionals who are trained in their safe use.

Until recently, chemical pesticides were the main weapon that pest-control technicians used to deter termites. The PCO would inject the chemicals into the soil around the house, creating a subterranean barrier of pesticide. Any termite attempting to cross the barrier would ingest the pesticide and die. That barrier technique was the state-of-the art in termite control, but it also presented a number of problems that concerned homeowners, environmentalists, and pest-control experts.

While the barrier prevented termites from attacking the house, it did nothing to destroy the source of termite infestation — the nest. Eventually, other termites would emerge to replace their fallen comrades. It became necessary then to add more pesticide periodically in order to maintain the barrier's potency.

Environmentalists long have been concerned about the effects of any pesticide on the environment. They are aware, for example, that chemicals can travel through the ground to affect plants and vegetation. Pesticides also can penetrate deep into the ground to contaminate ground water.

Scientists have been working to find another way to fight termites. They developed a program that uses termite bait, which is effective against termites yet has low impact on the environment. The bait program is implemented in three phases.

In phase one the technician strategically places monitor stations in the ground around the home. The techni-

cian doesn't need to enter the home or drill holes in the structure to inject pesticide. The monitor stations contain termite food but no bait. They are designed to help evaluate the extent of termite problem. The technician checks the stations periodically for signs of termite activity. If termites are detected, the technician initiates phase two.

In phase two a special bait is placed in those stations with termite activity. The bait is an insect growth regulator, IGR, called hexaflumuron. Unlike other

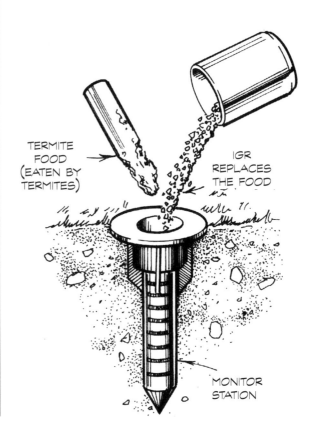

TERMITE FOOD (EATEN BY TERMITES)

IGR REPLACES THE FOOD

MONITOR STATION

pesticides, hexaflumuron does not permeate the ground; instead, the termites enter the station and feed on it. At the same time they deposit pheromones, or colony-specific scents that encourage other foraging workers to enter the bait stations to feed.

Having eaten the bait, the termites return to the nest apparently unharmed. However, they carry the IGR that they spread throughout the colony to the nonforaging soldiers, larvae, and small nymphs. Hexaflumuron does not kill the termites directly; instead, it disrupts their molting cycle by blocking the formation of chitin in their bodies. Unable to molt, the termites will die, and in a short time the termite nest will be eliminated.

Even though the colony is eliminated, it is possible that another colony may try to invade the area. To counter that threat, the pest-control technician leaves the stations in place and periodically checks them for signs of new infestation. That is phase three.

While termite bait is promising and is, in fact, the wave of the future in the termite-control arena, there is a downside to the technology. It may be months before the active-bait ingredient is distributed throughout a termite colony. For those who enjoy the "thrill of the kill," this can be a source of frustration.

The termite bait, hexaflumuron, is a natural agent rather than a pesticide. Natural agents are environmentally friendly and pose no threat to humans, birds or animals. Another such product is Bio-blast, a powder containing live spores of the insect-killing fungus Metarhizium anisopliae. The fungus has been shown to have great potential in fighting insect pests, but it needs further research and development before it can be used widely.

Some environmental groups suggest that homeowners can fight termites on their own by using nematodes. Nematodes, another natural agent, are tiny wormlike creatures that attack termites but will not harm people, plants, or pets. Nematodes are not available at the average home center but may be carried by some organic gardening supply companies. The only problem with do-it-yourself termite remedies is that it is difficult to evaluate their results. Since the termite colony is outside the house, how can you be sure that you've destroyed it? Usually, periodic follow-up inspections with sophisticated detectors are required.

While termite eradication is a job for a trained professional, the homeowner can do some things to make his home less inviting to termites. Eliminate wood-to-ground contact wherever possible. That means that wooden posts should rest on concrete blocks and wooden steps should be supported by a concrete slab. Also make sure that there is at least 6 inches of clearance between wood shingles or siding and the ground.

Termites thrive in moist soil. Make sure that the soil around your house is graded properly so that all rain water is

FILL CRACKS OR VOIDS IN THE FOUNDATION.

carried away from the foundation. Ventilate crawl spaces to reduce humidity and dampness. Covering the ground in the crawl space with polyethylene film also will help to control moisture.

REMOVE INFESTED STUMPS AND TREES NEAR YOUR HOUSE.

Screen all vents, including those in the attic and in crawl spaces, with 20-mesh noncorroding metal screening. Make certain that all gaps and cracks in the foundation are filled and sealed.

Finally, remove any wooden debris, including scrap lumber, tree limbs, and even sawdust from around the house. Stack firewood away from the house and remove tree stumps and dead trees. ⊕

CHECK ANY SECOND-HAND FURNITURE PRIOR TO PURCHASE.

SUMMER INSPECTION

SUMMER may seem more like a time for relaxation and play than for maintenance. Indeed, it is the ideal season to take time off for rest and vacation. However, some jobs around the house must be accomplished before you can relax completely.

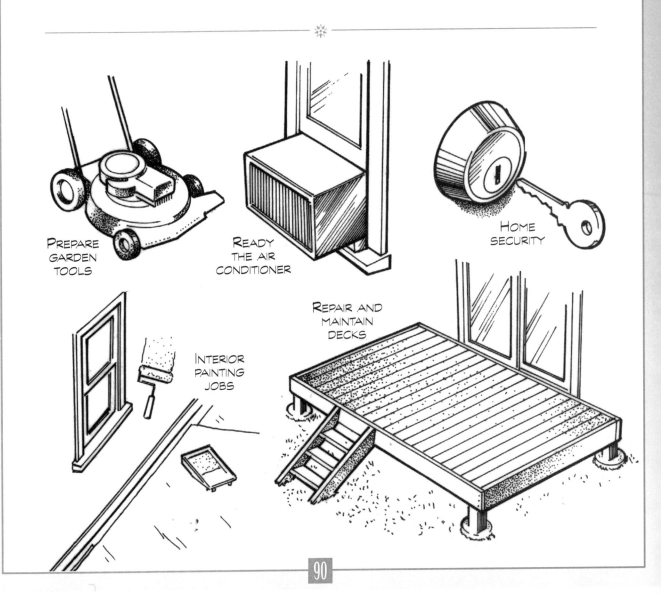

PREPARE
GARDEN
TOOLS

READY
THE AIR
CONDITIONER

HOME
SECURITY

INTERIOR
PAINTING
JOBS

REPAIR AND
MAINTAIN
DECKS

✓ First, it's important to **get the air conditioner ready** for the hot days ahead. Running it for extended periods of time can be expensive, and one way to cut energy costs is by **installing ceiling fans and a whole-house fan**.

✓ The lawn and garden will need attention, but before you can do any gardening chores, you will have to get the **lawn mower primed and ready** by cleaning the fuel tank, changing the oil, and replacing the filters. Sometimes it seems that maintaining a power mower may be more trouble than it's worth. If you have a large lawn, your only other option is to hire a garden service. If you have a small lawn, now is the time to consider buying a push mower.

✓ Summer is the time when leisure activities shift from indoors to outside. If outdoor cooking is likely to be a favorite activity, it will be necessary to **clean and prepare the barbecue** thoroughly. Also, you will want to give some **attention to your deck** and patio furniture. Do you have a fence around the perimeter of your property? Summer is a good time to **inspect the fence for possible damage**. If you have a **swimming pool**, it will require preparation and continual maintenance.

✓ Summer is a good time to tackle **indoor painting and refinishing projects** because you can work with the windows open and get good ventilation and air circulation.

✓ Naturally, you will want to take a vacation. But before you do, make sure that your home is secure from break-ins. Obviously, **home security** is a year-round concern, but statistics show that burglars are more active and break-ins are more common during the summer months. You will need to inspect all doors to be sure they have **strong locks**. You also will want to take adequate precautions to make sure your house looks occupied while you are away.

✓ Not all intruders will be human. Gardeners know that such animals as **deer and rabbits** can be a summertime nuisance as they forage through your garden for food. **Birds** also can become pests. So some time may have to be set aside for dealing with critters and pests.

✓ The major problem with working during the hot summer days is high **heat and humidity**. They can take a toll on the human body. Working hard on a hot summer day can bring on heat exhaustion or sunstroke.

Air Conditioner

Now is the time to inspect and clean your air conditioner and get it ready for the hot and humid days ahead. Care and preventive maintenance will keep the unit running efficiently and prevent malfunctions later on.

It will be helpful if you can identify the different components inside your unit and have some idea of their function. An air conditioner has a set of evaporator coils behind the front panel of the unit. Refrigerant circulates in the coils and changes from a liquid to a gas. When the refrigerant evaporates, it absorbs the heat from the surrounding air.

A blower, in the shape of a drum fan, also called a "squirrel cage," pulls the warm humid air from the room across the coils. The heat is absorbed from the air, and ambient moisture condenses and collects in a pan under the coils. The collected water flows by gravity to a second pan at the back of the unit. The blower pushes the cool, dry air back into the room. A metal barrier separates the evaporator coils and blower from the rest of the unit.

A compressor, centrally situated in the unit, pulls the refrigerant gas from

- **SCREWDRIVER**
- **VACUUM CLEANER WITH BRUSH AND CREVICE TOOL ATTACHMENTS**
- **MASKING TAPE AND PLASTIC BAGS**
- **PAINT BRUSH**
- **GARDEN HOSE**
- **COMPRESSED AIR**
- **OIL CAN WITH 10-20 NONDETERGENT MOTOR OIL**
- **FINE COMB (OPTIONAL)**
- **SANDPAPER**

the evaporator and compresses it back into a liquid. The liquid is pumped into the condenser coils, where it releases the captured heat into the surrounding air. A condenser fan, in front of the coils, draws air from the side vents and blows it across the condenser coils. That action cools the coils and pushes the released heat outdoors.

The condenser fan and the blower fan usually are powered by the same

motor. A common shaft that runs through the motor joins the fans.

Under the condenser coils is the other collector pan joined to the front pan by two tubes. In some units the collected water drains through a hole in the bottom of the pan. In other models it is picked up by a rotating ring around the condenser fan. The rotating "slinger" ring whips the water across the condenser coils. It cools the coils as it is pushed outside.

CLEANING & MAINTENANCE: Preventive maintenance consists of removing the unit from its housing — sometimes called the "sleeve" — cleaning the components and lubricating a few moving parts. You'll need only a few basic hand tools and a vacuum cleaner for that task.

Start by unplugging the air conditioner. Then remove the front grill and filter. The filter traps dirt, dust, and pollen and keeps it from collecting on

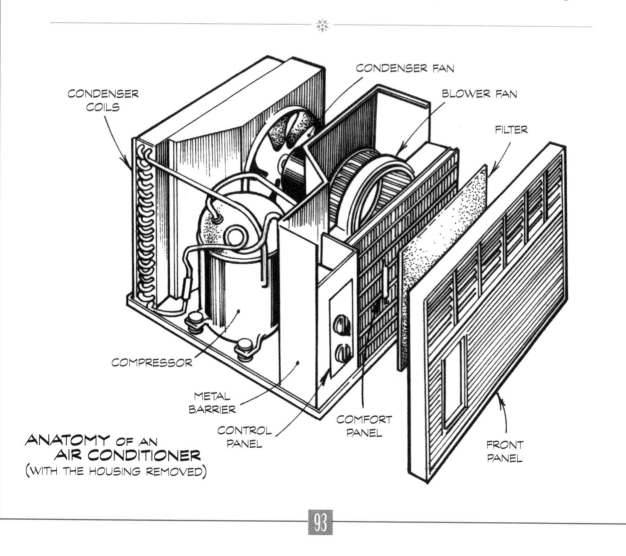

ANATOMY OF AN
AIR CONDITIONER
(WITH THE HOUSING REMOVED)

CONDENSER COILS

CONDENSER FAN

BLOWER FAN

FILTER

COMPRESSOR

METAL BARRIER

CONTROL PANEL

COMFORT PANEL

FRONT PANEL

the evaporator coils. A clogged filter will obstruct proper air circulation and impede operating efficiency. If the filter is dirty but in good condition, wash it with soap and water. Replace the filter if it's deteriorated. If you cannot replace it with an exact duplicate, you usually can buy a utility filter, which is available at home centers or appliance stores and can be cut to fit with a pair of scissors.

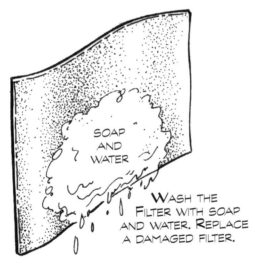

WASH THE FILTER WITH SOAP AND WATER. REPLACE A DAMAGED FILTER.

Remove the air conditioner from the window. Most air conditioners are heavy, so enlist the aid of a helper if necessary. Slide the unit out of its housing. With some units the housing is held in place with a few screws; remove the screws and set them aside.

You'll find that it's easier to give the appliance a thorough cleaning if you take it outside and place it on a couple of saw horses. Alternatively, you can rest the unit on 2 x 4s. Use a vacuum fitted with the crevice tool to clean dust and loose debris that may have accumulated around the components.

Remove stubborn dirt, grease, and grime with soap and water, but first seal the compressor, the electrical controls, and the fan motor with plastic bags. Use plenty of tape so that the plastic shields are completely watertight. Then use a paint brush to scrub the coils, fan blades, and collector pans with the warm, soapy water.

Rinse the appliance using a garden hose with a fine spray. Allow all the water to drain and the moisture to evaporate. You can hasten the drying process by blowing on the unit with compressed air. If you don't have an air compressor you can use a can of compressed air, which is available at hardware stores or photo supply stores. When the unit is thoroughly dry, remove the plastic shields and tape from the components.

Next, lubricate the fan motor with a few drops of 10-20 nondetergent motor oil (this is not necessary if the motor has sealed bearings). If your unit has a drain hole in the collector pan, make sure that it is open and free of debris.

Finally, examine the cooling fins on the condenser coils. Many units have a

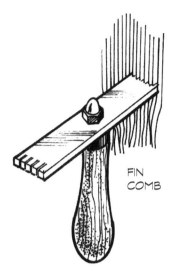

USE A FIN COMB OR A PUTTY KNIFE TO STRAIGHTEN THE CONDENSER FINS.

grid of soft aluminum fins designed to dissipate heat quickly. To be effective, there must be some space between each fin so that air can circulate. Unfortunately, the fins bend easily, and it's not uncommon to find large sections mashed together. You can straighten bent fins by drawing a screw-driver through the crushed sections, or you can purchase a fin comb at local appliance supply stores.

Before replacing the appliance in the window, examine the housing for signs of rust or corrosion. These should be removed with fine sandpaper, then primed and painted. Inspect the window sill and vacuum any accumulated dust and dirt. Now install the unit in the window. Most people assume that all air conditioners should be pitched so that the back of the unit is slightly lower than the front. That is true of units with a drain hole in the collector pans, but those units that remove water with the "slinger" ring should be perfectly level. If you're in doubt, check your owner's manual for installation instructions.

Install new foam insulation around the window, and don't forget to plug the unit in. ⊕

Ceiling Fans

Fans were the earliest form of cooling devices. Paintings on tomb walls show that the ancient Egyptians employed servants to wave palm branches to provide cooling breezes on hot days. The Japanese developed the folding fan, the Akomeogi, during the sixth century. Portuguese traders introduced it to the west in the 16th century and soon both men and women throughout the continent adopted it. By 1750, more than 150 fan makers plied their trade in Paris alone. In India, where the climate is often hot and humid, the punkah was developed. This was a cloth covered frame, which swung back and forth when a servant pulled on a cord. It was used to cool an entire room.

However, those were muscle-powered fans. Creative minds began to speculate on the possibility of mechanizing the fan. Thomas Jefferson designed a fan powered by a pendulum and clock mechanism. His notebooks contain detailed drawings and descriptions of such a fan, but there is no physical evidence that he ever built it.

This was before the introduction of

- **CLEANING CLOTHS**
- **SCREWDRIVER**

electrical power. In 1882, Thomas Edison developed the first practical system for providing electricity to homes and industry. Engineers now could attach an electric motor to the fan and suddenly an idea that seemed like a vague dream became a reality. In that same year Philip Diehl, considered to be the father of modern ceiling fan, introduced "The Diehl Electric Fan." Later he combined the electric chandelier and the fan into a single appliance which he called "The Diehl Electrolier."

By the late 1920s almost every restaurant, ice cream parlor, and fashionable dining room had at least one ceiling fan. A decade later the situation had changed. Air conditioning was developed, and although it consumed enormous quantities of power, it was affordable because electricity was relatively cheap. By the 1950s, the ceiling fan had gone the way of the horse-drawn buggy.

Two decades later, in the 1970s the ceiling fan started to make a comeback. The nation was hit with an energy crunch, and air conditioning was no longer cost-effective.

Today people recognize that like insulation and weather stripping, a ceiling fan can be an energy conservation investment. That's because ceiling fans use less power than air conditioners. Research shows that individuals remained comfortable in ambient temperatures between 72 degrees and 86 degrees when a ceiling fan was used to circulate the air.

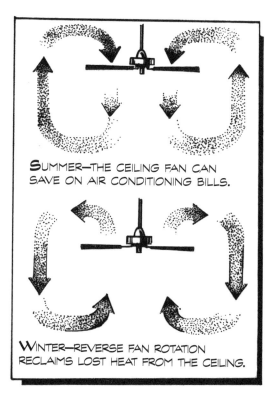

SUMMER—THE CEILING FAN CAN SAVE ON AIR CONDITIONING BILLS.

WINTER—REVERSE FAN ROTATION RECLAIMS LOST HEAT FROM THE CEILING.

Above 86 degrees, the fan alone is not effective; but operating with an air conditioner it can be a cost-effective way to cool your home. A ceiling fan working with an air conditioner on a low setting can provide the same comfort at less cost than the same air conditioner on a high setting. In cold weather the ceiling fan can operate in reverse to circulate warm air trapped near the ceiling and save from 5 percent to 10 percent of heating costs.

Fans are available in different sizes. The size is the span between tips of the blades. The most popular fan sizes are 32 inch, 38 inch, 42 inch, 44 inch, 52 inch. For maximum operating efficiency, match the fan size to the room size. A 32-inch fan will provide efficient air circulation in rooms up to 64 square feet, a 38-inch fan in rooms up to 96 square feet, a 42-inch fan in rooms up to 144 square feet, a 44-inch fan in rooms up to 225 square feet, a 52-inch fan in rooms up to 400 square feet. For larger areas, two or more fans may be needed. Never downsize a fan. A fan that is too small will have to work harder and use more electricity to cool a large room. When in doubt go up to the next larger fan size.

POSITIONING OF FANS: Most homeowners position the fan in the center of the ceiling. Used as a decorating accent, the fan can be positioned in a

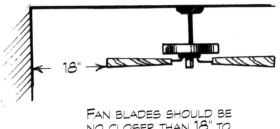

18"

FAN BLADES SHOULD BE
NO CLOSER THAN 18" TO
THE WALL.

LOW PROFILE

FOR SAFETY REASONS THE FAN
BLADES SHOULD BE AT LEAST 7
FEET AWAY FROM THE FLOOR. A
LOW PROFILE FAN IS AVAILABLE
FOR ROOMS WITH LOW CEILINGS.

corner, but the blades should be no closer than 18 inches to the wall. That distance will allow sufficient clearance for proper air circulation. In the bedroom the ideal location for the ceiling fan is over the foot of the bed, never directly over the head of the bed. A dining-room fan should have a reversing switch that allows the fan to create an updraft during dining. A down draft would cool hot food prematurely.

A ceiling fan cools and circulates room air most efficiently when the blades are 8 feet to 9 feet above the floor. For rooms with high ceilings, extension poles — available in lengths between 1 feet to 6 feet — can be attached between the ceiling mount and the fan.

For safety reasons, the fan blades should be at least 7 feet away from the floor. A low-profile fan, with the blades 8 inches from the ceiling, is available for rooms with low ceilings.

Some fans are controlled by a simple pull chain or wall switch, but other,

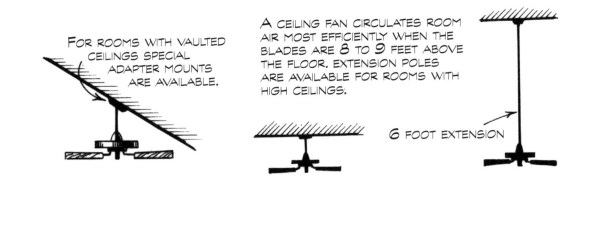

FOR ROOMS WITH VAULTED
CEILINGS SPECIAL
ADAPTER MOUNTS
ARE AVAILABLE.

A CEILING FAN CIRCULATES ROOM
AIR MOST EFFICIENTLY WHEN THE
BLADES ARE 8 TO 9 FEET ABOVE
THE FLOOR. EXTENSION POLES
ARE AVAILABLE FOR ROOMS WITH
HIGH CEILINGS.

6 FOOT EXTENSION

more sophisticated control devices, are also available. Wall controls include: fan/light control switches, multiple fan speed controls, and a three-speed-stepped control switch. Those switches shouldn't be confused with the ordinary household dimmer switch, which only should be used for incandescent lights. A wireless remote control, similar to those found on television sets, also is available.

Well-designed fan motors have sealed bearings so that they require no lubrication or maintenance. However, vibrations sometimes can cause the screws on the blade mounts or motor housing to work loose. That results in noisy fan operation. The remedy is simple: Tighten any loose screws with a screwdriver. Do not overtighten. Before turning on the fan, spin the blades by hand to be sure they rotate freely.

The rotating blades usually pick up dust and dirt, so periodic cleaning is a must. Clean the blades and housing with a mild detergent. Do not use abrasive agents because they can mar the finish. It's also a good idea to protect wooden fan blades with a light coat of furniture polish. ⊕

HOUSEHOLD HELPS • STORAGE

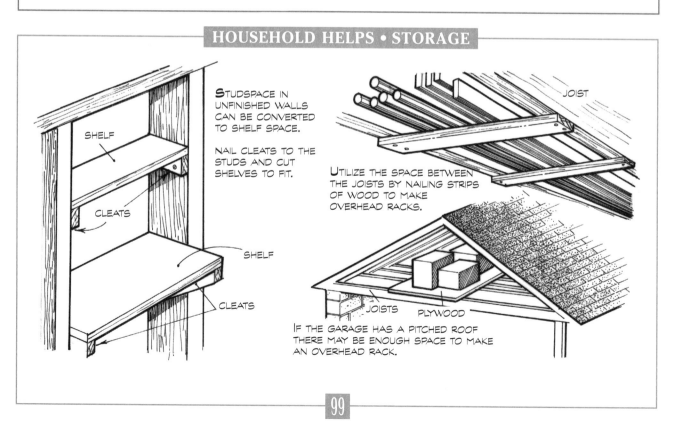

SHELF

CLEATS

SHELF

CLEATS

Studspace in unfinished walls can be converted to shelf space.

Nail cleats to the studs and cut shelves to fit.

JOIST

Utilize the space between the joists by nailing strips of wood to make overhead racks.

JOISTS   PLYWOOD

If the garage has a pitched roof there may be enough space to make an overhead rack.

Cooling the House

During the summer months it seems that the only way to keep the house cool is by running the air conditioner. Unfortunately, many homeowners have found that using their air conditioners for lengthy periods can drive up the electric bill. In addition, the increased energy consumption of all the air conditioners in a community can have a negative effect on the environment, because it requires the utility company to burn more fuel to generate additional power.

Fortunately, you can keep your house cool in other ways without using the air conditioner. They are more economical and environmentally friendly because they use shade to block the rays of the sun and ventilation to pull the hot air from the house. They will not eliminate the need for air conditioning, but they can reduce the time you run it and thereby help to cut your electric bill.

To know how to use shading effectively, it is helpful to understand that the summer sun heats your house. In the morning the sun assaults the east side of the house first. Its effects will not be felt immediately because sunrise is the coolest part of the day. Unless the house has retained heat from the previous day, it will take time before the sun's heat can penetrate through the insulation in the walls to the interior. By late morning, however, that heat can be felt inside.

At noon the sun is almost directly overhead. If the house is properly designed, the eaves will keep the sun's rays from hitting the walls. The roof, however, has no protection, and it will bear the brunt of the sun's intensity. On a hot summer day, roof temperatures can soar to well over 160 degrees. Inside the attic can feel like an oven. If the attic floor has enough insulation, it will take time before that heat can drop below into the living quarters.

In the afternoon, the sun works its way down into the western horizon and the wall facing that direction begins to heat up. The outside temperature will peak about 4 p.m., then it will start to drop. However, the air will continue to feel hot for hours afterward, because of the heat absorbed in the walls. This sensation of heat is exacerbated by the

COOLING THE HOUSE

humidity, which continues to rise in the early evening.

One way to keep the house cool is by shading it from the sun and blocking the rays before they penetrate inside. The eastern and western walls should have the most protection because they are exposed to most of the sun's radiation. While the heat can penetrate through the walls, the most direct route to the interior is through the windows.

A number of devices are available that can be fitted across the windows to block the sun's rays. Shades, blinds, and curtains are the most popular because they are relatively inexpensive and easy to install. Ideally, their outerfacing

should be light colored to reflect the rays and heat away from the window. Dark colors, on the other hand, capture the radiation and draw it inside. The disadvantage to shades and blinds is that when they are closed, they block the view and they stop cool breezes from entering through the windows.

Other shading alternatives block the sunlight yet allow you to look out the windows. One is called shade cloth. It is screening made of aluminum or fiberglass, and it can effectively block up to 75 percent of the sunlight. Another option is a tinted plastic film that can be applied directly to the windows. It is available in different densities so that it

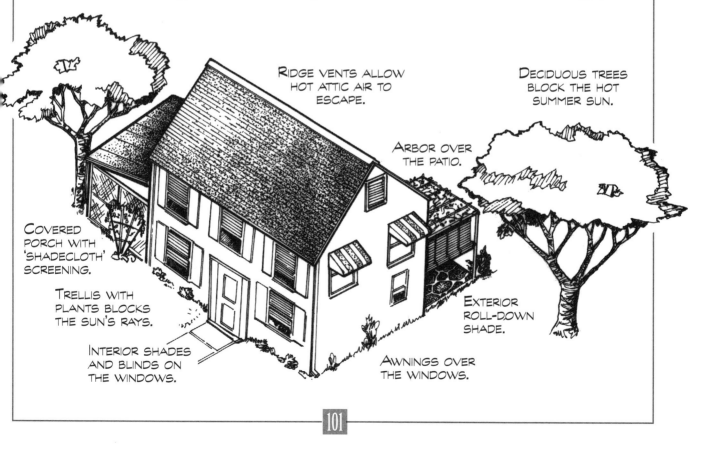

RIDGE VENTS ALLOW HOT ATTIC AIR TO ESCAPE.

DECIDUOUS TREES BLOCK THE HOT SUMMER SUN.

ARBOR OVER THE PATIO.

COVERED PORCH WITH 'SHADECLOTH' SCREENING.

TRELLIS WITH PLANTS BLOCKS THE SUN'S RAYS.

EXTERIOR ROLL-DOWN SHADE.

INTERIOR SHADES AND BLINDS ON THE WINDOWS.

AWNINGS OVER THE WINDOWS.

COOLING THE HOUSE

can block or reflect out the sun's rays. Those products are readily available in most southern states, but they may be difficult to find in northeastern regions except in specialty shops or well-stocked home centers.

Awnings are another shading option. They are more expensive than blinds or shades, but they offer shade without obstructing the view or hindering the cooling breezes. In order to be effective, they should extend about halfway down the window and have side panels.

No matter what type of shades you install, remember to place them on the east-facing windows to block the morning sun and the west-facing windows to block the evening sun. During the winter months the shades, blinds or awnings should be opened or removed to gain the maximum heat from the sun's rays.

Landscaping can be another effective shading strategy. Landscaping uses trees, bushes and large shrubs to block the sun. It takes time to reap the benefits from that technique — after all, large trees do not grow overnight — but in many ways it can the most effective and satisfying shading method. The trees and shrubs will block the sun's rays before they hit the house, so that the radiated heat will not penetrate into the walls or roof. In addition, landscaping will make your yard cooler and more attractive.

When drawing up your landscape plan, you should consider several factors. The trees and shrubs should be positioned so that they shade the house in the summer yet do not block the winter sun. The plants should be of different heights, moderate and tall. The moderate trees will block the late-morning and early-evening sun, while the tall trees will cast shade over the roof at midday. Large trees should be broadleaf deciduous trees, which lose their leaves in the winter.

Also consider the storm conditions indigenous to your area. Some trees do not weather well in storms with high winds. Consult with the experts at your local nursery to find out which trees are best for your area.

Ventilation is important in keeping the house cool because it flushes out the hot air and replaces it with cooler air. It is particularly important in the attic, where most hot air collects. The cupola was an early device used to ventilate attics before the invention of fans or air conditioners. Today it has been replaced by the ridge vent, a venting device that allows hot air to escape at the highest point in the attic. Other effective ventilators are gable vents and roof vents. To achieve maximum air circulation, consider installing a whole-house fan in the attic. ⊕

Whole-House Fan

Installing a whole-house fan can help cool a house because it will evacuate the hot attic air and draw in cooler, replacement air from the outside. Such a fan is most effective when the outside air is cooler than the inside, and the relative humidity is less then 60 percent.

Whole-house fans have a cubic-feet-per-minute, or CFM, rating. The rating will give you some idea of the unit's ability to circulate air. Ideally, a whole-house fan should change the air in the house every two minutes. Before buying the fan, you will have to estimate the volume of living space in your house so that you know how much air the fan will have to circulate. That may sound complicated, but it's a simple matter of multiplying the length by the width and height of each room and then adding the totals together. Do not include the basement in your calculations because the fan will cool only those rooms above ground level.

Once you've calculated your home's volume, multiply the number by .33 to obtain the recommended fan rating. Thus a house that has 12,800 cubic feet of space will need a fan with a rating of 4,224 CFM.

Your attic may have some roof vents installed already. For a whole-house fan you may have to add more. Calculate the venting area by dividing the fan's rating by 750. Thus 4,224 CFM divided by 750 requires 5.6 square feet of unrestricted vent area.

TOOL BOX

- COAT HANGER
- STEEL TAPE MEASURE
- HANDSAW
- MASKING TAPE
- SCREWDRIVER
- ADJUSTABLE WRENCH
- WIRE STRIPPERS AND SOLDERLESS CONNECTORS (NOT NECESSARY IF THE ELECTRICAL HOOK-UP IS TO BE MADE BY AND ELECTRICIAN)
- UTILITY KNIFE

WHOLE-HOUSE FAN

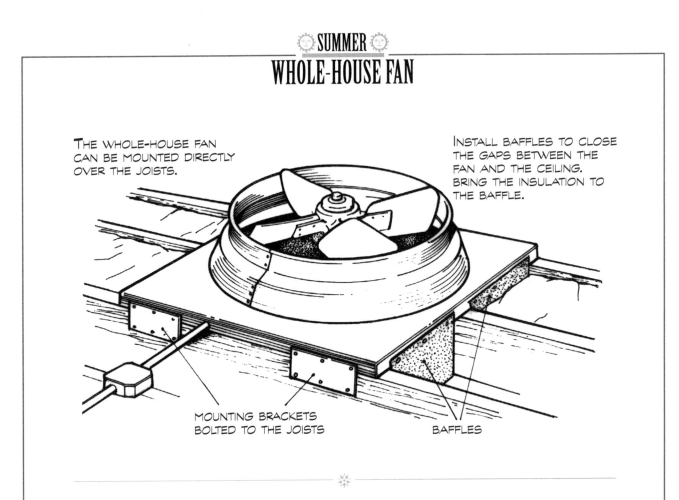

THE WHOLE-HOUSE FAN CAN BE MOUNTED DIRECTLY OVER THE JOISTS.

INSTALL BAFFLES TO CLOSE THE GAPS BETWEEN THE FAN AND THE CEILING. BRING THE INSULATION TO THE BAFFLE.

MOUNTING BRACKETS BOLTED TO THE JOISTS

BAFFLES

INSTALLATION: It is not difficult to install a whole-house fan. The procedure requires cutting a hole in the attic floor and mounting the unit across the joists. You will, however, be working in the attic, so you should keep in mind a number of safety pointers. Since the attic is apt to be dark, rig up a work light so that you can see what you're doing. Place wide planks across the joists so that you'll have a secure working platform. When working with attic insulation, wear long sleeves, gloves and a dust mask. Finally, remember that the attic can get very hot during summer. Watch the temperature and take breaks to avoid heat stroke.

The best location for the fan is over a central hallway. Find the center of the hall and then poke a wire, such as a straightened coat hanger, up through the ceiling into the attic above. In the attic locate the wire and pull back the insulation to make sure that there are no electrical wires or obstructions in the location. Measure the space between the joists and the roof. At least 20 inches of clearance should be between them.

Next determine which joist will be centered directly under the fan. Most likely it will be the one closest to the protruding wire. You'll want to mark it so that you can pinpoint its location from the hallway below. The easiest way to do that is by cutting two narrow holes about 2 inches by 8 inches on either side of the joist.

CUTTING THE CEILING AIR INTAKE HOLE: The next step is to cut an air intake hole in the ceiling above the hallway. Most fan kits include a cardboard template to help you position and cut the hole. Return to the hallway and position the template so the center lines align with the center joist. Hold it in place with tacks or masking tape,

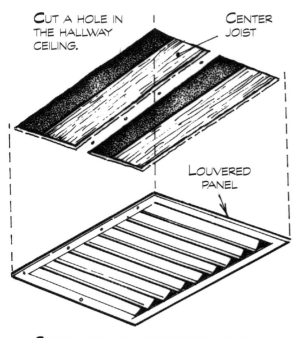

Cut a hole in the hallway ceiling.

Center joist

Louvered panel

Screw the louvered panel to the joists or attach it to the drywall with hollow-wall anchors.

then cut completely around the perimeter with a drywall saw. Protect your face and eyes from the falling debris and dust with a dust mask and goggles.

If the ceiling panel is nailed to the center joist, it will remain in place after the cuts are completed. Remove it by making cuts on either side of the joist. This will divide the panel in two pieces and leave a narrow strip nailed to the joist. Check the installation instructions to see if this narrow strip is required as a stabilizer for the louvered vent; if not remove it.

Consult the manufacturer's instructions for assembly details for your fan. Usually it's necessary to bolt mounting brackets to the fan housing before bringing the unit to the attic. Lift the assembled fan into the attic through the newly cut hole in the ceiling. Raising the fan into place is a two-person job, with one person in the attic to help lift and guide the fan into place.

ELECTRICAL HOOKUP: The most difficult part of the installation may be hooking up the electrical controls. Before attempting to make any electrical connections, check the local electrical codes to see if a licensed electrician must perform the work. Even if the local code permits you to do the electrical work yourself, do not attempt it if you are inexperienced or unsure when working around electricity. Remember also to shut off all power before working on any circuit.

In most cases the hookup will require running a new cable from the fan controls directly to the electrical service panel. Sometimes you can tap directly into an existing circuit in a nearby junction box. Make sure, however, that the circuit is not controlled by a three-way switch and that the fan motor will not overload it.

When the controls are connected, you can position the fan on the joists and bolt the mounting brackets to them. There will be gaps between the bottom of the fan frame and the ceiling. Close them by installing cardboard baffles — they should be included in the fan package — directly to the fan frame. Then cut the floor insulation to fit up against the baffles. The insulation should not come over the fan housing or blades.

Finally, install the louver panel in the hallway ceiling. It can be screwed to the joists or attached to the drywall ceiling with spring loaded hollow-wall anchors.

When operating your fan be sure to open the windows; otherwise, backdrafting — drawing exhaust gases from the chimney or other exhaust vents — will occur. ⊕

HOUSEHOLD HELPS • PLANES

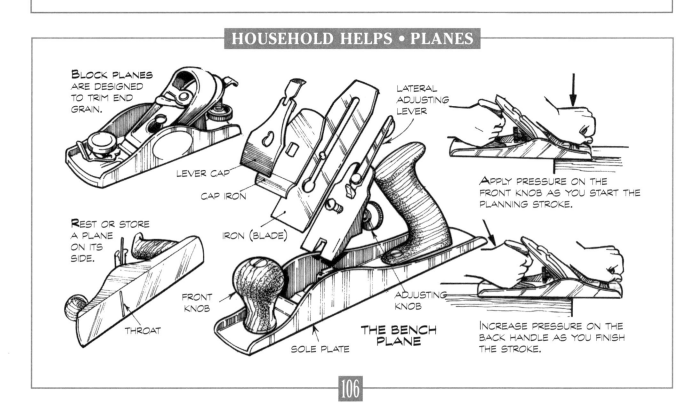

BLOCK PLANES ARE DESIGNED TO TRIM END GRAIN.

LEVER CAP

CAP IRON

REST OR STORE A PLANE ON ITS SIDE.

IRON (BLADE)

THROAT

FRONT KNOB

SOLE PLATE

THE BENCH PLANE

LATERAL ADJUSTING LEVER

APPLY PRESSURE ON THE FRONT KNOB AS YOU START THE PLANNING STROKE.

ADJUSTING KNOB

INCREASE PRESSURE ON THE BACK HANDLE AS YOU FINISH THE STROKE.

Lawn Mower

Cutting the grass for the first time means going to the garage, pulling out the lawn mower, dusting it off, and trying to start it. If the machine starts, the average homeowner assumes that his troubles are over, and the mower will go through the summer without problems. That is not necessarily so. However, an hour or two of preventive maintenance at the beginning of the season can save heartaches and possible repair bills later on.

Gas Lawn Mowers

Since you'll be working with gasoline and solvents, it's best to work on your mower outdoors. If possible, keep a small fire extinguisher handy. Before doing any maintenance, disconnect the sparkplug cable and tape it out of the way. That will prevent any accidental start-ups during the maintenance routine.

At the end of the summer, you should have emptied the gas tank before putting the mower into storage. Gasoline left in the tank usually evaporates, leaving a gummy deposit behind. Clean the tank by flushing it with a little fresh gasoline.

Next clean the exterior of the mower. You'll want to remove last year's dirt and any dust that may have accumulated during the fall and winter months. Make sure that the cooling fins on the engine are clean and free of grass and debris. Cleaning the mower beforehand will keep any dirt from entering the engine while you're working on it.

INSPECTING & REPLACING THE SPARK PLUG: The spark plug supplies the spark necessary for igniting the

TOOL BOX

- **SCREWDRIVER**
- **PUTTY KNIFE**
- **WIRE BRUSH**
- **SOCKET WRENCH WITH SOCKETS**
- **WIRE FEELER GAUGE**
- **FILE**
- **30-WEIGHT MOTOR OIL**

GAP SPARK PLUGS WITH A WIRE FEELER GAUGE.

fuel-air mixture that powers the engine. It is essential that the plug be in good condition. Remove the plug with a ratchet-handle wrench fitted with a deep-well socket. Once you have removed the plug, examine the electrodes for signs of wear. Plugs with black, oil-coated electrodes indicate an engine with a clogged air filter or a weak ignition. Worn electrodes and chalky deposits are signs of an engine with dirty cooling fins or a carburetor with too-lean settings. Those conditions should be corrected before attempting to use the mower for the summer.

Electrodes with light brown or tan deposits and slight wear are normal. While plugs with normal wear can be regapped and replaced, it is better to install a new one and keep the old one for a spare. Replace the plug with one that meets the specifications listed in your owner's manual. Before installing the new plug, check the electrode gap

with a wire feeler gauge. Make gap adjustments with care; bend the side or ground electrode and do not attempt to alter the center electrode. Some engines call for a .025-inch gap; others require a .030-inch gap. So look in your manual for your engine specifications. Install the plug and tighten it by hand; then give it an additional one-sixteenth turn with the wrench.

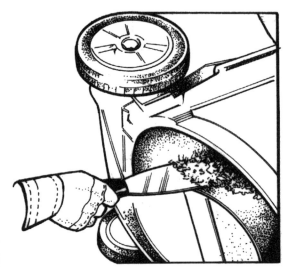

SCRAPE AWAY ACCUMULATED GRASS AND DIRT FROM THE UNDERSIDE.

TIGHTEN EACH WHEEL NUT WITH A SOCKET WRENCH.

With the spark plug in place, inspect the spark plug cable. If it's cracked or split, it should be replaced. Depending upon your mower, it may be a job for a professional serviceman. Assuming, however, that the cable is in good condition, continue the maintenance inspection but do not connect the cable to the plug yet.

CLEANING & INSPECTING THE MOWER DECK: Turn the mower on its side and clean the underside of the mower deck. Remove caked grass and dirt with a stiff putty knife and a wire brush; then check to make sure that the engine mounts are tight. Loose mounting bolts can contribute to vibrations that will shorten the life of your mower. Now carefully examine the cutting blade. A

TO REMOVE THE BLADE, USE A WRENCH AND TURN THE MOUNTING BOLT CLOCKWISE. WEDGE A WOOD BLOCK BETWEEN THE BLADE AND HOUSING TO KEEP THE BLADE FROM TURNING.

blade that is bent or cracked should be replaced. Also, a blade with worn vacuum/lift wings — the triangular sections of the blade opposite the cutting edges — should be discarded. A dull blade usually can be sharpened and reused.

To sharpen the blade, clamp it in a vise and use a medium-grade flat file. File along the cutting edge in one direction only. Be careful to maintain the angle of the cutting edge, which is usually 30 degrees. Sharpen both cutting edges on the blade to maintain blade balance. Once the blade is sharp and in balance, you can remount it. While the mower is still on its side, check the wheels. Make sure that each wheel nut is tight and the wheels are secure on their axles.

CABLES, AIR & OIL FILTERS: Now turn the mower right-side up and examine the starter cord. A cord that is worn or frayed can break and should be replaced. Usually, that job should be left to a professional. Next lubricate the throttle and drive cables by applying a light coating of 30-weight oil with a clean cloth. That step will prevent the controls from sticking during mower operation.

Inspect the air filter. If your mower has an oil-impregnated foam filter, you should clean it. Detach the air filter unit; separate the parts and wipe them clean. Wash the foam element in detergent and water, and squeeze it dry. Apply new oil, SAE-30 weight, to the filter and replace it in the filter unit. Before installing the unit on the carburetor, check the gasket on the filter housing. A worn or cracked gasket should be replaced. If your lawn mower has a paper filter, replace it. Paper elements cannot be cleaned, nor should they be oiled.

Now change the engine oil. Some mowers have a drain plug on the underside of the engine. With other mowers it may be necessary to remove the dipstick or filler plug and tip the mower on its side to drain the oil. Collect the oil in a suitable container and remember to dispose of it properly. Refill the crankcase with clean oil. Check your owner's manual to find the correct oil for your mower.

Fill the fuel tank with fresh gas, as recommended by the manufacturer. Then reconnect the spark plug cable to the spark plug and start the engine.

Push Lawn Mowers

Not all homeowners use power mowers to manicure their lawns. A few people still use the old-fashioned push mowers — also called "hand mowers" and "manual reel mowers" — for this chore. Push mowers have four, five, or six blades that are mounted in a horizontal reel assembly, which is linked to the wheels with a pinion gear that meshes within a larger gear in the wheel side plate. Pushing the mower rotates the wheels, causing the blades to turn.

Push mowers may seem like an archaic tool, but some compelling reasons justify using them. Since they are muscle-powered, they are quieter and more environmentally friendly than the power units. There's no engine to maintain, fuel to buy and store, or exhaust fumes to breathe. They require no maintenance other than occasionally sharpening the blades or adjusting the cutting bar and roller. They are safe to operate because the cutting blades stop rotating the instant you decide to stop pushing.

Push mowers are ideal for the homeowner with a small — a quarter-acre or less — flat lawn. Even though pushing a hand mower hasn't achieved the status of working out at a trendy gym, you still can use one for a light workout.

If you haven't used a push mower in a long time, you may be surprised to find that newer models — yes, they are still being manufactured — are lightweight and easier to maneuver than the old-fashioned mowers that granddad used. Lightweight alloys and plastics have replaced cast iron, steel, and heavy oak.

Push mowers are relatively inexpensive, between $65 to $200, depending on the width of the reel — cutting width ranges from 14 inches to 18 inches — and the number of cutting blades. The better models have ball bearings supporting the reel shaft, which minimize shaft wear and allow the reel to spin with less friction.

Lawn experts recommend buying a model with no fewer than five blades. The additional blades cut the grass evenly and eliminate wavy patterns that may appear with four-bladed models. The only optional equipment for the push mower is a grass catcher. These have canvas- or plastic-covered wire frames that hook onto to the back of the mower.

Most push mowers cannot be set to cut grass higher than 1 1/2 inches, so they are not good for cutting tall, dense grass. Most models cannot cut closer than 3 inches around obstacles.

You can purchase a push mower at garden centers, home centers, or large hardware stores. Occasionally, you may run across one at a flea market or garage sale. ⊕

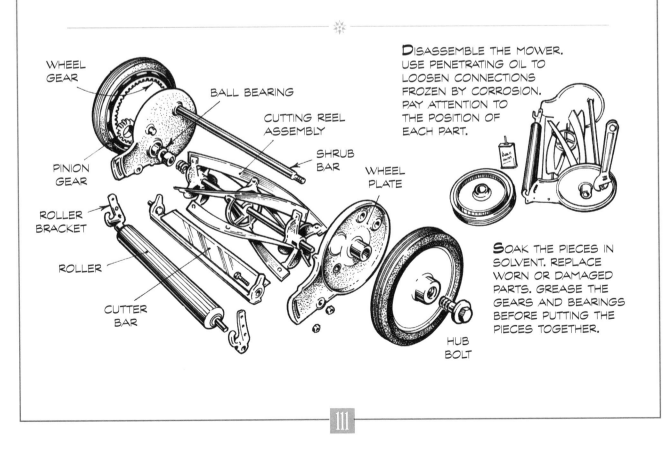

WHEEL GEAR

BALL BEARING

CUTTING REEL ASSEMBLY

PINION GEAR

SHRUB BAR

ROLLER BRACKET

ROLLER

CUTTER BAR

WHEEL PLATE

HUB BOLT

DISASSEMBLE THE MOWER. USE PENETRATING OIL TO LOOSEN CONNECTIONS FROZEN BY CORROSION. PAY ATTENTION TO THE POSITION OF EACH PART.

SOAK THE PIECES IN SOLVENT. REPLACE WORN OR DAMAGED PARTS. GREASE THE GEARS AND BEARINGS BEFORE PUTTING THE PIECES TOGETHER.

The Gas Grill

Years ago, outdoor cooking involved lighting a pile of charcoal in a brick or stone hearth. For those who didn't have a masonry pit or who wanted to take their barbecue to a favorite vacation spot, manufacturers offered a portable charcoal grill. Eventually, designers developed a gas grill that dispensed with the charcoal yet still offered the full flavor of outdoor cooking.

At first consumers viewed the gas grill with some skepticism. Some thought that it was little more than a kitchen range relocated to the backyard. People wondered how the gas flame could cook food and give it the smoky taste characteristic of charcoal fires. Actually, it's not the flame but the drippings from the food that produce that aroma and flavor.

Briefly, here is how a gas grill works. Gas flows from a storage tank to the unit. A shut-off valve regulates the flow of gas. When the valve is opened, gas flows through orifices into venturi tubes where it is mixed with air. The gas-and-air mixture travels to the burners and exits from burner ports, where

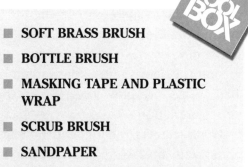

TOOL BOX

- ■ **SOFT BRASS BRUSH**
- ■ **BOTTLE BRUSH**
- ■ **MASKING TAPE AND PLASTIC WRAP**
- ■ **SCRUB BRUSH**
- ■ **SANDPAPER**
- ■ **PAINT BRUSH, PRIMER, PAINT**

it is ignited. Most grills have piezo electric igniters capable of generating a spark to light the gas and air. The electric igniter may operate with either a push button or a rotary knob. While both generate a spark, the rotary igniters are easier to use and are more likely to light on the first try.

Situated above the burner is the heat distributor, a rack with either lava rocks, ceramic briquettes, or metal triangles. When drippings from the food fall onto the heat distributor, they are vaporized into aromatic smoke. It is the smoke that bastes the food above and gives it the characteristic flavor of outdoor cooking.

THE GAS GRILL

For most homeowners gas grills offer the flavor of outdoor cooking without the bother of buying charcoal or trying to light it. They are generally easy to start up; they reach warm-up temperature fast, and some have extras like shelves and even side burners.

Gas grills require yearly maintenance if they are to provide safe and reliable service. Start by inspecting the lava rocks or ceramic briquettes on the heat distribution grid. They absorb food drippings and grease that might otherwise fall onto the burners. They can, however, become coated with excess grease and lose their absorbency. It's simple to clean them. When the grill is cold, turn the rocks over so that the greasy side faces the burner. Ignite the flame, turn the heat control to high, then close the cover. In about 15 minutes the grease will be burned off, and the briquettes will be serviceable again.

Allow the grill to cool; then remove the cooking grids. Scrub them with a soft brass brush to remove grease and food deposits. Brushes made for that purpose are available at home centers. You also can use oven cleaner on grids that have heavy deposits food or grease. Spray it on and wait about 30 minutes; then hose it off. That should loosen the deposits enough so that they can be scraped off.

Next remove the burner and venturi assembly. They can become clogged

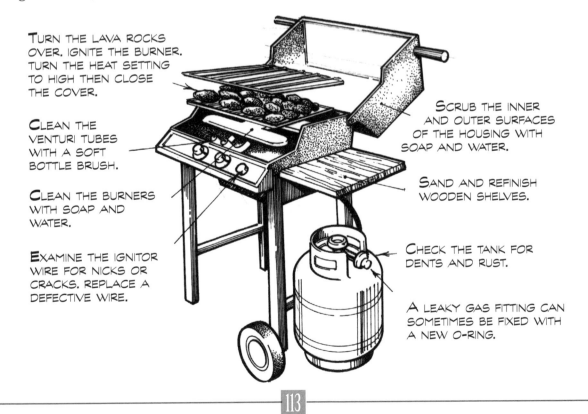

TURN THE LAVA ROCKS OVER. IGNITE THE BURNER. TURN THE HEAT SETTING TO HIGH THEN CLOSE THE COVER.

CLEAN THE VENTURI TUBES WITH A SOFT BOTTLE BRUSH.

CLEAN THE BURNERS WITH SOAP AND WATER.

EXAMINE THE IGNITOR WIRE FOR NICKS OR CRACKS. REPLACE A DEFECTIVE WIRE.

SCRUB THE INNER AND OUTER SURFACES OF THE HOUSING WITH SOAP AND WATER.

SAND AND REFINISH WOODEN SHELVES.

CHECK THE TANK FOR DENTS AND RUST.

A LEAKY GAS FITTING CAN SOMETIMES BE FIXED WITH A NEW O-RING.

with grease, dirt, and even spider webs. On some grills the burners may lift right out, but in most cases you'll have to loosen a retaining clip near the grill housing. Clean the assembly with a soft brush and soap and water. Clean the inside of the venturi tubes with a soft bottle brush. Dry the assembly off; then carefully inspect it for minute holes caused by rust or corrosion. Replace all defective pieces.

Examine the igniter wire for cuts or nicks. Those imperfections may seem minor, but they could bleed electricity from the wire and cause a shock hazard. It's best to replace the wire or the entire igniter if you find defects.

Inspect the gas orifices for blockage. If the openings appear clogged, clear them with a wooden toothpick. Do not use a metal wire; you could damage the orifice openings.

While you have the burner assembly disconnected, you can clean the grill housing. First wrap gas orifices with plastic wrap. That will keep water from entering and possibly corroding them. Scrub the inner and outer surfaces of the housing with a scrub brush and warm soapy water. Use a garden hose to rinse, and then dry the grill with a towel. Examine the outside surface of the housing for chips in the paint finish. You can touch them up with spray paint made especially for high-temperature applications. When the paint is dry, replace the burner assembly.

Once the grill is clean with all the parts in place, turn your attention to the gas line. First clean off any dirt from the line, tank, and fittings. Then test their condition by brushing on a solution of soapy water. The solution will start to bubble if there are any leaks. Leaks around the fittings sometimes can be corrected by tightening the fitting, coating the threads with pipe sealant, or by replacing the O-ring. If those attempts fail, it may be necessary to replace the entire fitting.

Check the propane tank for dents and rust. A large dent can decrease the tank's internal volume and cause the gas to vent through the pressure relief valve, creating a fire hazard. Rust on the tank's surface may not be cause for concern provided that it hasn't eaten into the metal. However, rust spots should be sanded down to the bare metal, then primed and painted. Remember always to store the propane tank outdoors, away from direct sunlight, because warm temperatures can cause the gas to expand inside the tank, forcing it through the relief valve.

After you've performed this maintenance routine, you'll want to keep your grill in good condition by protecting it with a cover. ⊕

Fixing Hoses

Few homeowners give thought to their garden hose until they need to water the lawn and garden. Then leaks and cracks will show up when water is forced through the hose. Most likely the damage developed during the winter months because the hose was not stored properly. For example, a hose can deteriorate if it is left outside during the winter months. Water remaining in the coils is apt to freeze, expand and crack the hose.

Even if the hose is brought indoors, it still can be damaged if it was left to hang on a nail. A nail puts creases in the hose that eventually dry and crack. Ideally, a hose should be drained and wrapped around a reel or at least placed on the floor in a neat coil.

A rubber hose also can deteriorate if it is stored in the same room with an electrical appliance. The electric motor in the appliance generates ozone, an allotropic form of oxygen, that can attack the rubber.

Of course, it is too late to worry about storing the garden hose now, but keep these tips in mind for the end of the season. Now the problem is what to do about a hose that leaks whenever you use it.

Leaks around connections, where the hose is joined to a faucet or a spray nozzle, are easy to correct. They occur because the washer in the coupling has deteriorated. Pry out the old washer and replace it with a new one.

TOOL BOX

- **UTILITY KNIFE**
- **ELECTRICAL TAPE**

Leaks in the body of the hose are more difficult to repair. Before making any repairs, carefully examine the entire hose. One or two cracks can be fixed, but several indicate that the hose is badly deteriorated and probably not worth saving.

You can repair a damaged section in a hose in two ways. A temporary fix can be made with electrical tape. First clean and dry the hose. Wrap the tape around the damaged section, stretching the

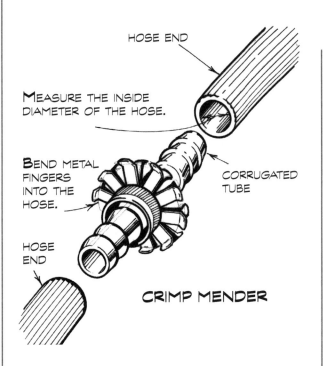

HOSE END

MEASURE THE INSIDE DIAMETER OF THE HOSE.

CORRUGATED TUBE

BEND METAL FINGERS INTO THE HOSE.

HOSE END

CRIMP MENDER

tape as you wrap. Do not stretch the first or the last few turns of the tape; otherwise the tape eventually will unravel.

A more permanent repair can be made by replacing the damaged section with a metal hose mender. Hardware stores and home centers stock three basic types: crimp menders, collar menders, and bushing-coupler menders. All work well, but before you buy one, measure the inside diameter of the hose. It will be either 1/2-, 5/8-, or 3/4 inches wide. Purchase a mender that fits that diameter.

The first step in installing a mender is to cut out the damaged section of the hose with a utility knife. Make sure the cut ends are perpendicular to the length of the hose. The mender will replace the damaged section and join the two lengths together.

USING A CRIMP MENDER: With the crimp-type hose mender, the hose lengths are joined by a corrugated tube that fits between them. The mender has metal fingers that grip the hose to keep it from separating. To install the crimp mender, insert one end of the corrugated tube into the hose; then place it on an anvil or wooden block. Hammer down the metal fingers so that they grip the hose. Rotate the piece to tap all the fingers into place. Push the other length of hose onto the opposite end of the tube and repeat the crimping procedure.

USING A COLLAR MENDER: Collar menders also have a corrugated tube to join the hose together. The pieces are held together with a saddle, two pieces of molded plastic that are screwed in place over the joint.

USING A BUSHING-COUPLER MENDER: The bushing-coupler mender consists of two couplings each with its own metal tube, called a bushing. One coupling is attached to each end of the hose. First, the bushing, a tapered metal tube, is inserted in the end of the hose. The hose coupling fits over it, and the two are locked together by twisting the bushing in place. You must use a special key, which is included in the mending kit, to turn the bushing.

The installation procedure is repeated on the other section of hose. The two sections are then joined by screwing the couplings together. In essence the mender makes one long hose into two shorter hoses that are joined by mating the couplers.

Those repairs are easy to make on rubber hoses because they are relatively flexible. Plastic hoses, on the other hand, are often stiff and difficult to work with. Try dipping the hose end into hot water for a few minutes, which should soften it and make it more pliable.

Now that the hose is repaired, keep it in good condition by draining and coiling it each time you use it. Straighten out any kinks immediately; otherwise, they will crease the hose and cause it to crack. ⊕

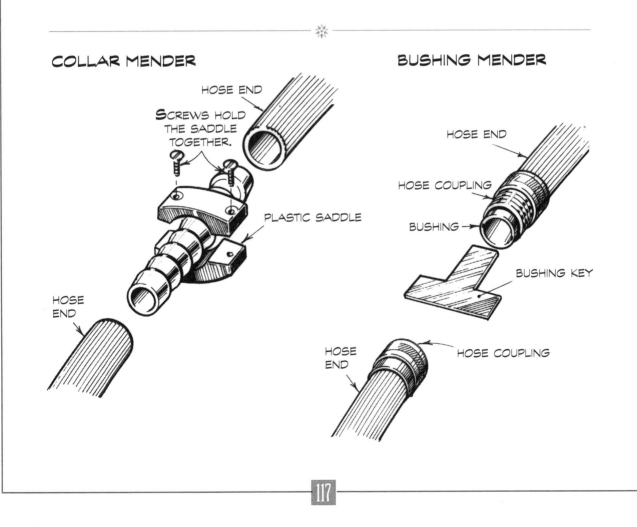

COLLAR MENDER

HOSE END

SCREWS HOLD THE SADDLE TOGETHER.

PLASTIC SADDLE

HOSE END

BUSHING MENDER

HOSE END

HOSE COUPLING

BUSHING

BUSHING KEY

HOSE END

HOSE COUPLING

Decks

Most decks are constructed of such moisture and rot-resistant woods as redwood, cedar, or pressure-treated pine. Even so, weather, shifting ground conditions, and human activity can exact a toll on a deck. Even one treated with stains and preservatives must have the finish renewed periodically. It is impossible to cover all the problems that can occur, but the following will serve as a guide for most situations.

Start by crawling around and under the deck. Inspect the joists, fastenings, deck boards, railings, and steps for signs of rot and structural damage. Inspect the top edge of the joists where the deck boards are attached. Often moisture collects here, resulting in rot. You may have to pry up some of the deck boards to expose the damaged area. If only the top of the joist is damaged, then you can leave it in place and reinforce it with a "partner." The partner is a new piece of 2 x 4 or 2 x 6 that is nailed to a damaged joist. Before attaching that piece, liberally coat the rotted area of the joist with wood preservative. It will seal the wood and halt further rot by killing any fungus.

Next align the top edges of the partner with the joist, then secure it in place with 10d galvanized nails or 3-inch galvanized deck screws.

JOIST REPAIR: Inspect the ends of the joists. The end grain soaks up moisture readily and becomes a prime target for rot. Most decks have a band, or rim, joist nailed to the ends of the deck

TOOL BOX

- **WOOD PRESERVATIVE**
- **CIRCULAR SAW**
- **HAMMER AND 10D DECK NAILS**
- **TAPE MEASURE**
- **COMBINATION SQUARE**
- **ELECTRIC DRILL WITH BITS**
- **CAULKING GUN WITH CAULK COMPOUND**
- **PRY BAR**
- **BELT SANDER**
- **BAR CLAMP**
- **SCREWDRIVER**

joists. It probably will be damaged also. The most effective solution is to saw off the rotted ends of the deck joists and nail a new band joist in place. Be aware, however, that it will shorten your deck by a couple of inches.

LEDGER REPAIR: A more serious problem occurs at the ledger board. The ledger board is the joist that's bolted to the house. The deck joists are nailed to it at right angles. Frequently, water seeps behind the ledger, causing it to rot. Usually, the ends of deck joists are damaged also. You'll have to replace the ledger and trim the rot off the ends of the joists. Some building authorities consider that a structural fix requires a permit. So check with local codes before proceeding.

Expose the ledger and the joists by removing a few deck boards. Since you'll be cutting the joists from a support member, it's a good idea to prop up the deck with a temporary support. Run a 2 x 6 on edge under the joists and support it with 4 x 4s.

Next trim the joists with a reciprocating or circular saw and coat the ends with wood preservative. Trimming the end of the joist shortens it by a couple of inches. It is important that you shorten each joist to the same length, so measure carefully. Now cut a new ledge board out of pressure-treated lumber to

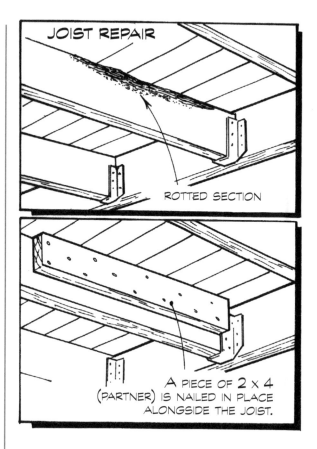

JOIST REPAIR

ROTTED SECTION

A PIECE OF 2 x 4 (PARTNER) IS NAILED IN PLACE ALONGSIDE THE JOIST.

the exact size of the old one. Since the joists are now shorter, they won't reach the ledger. An easy way to bridge the gap is by sandwiching two ledger boards together.

Bolt the new board to the house. You can use the old board as a pattern to drill new bolt holes. Seal around the ledger with caulking compound and install flashing to fit under the house siding and over the ledger. Attach the joists to the ledger with joist hangers and then replace the deck boards.

Inspect the deck boards next. Some of them may be cracked or broken and should be replaced. Others may be cupped or warped. Sometimes you can correct that by prying the board up and turning it over. Use galvanized deck screws to pull the board flat and secure it to the joists. However, if the board is distorted severely, it must be replaced. If the deck boards are rough and splintered from weathering, you can smooth them by sanding. First, countersink the deck nails below the surface with a nail set. A belt sander will quickly smooth the surface of the deck. Wear a dust mask. Sand in the direction of the grain and keep the sander moving to avoid gouging the wood.

If your deck has stairs, inspect them. Check the treads for cracks or splits and replace them, if necessary. The easiest way to remove a damaged tread is to saw it in two with a handsaw and then pry the pieces away from the stringer with a pry bar. Cut a new tread and treat it with wood preservative. Slide it into place in the stringer slots and secure it with galvanized nails or deck screws.

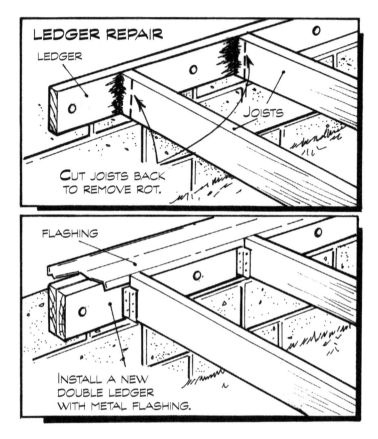

LEDGER REPAIR

LEDGER

JOISTS

CUT JOISTS BACK TO REMOVE ROT.

FLASHING

INSTALL A NEW DOUBLE LEDGER WITH METAL FLASHING.

Sometimes frost heaving or ground settling can cause the stringers to spread apart and separate from the treads. Use a long bar clamp to draw the stringers together and fasten them to the treads with galvanized deck screws.

REPAIRING RAIL POSTS: Next turn your attention to the deck railings. Smooth splintered railings with a sanding block or an orbital sander. On many decks the railing support posts are only

RAILING POSTS

LAG BOLT

WASHER

SECURE POSTS WITH LAG BOLTS.

DOUBLE-BORE HOLES TO SINK BOLT HEADS BELOW THE SURFACE.

nailed in place. Check to make sure that they are secure; if not, you can renail them. An even better way to stabilize them is with lagbolts. Bore pilot holes for the lagbolts and counter-bore holes in the posts so that the lagbolt heads and washers will sink below the surface.

Once the deck is structurally sound, examine the finish. You can remove stains and weathering with a deck brightener — actually a wood bleach — change the color with stain, and finally preserve it with deck sealer. Before applying any of those products, read the labels to make sure that they are compatible with the wood in your deck. And remember to wear gloves and eye protection when applicable. ⊕

Fence Repair

Many homeowners have wooden fences around their homes. Fences take a lot of abuse, and sooner or later they need some repair work. Before starting any repair, it's a good idea to look over the entire fence and evaluate the extent of damage. What may seem like a minor problem may in fact be more extensive. For example, a rotted picket may be an isolated problem, or the wood rot may extend to neighboring pickets or even the support members. Careful investigation may reveal that it will be better to rebuild the fence rather than to attempt repairing a section at a time.

GATE REPAIR: The first part of the fence that usually develops problems is the gate. It may sag, bind, drag, or pull away from the support post. A gate will sag when its frame becomes distorted and is no longer square. An easy way to true it up is by attaching a threaded rod at opposite corners of the gate and pulling them together with a turnbuckle. A turnbuckle is a steel sleeve with a central slot and a threaded hole at either end. Thread the rods into the turnbuckle holes, insert a screwdriver into the

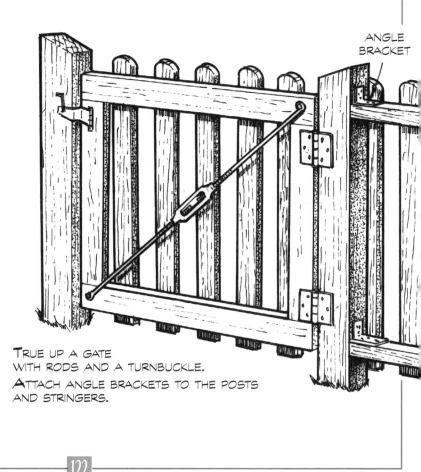

ANGLE BRACKET

TRUE UP A GATE
WITH RODS AND A TURNBUCKLE.
ATTACH ANGLE BRACKETS TO THE POSTS
AND STRINGERS.

FENCE REPAIR

- **TURNBUCKLE**
- **SCREWDRIVER**
- **WOOD PLANE**
- **PAINTBRUSH AND PAINT**
- **ELECTRIC DRILL WITH BITS**
- **SLEDGE HAMMER**
- **CONCRETE TROWEL**
- **WRENCHES (TWO REQUIRED)**

slot, and twist the turnbuckles around. That will draw the rods together and pull the gate frame into alignment.

The gate will bind against the latch post if it is out of alignment or if the frame absorbs moisture and swells. To correct the problem, remove the gate from its hinges and plane some wood from the latch side. Seal and paint those edges before rehanging the gate.

A gate that sees a lot of use eventually can sag, jam against the latch post, and rub against the ground. It also can pull the hinge post out of alignment, causing it to separate from the fence frame. To correct the problem, push the post back against the frame, attach wooden braces to hold it in place, and secure it to the framework with steel angle — also called "L" — brackets. You also can cut about a half inch off the horizontal framing members, called "stringers," before attaching the angle brackets, which will pull the gate slightly out of plumb and raise it away from the ground. You may have to realign the latch mechanism after you make the repair.

Sometimes the hinges may work loose on the gate. That can happen if the wood around the hinge screws expands enough so that the screws no longer bite into the wood. Remove the hinges and drill out the holes with a 1/4-inch bit. Drive short lengths of dowel into the holes; then drill pilot holes for the screws and remount the hinges.

FENCE POST REPAIR: Gate problems are relatively minor compared to those of fence posts. The posts support the entire fence. If one or two posts loosen or start to wobble, the structural integrity of the entire fence will be threatened. Fixing a loose fence post is not necessarily a major task, however. Often the post can be firmed up by driving pressure-treated wedges into the ground around the base of the post. Some posts may be pushed upward by frost heaves. You can drive them back into the ground with a sledge hammer.

If the post is set in dirt, you can give it a more secure foundation with concrete. First, attach wooden braces to

PRESSURE-TREATED WEDGE

FIX A WOBBLY POST BY POUNDING PRESSURE-TREATED WEDGES IN THE GROUND NEAR THE BASE OF THE POST.

the post to hold in it place. Then dig a hole around the base 8 inches to 12 inches in diameter. Pour concrete into the hole until it rises above the ground level. Shape the surface of the concrete with a trowel so that rain water will run away from the post onto the surrounding ground.

Wobbly posts that are set in concrete can be firmed up by reinforcing the foundation. Pound the concrete further into the ground with a sledgehammer and then pour at least 6 inches of new concrete over it.

Posts that are partially rotted or decayed often can be salvaged by bolting new lumber to the post. For example, a post with a decayed base can be rescued by driving a shorter post into the ground next to it. After the two posts are bolted together, the decayed section can be removed. Be sure, however, that the bolts run through solid wood.

Fence posts that are structurally unsound must be replaced. Before they can be removed, however, the fence sections must be detached from the post and shifted away. Pull all the nails that fasten the stringers to the posts; then swing the fence sections at least two feet away. Prop the free ends of those sections up on wood blocks to

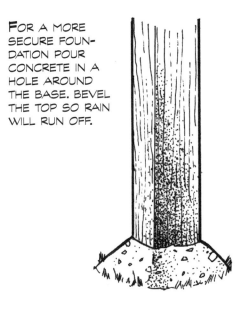

FOR A MORE SECURE FOUNDATION POUR CONCRETE IN A HOLE AROUND THE BASE. BEVEL THE TOP SO RAIN WILL RUN OFF.

keep them from pulling off the other posts. You can now replace the damaged post. If the original post is set in concrete, be careful when removing it; it can weigh 100 pounds or more.

If your fence is in good condition, you can do a number of things to keep it looking good. First remove all debris, piles of leaves, sticks, or lumber that are stacked against the fence. They collect moisture and attract insects, particularly termites, that can damage the fence.

Water collecting under the base of the fence eventually will cause damage.

The best way to prevent that is by making a drainage path under the fence. Dig a shallow trench under the fence and fill it with gravel or crushed stone.

Water also can penetrate into the tops of the fence posts where the end grain is exposed. That will cause them to rot or crack prematurely. Make sure that all the post ends are cut to a slant or else topped with wooden or metal caps to repel water.

Finally, stain or paint your fence often — especially after making repairs — to keep it looking good and protect it from the elements. ⊕

HOUSEHOLD HELPS • SAWS

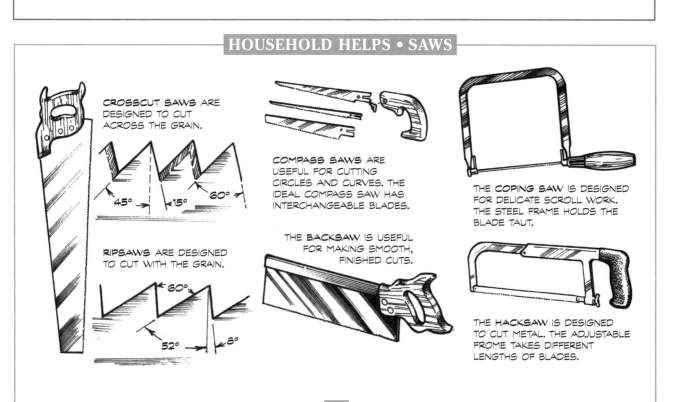

CROSSCUT SAWS ARE DESIGNED TO CUT ACROSS THE GRAIN.

45°   15°   60°

RIPSAWS ARE DESIGNED TO CUT WITH THE GRAIN.

60°   52°   8°

COMPASS SAWS ARE USEFUL FOR CUTTING CIRCLES AND CURVES. THE IDEAL COMPASS SAW HAS INTERCHANGEABLE BLADES.

THE BACKSAW IS USEFUL FOR MAKING SMOOTH, FINISHED CUTS.

THE COPING SAW IS DESIGNED FOR DELICATE SCROLL WORK. THE STEEL FRAME HOLDS THE BLADE TAUT.

THE HACKSAW IS DESIGNED TO CUT METAL. THE ADJUSTABLE FROME TAKES DIFFERENT LENGTHS OF BLADES.

Swimming Pools

Swimming pools can make a hot summer more pleasant, but they do require attention and maintenance to keep them safe and clean. Whether you choose to do those chores yourself or hire a professional, you should have some understanding of the swimming pool system. Knowledge of the basics can help you to solve simple problems and prevent costly service calls.

The pool system is designed to circulate, filter, and disinfect the water to improve its clarity and quality. Water clarity refers to the visibility of the water — that is, how transparent it is. Water becomes dark and murky with quantities of dirt and debris suspended in it. Proper filtration can remove those particles and improve water clarity.

The quality of the water is determined by the amount of contaminants — bacteria and other biological organisms — in it. Most people assume that clarity and quality go hand in hand; if the water is crystal clear, then it must also be free of contaminants. That, however, is not also the case. Biological contaminants are virtually invisible; so they may be present in significant amounts even though the water looks pristine and clear.

THE CIRCULATION SYSTEM: Swimming pools are equipped with a circulation system designed to remove dirt and debris by drawing water from the pool, forcing it through a filter, then returning it to the pool. The water is pulled from the pool through outlets. There are two types of pool outlets: surface skimmers and the main drain.

Leaves, pollen, and dirt usually collect and float on the surface of the water. Surface skimmers suck water from the surface and capture the debris before it becomes saturated with water and sinks to the bottom. Your pool should have at least one surface skimmer for every 500 square feet of water surface, and one should be positioned on the downwind side.

The main drain is a single outlet positioned underwater at the deepest part of the pool. It suctions the water and all the debris at the bottom. It is also used to drain the pool when necessary.

The heart of the system is the pump. The most common pool pump is the centrifugal pump. An electric motor attached to the pump spins impeller blades, which capture the water and use centrifugal force to push it through the system.

Proper pump size is essential if the system is to filter the water effectively. A good pump should be strong enough to recycle all the water in the pool, called a turnover, six to eight times a day. If the pump is too small, it cannot effect sufficient turnover, while a large pump could cause damage by forcing too much water through the system. Most pool dealers have tables based on

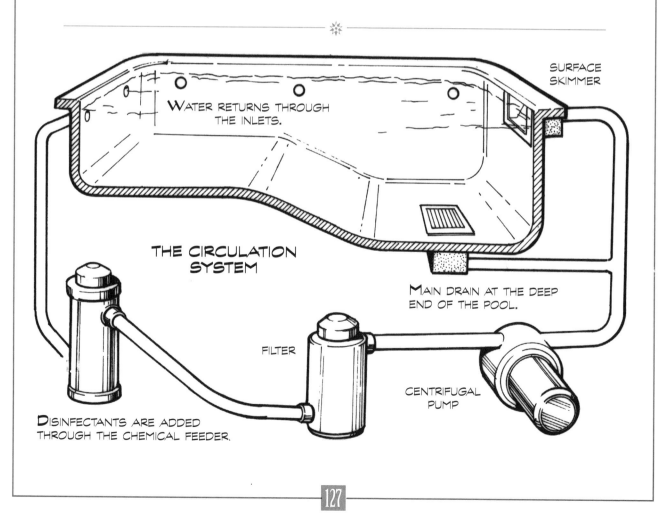

SURFACE SKIMMER

WATER RETURNS THROUGH THE INLETS.

THE CIRCULATION SYSTEM

MAIN DRAIN AT THE DEEP END OF THE POOL.

FILTER

CENTRIFUGAL PUMP

DISINFECTANTS ARE ADDED THROUGH THE CHEMICAL FEEDER.

pump performance curves. They can help you select the proper size pump for your pool.

CHOOSING FILTERS: The pump pushes the water through a filter, which removes dirt, hair, pollen, and other small particles. Generally, the water enters through the top of the filter and travels through the filtration media to the bottom, where it exits as clean water. Water filtration is important, so it's a good idea to buy the best filter you can afford. Basically, three types of filtration media are available: sand; diatomaceous earth, or DE; and synthetic fibers.

Sand is the most common filter media. Sand filters are easy to maintain, and they work well for most pool applications. Most sand filters have high-rate elements that use the entire depth of the sand to remove particles, in contrast with other media, such as diatomaceous earth, that use only the surface of the medium to capture particles. Sand filters can be cleaned by backwashing; the flow of water is reversed so that the accumulated sediment is pushed from the filter and flushed out as waste. Unfortunately, the backwashing process wastes water.

DE filters use granules composed of the skeletal remains of fossilized marine life, frequently referred to as diatoms, to clean the water. The individual granules are extremely porous with numerous cracks and crevasses. They are able to trap a great deal of dirt to produce clear water. DE cannot be backwashed. It must be removed when it becomes clogged with sediment — about once a week — and replaced with fresh DE.

Special regenerative DE filters allow you to agitate the unit and circulate the DE. That action puts fresh material near the septa, the filter screen, so that these filters do not have to be changed as often as the conventional DE filters.

Be sure to wear a protective mask when you handle DE because it can be a lung irritant. Most pool owners dispose of the dirty DE in the household trash, but some communities require that DE be bagged and deposited in a special disposal system.

Cartridge filters have a pleated synthetic fabric element to trap dirt and debris. Those filters cannot be backwashed, but they can be cleaned by hand — usually. Many pool owners find that it easier just to replace the element. When opening the filter housing, it's important to check the lid, gaskets, and O-rings. Lubricate them regularly and replace them if they are worn or cracked.

After the water leaves the filter, it is pumped through a chemical feeder. It will introduce the chemicals to improve

the water quality. Finally, the filtered and disinfected water will return to the pool through pool inlets. The inlets may be positioned on the sides of the pool or on the bottom, but they must be in strategic locations to ensure that the chemicals are distributed evenly throughout the pool.

WATER TESTING & CHEMICAL TREATMENTS: Proper pool maintenance requires more than simply adequate filtration. Chemical treatment, pH balance, water testing, and vacuuming should also be part of the maintenance schedule.

The circulation and filtration systems are designed to recycle the pool water so that it can filter out the dirt and debris and make the water clearer. Water that is clear and transparent can be deceptive, however. Even though it looks clean, it may still harbor germs and algae. To remove those contaminants, you need to treat the water with disinfectants.

Before adding any chemicals to the water, it's important to test it. Test kits, which are available at pool dealers for around $10, are designed to analyze the following: pH levels, amounts of pool disinfectant, calcium hardness, and sometimes the cyanuric acid levels.

Testing the water is a relatively simple procedure. Essentially, it consists of collecting a water sample and then adding a reagent, which will cause the sample to turn color. The colored water sample is then matched to a color chart provided in the kit. Even though the testing procedure is simple and straightforward, it's possible to obtain inaccurate readings if you are careless.

To get the most accurate results, keep all the vials and test tubes impeccably clean. Obtain the water sample by reaching at least 12 inches below the water surface and away from any inlets. Mix the reagents with the samples by gently swirling the vials; do not shake the containers. The reagents are sensitive to heat and light; store them in a cool, dry place — not by the poolside. Since reagents have a short shelf life, it's best to mark them with the date of purchase and dispose of them within six months of that date. Keep in mind that not all reagents are the same, so do not interchange brands. Finally, remember to wash your hands before and after making the test.

One important test to make is the pH reading. It measures the level of acidity or alkalinity in the water. The pH scale ranges from 0 to 14. Ideally, the pH level should be balanced between 7.2 and 7.6.

A reading of 1 would indicate a strong acid level in the water. Too much acidity can cause the disinfectant

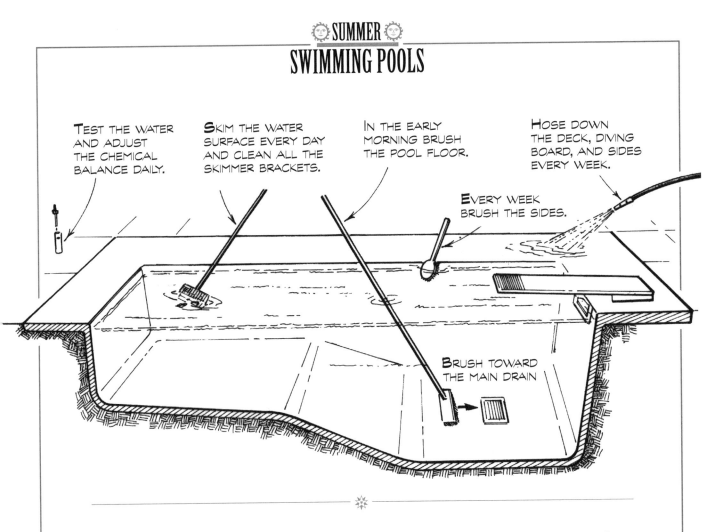

TEST THE WATER AND ADJUST THE CHEMICAL BALANCE DAILY.

SKIM THE WATER SURFACE EVERY DAY AND CLEAN ALL THE SKIMMER BRACKETS.

IN THE EARLY MORNING BRUSH THE POOL FLOOR.

HOSE DOWN THE DECK, DIVING BOARD, AND SIDES EVERY WEEK.

EVERY WEEK BRUSH THE SIDES.

BRUSH TOWARD THE MAIN DRAIN

chemicals to become unstable. The acid could also etch the pool walls and corrode the metal fittings in the circulation system. Generally acidity is not a problem because most halogen-based disinfectants tend to raise the pH level, although in extreme cases sodium bicarbonate — baking soda — can be added to neutralize the acidity.

A reading at the other extreme of the scale, 13 or 14, would indicate a high alkaline content. Alkaline water will retard the effectiveness of the disinfectant, so it would not be able to kill the germs in the pool water properly. To counter alkalinity, you can add a neutralizer, such as muriatic acid or sodium bisulfate, to the water.

The germs in the water can be killed with chemical disinfectants. The most popular compounds are members of the halogen family: chlorine, bromine, and iodine. Most people are familiar with chlorine because it is frequently used to treat drinking water. While it is available in gas — designed for commercial applications — liquid, or dry form, the latter is safer, more stable, and easier to use than either the liquid or gas.

Calcium hypochlorite, also called Cal Hypo, and lithium hypochlorite are two popular dry chlorine chemicals designed for pools. Those chemicals are relatively stable and have a long shelf life. Both compounds tend to raise the pH level of the water. Some formulations have buffers, such as cyanuric acid, to keep them from breaking down in the sunlight. The problem with cyanuric acid is that it is difficult to remove once it's introduced into the water.

While those chemicals are safe to use, it is important to store them in a cool, dry place away from other substances. Some formulations can react with organic materials — soda, oil, soap or even sweat — and cause combustion.

Some people object to adding chlorine compounds to their pool water because they feel it causes eye irritation and gives off an unpleasant odor. Actually, it is not the chlorine that is at fault. When chlorine combines with the ammonia in pool water, it forms chromides. They cause the irritations and offensive odors. The solution to the problem, ironically, is to add more chlorine. That treatment, called superchlorination, involves adding three to four times the usual dosage of chlorine once a week before sunrise or after sundown.

Bromine and iodine are also effective as disinfectants; they are also less likely to combine with ammonia and form eye-irritating compounds. Bromine is available in stick form, so it can be handled in the same manner as dry chlorine. Iodine is available in dry form; typical formulations also include other chemicals, such as potassium and sypochlorite, to help make the iodine water soluble. As a disinfectant, iodine remains active longer than chlorine, but it is not so effective in fighting algae.

MAINTENANCE: In addition to filtering the water and adding the proper chemicals, it is important to set up a regular maintenance schedule to avoid problems and protect the pool. Daily chores should include skimming the water surface to remove floating debris. After skimming remove and clean all the skimmer baskets. Another daily chore includes testing and adjusting the chemical balance of the water. Also test it several times on those days when the pool is filled with a number of active swimmers. In the early hours of the morning, when the dirt particles have had a chance to settle to the bottom, brush the pool floor. Always brush toward the main drain.

Weekly chores include vacuuming and brushing the sides, particularly around the water line, of the pools. The filter also should be cleaned or backwashed. In addition to the pool, the deck, diving board, and sides should also be hosed down and cleaned every week. ⊕

Home Security

Many homeowners become complacent about home security because they feel they have nothing worth stealing. What they fail to realize is that the majority of burglars have no way of knowing exactly what is inside any home. Most break into a house, expecting to get lucky. Given enough time, a burglar will tear into a house, ripping apart upholstery, breaking up cabinets, and even pulling pictures from the walls, looking for salable items. Thus it may cost more to repair the damage than to replace the stolen items.

Only a small percentage of burglaries are the result of careful planning and execution by seasoned professionals. The majority of break-ins are perpetrated by individuals — most burglars work alone, but a few have one or more partners — in need of money, who drive around looking for likely targets.

What makes any house a good target for a break-in? A number of studies, usually based on interviews with actual burglars, have been conducted by different agencies and organizations. Since many burglars have their own individual methods and preferences, the results are far from conclusive, but a number of important factors are evident nevertheless.

One factor that influences many burglars is location. They usually operate within 5 to 10 miles of their home. As they scout out neighborhoods for possible targets, they look for areas near major traffic arteries, expressways, or throughways that may offer access to a quick getaway. Usually, they avoid houses on dead-end streets, cul-de-sacs, or circles.

There is some debate on the effectiveness of street lighting in deterring break-ins. Most law-enforcement agencies maintain that homes on well-lighted streets are less likely to be burglarized than those on dark streets. Some studies have shown that street lights are not a significant factor, because a surprising number of break-ins occur during the daytime, when the occupants are at work and in school.

When discussing potential targets, some burglars indicated a preference for corner houses, while others chose homes in the middle of the street; some picked secluded houses, and some preferred houses on busy streets. All burglars, however, agreed that unoccupied houses were prime targets. Thus it behooves any homeowner to make his house look occupied even when he is out.

If you are away from home for long periods you might want to consider having a house sitter drop by at different times. College students, retirees, and elderly relatives or others who have flexible schedules are possible candidates. It also may be possible to prevail on a trusted neighbor who spends most of the time at home to come over during the day to open the curtains, draw the blinds, or raise a few window shades.

You also can set up props to create the illusion of activity around the house. Positioned on the front porch, objects like a child's tricycle, a snow

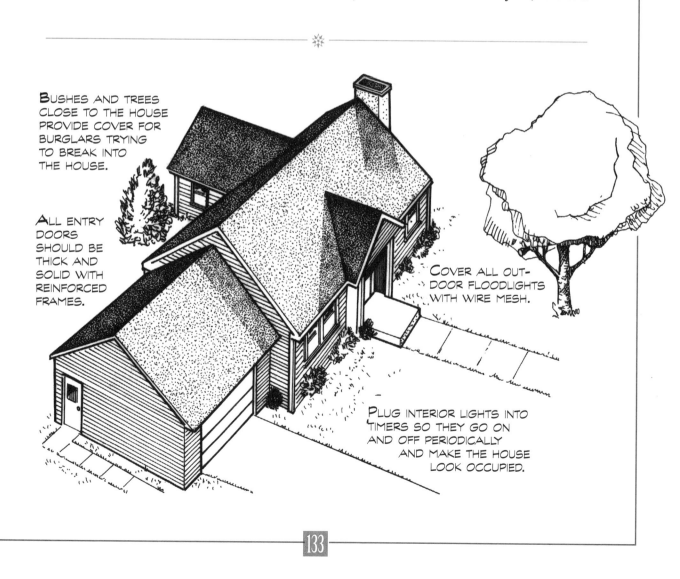

BUSHES AND TREES CLOSE TO THE HOUSE PROVIDE COVER FOR BURGLARS TRYING TO BREAK INTO THE HOUSE.

ALL ENTRY DOORS SHOULD BE THICK AND SOLID WITH REINFORCED FRAMES.

COVER ALL OUTDOOR FLOODLIGHTS WITH WIRE MESH.

PLUG INTERIOR LIGHTS INTO TIMERS SO THEY GO ON AND OFF PERIODICALLY AND MAKE THE HOUSE LOOK OCCUPIED.

shovel in the winter, or a garden rake suggest that someone is in the house and may step outside to retrieve them at any moment. Props are not as effective as a human presence, but they might cause a burglar to think twice about breaking into your home. When choosing props, select items that are not so valuable or attractive as to invite theft themselves.

Remember to stop all deliveries if you intend to be away for extended periods of time. Have a neighbor pick up the mail every day and arrange to have someone mow the lawn in the summer and shovel the walk in the winter.

Your home never should be totally dark at night. It's best to install timers around the house to turn interior lights on and off periodically. Exterior lights should also be regulated by timers or photosensitive activators. All exterior lights should be protected by wire guards so that burglars or vandals cannot smash and thus disable them.

The effectiveness of home burglar alarms is still open to debate. It largely depends on the system itself. It seems that an alarm system with lights and sirens may not be so effective as a system that's connected to a law-enforcement agency. Burglars themselves give alarms mixed reviews. Most say they may enter a house with an alarm, but they will retreat if they trip it.

Another theft-deterrent strategy involves marking valuable items by engraving an identification number on them. Often local police stations will lend the homeowner an electric engraving tool for marking. That ploy, however, draws mixed reactions. Most insurance companies, for example, point out that the engraved items are no more likely to be recovered than nonengraved items after a burglary.

Perhaps the best deterrent against burglary is a network of watchful neighbors. Unfortunately, most people, particularly in large cities, feel that it is in their best interest to mind their own business. Hence they often ignore strangers and suspicious vehicles in the area. ⊕

Locks

In colonial times homeowners were rather casual about securing their homes. The lock on the front door consisted of a large wooden bolt, which could be opened from the outside by pulling a drawstring. At night the owner would lock the door by pulling the string inside.

As the population increased, so did burglary and theft, and the demand arose for more sophisticated and effective locks. In an effort to meet that need, local craftsmen and blacksmiths started manufacturing locks. The locks of the 18th and early 19th centuries were handmade and were often quite cumbersome, some weighing as much as five pounds. In 1865, Linus Yale Jr. invented a lock that was simple and compact and could be mass-produced on automatic machinery.

Yale's design consisted of a cylinder with an internal rotating plug. When the key was inserted in the cylinder, it raised a number of small pins, called tumblers, so that the internal plug could rotate and release the bolt. Most of the locks manufactured today are based on the early Yale design. It would seem, then, that these locks are all the same. That, however, is not the case; locks differ greatly in the amount of security they offer. With break-ins increasing, it is important that you have the most effective lock on your doors to protect your home and person.

Today most home builders routinely install a key-in-knob lock on newly con-

A SOLID DOOR WITH A STRONG LOCK CAN BE FORCED OPEN BY PUSHING THE JAMB AWAY FROM THE DOOR. INSERT A SPACER BLOCK IN THE GAP BETWEEN THE JAMB AND THE STUD.

JAMB

STUD GAP

PRY BAR

BOLT

JAMB

SPACER BLOCK

WINDOW LOCKS

REPLACE CLAMSHELL LATCHES WITH KEY-TURNBUCKLE LOCKS.

SECURITY BOLT PASSES THROUGH BOTH SASHES. USE A KEY TO INSERT AND REMOVE THE BOLT.

ROD LOCKS ARE SIMILAR TO SECURITY BOLTS. THE ROD PASSES THROUGH BOTH SASHES. IT CAN BE LOCKED IN PLACE WITH A SET SCREW.

structed homes. Those locks are particularly vulnerable to break-ins for two reasons. First, the lock is contained in the knob, and an aggressive burglar can remove the lock by wrenching off the knob. He can then push back the bolt and open the door. The other weak feature is a spring-bolt that easily can be pushed back by inserting a shim — a thin piece of metal or plastic — between the door and the jamb. If you have such a lock on your door, consider installing an additional, stronger

- **ELECTRIC DRILL**
- **HOLE SAW**
- **SPADE BIT**
- **1/8-INCH DRILL BIT**
- **SCREWDRIVER**

lock. This lock should be a minimum of 6 inches away from the key-in-knob lock.

A good choice for a supplementary door lock is an internal — internal because it fits within the door — deadbolt lock. It consists of a cylinder, a cylinder guard, a bolt, and a thumbturn. The cylinder, mounted on the exterior of the door, houses the locking mechanism. Burglars often attack cylinder locks by gripping and turning the cylinder with a wrench. That forces the bolt back. The cylinder guard, a tapered, rotating ring, covers the cylinder and makes it almost impossible to grip or turn it.

The bolt is a metal rod that extends from the door into the strike plate on the jamb. It should be made of hardened steel and have a 1-inch throw. A 1-inch throw means that the bolt extends 1 inch past the edge of the door. The extra length thwarts a burglar who attempts to clear the bolt by wedging a pry bar between the door and the jamb.

On the interior side of the door, a thumb-turn allows you to open the lock by flipping the thumb lever. If the door has glass panels, an intruder easily can break the glass, reach in, and unlock the door. Here it's best to install a deadbolt with key-turn. The lock can be operated from either side only with a key. Some communities ban this type of lock because it can prevent exit as well as entrance, which could be hazardous in a fire. It's essential then to have a spare key nearby.

DEADBOLT INSTALLATION: To install an internal deadbolt lock, you'll have to drill two holes: one through the face of the door and another, perpendicular to the first, through the edge of the door. The first hole is a large one, so you'll need a hole saw. For the second hole you can use a spade bit.

You'll also have to mortise the edge of the door and the jamb to receive the bolt mount and the strike plate. Usually, the lock comes with instructions and a template to help you align the holes properly. Installation is not especially difficult, but it's important to drill the holes precisely; novice do-it-yourselfers may find that challenging. Fortunately, another lock provides equal security and is easier to install — the surface-mounted deadbolt.

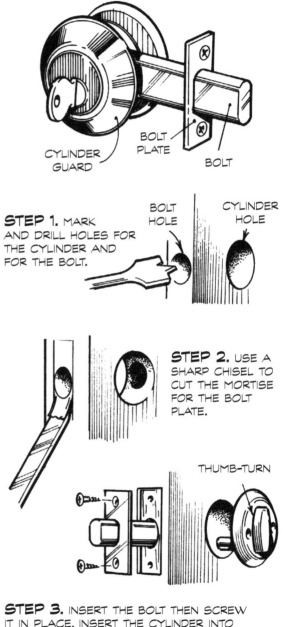

INSTALLING A DEADBOLT LOCK

CYLINDER GUARD

BOLT PLATE

BOLT

STEP 1. MARK AND DRILL HOLES FOR THE CYLINDER AND FOR THE BOLT.

BOLT HOLE

CYLINDER HOLE

STEP 2. USE A SHARP CHISEL TO CUT THE MORTISE FOR THE BOLT PLATE.

THUMB-TURN

STEP 3. INSERT THE BOLT THEN SCREW IT IN PLACE. INSERT THE CYLINDER INTO HOLE ON OUTSIDE OF DOOR. INSTALL THE THUMB-TURN. SECURE IT WITH SCREWS.

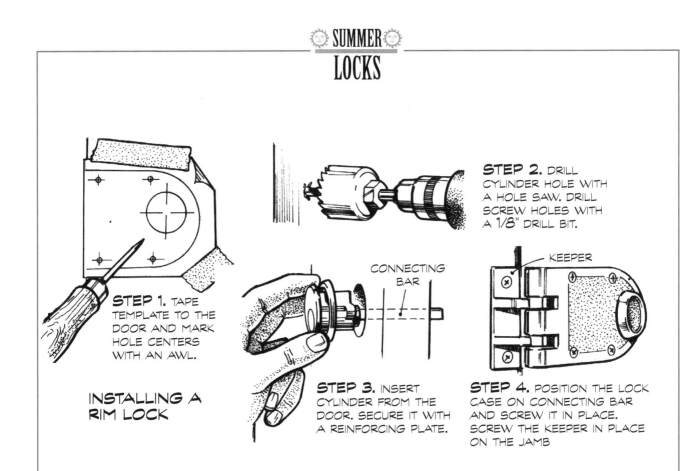

STEP 2. DRILL CYLINDER HOLE WITH A HOLE SAW. DRILL SCREW HOLES WITH A 1/8" DRILL BIT.

STEP 1. TAPE TEMPLATE TO THE DOOR AND MARK HOLE CENTERS WITH AN AWL.

INSTALLING A RIM LOCK

CONNECTING BAR

STEP 3. INSERT CYLINDER FROM THE DOOR. SECURE IT WITH A REINFORCING PLATE.

KEEPER

STEP 4. POSITION THE LOCK CASE ON CONNECTING BAR AND SCREW IT IN PLACE. SCREW THE KEEPER IN PLACE ON THE JAMB

RIM-LOCK INSTALLATION: The surface-mounted deadbolt, sometimes called a rim lock, is mounted on the interior face of the door. The locking cylinder is fitted into the exterior of the door. A drive bar connects the cylinder plug to the lock. The locking bolts are two steel rods that drop vertically through holes in the keeper — similar to the strike plate — mounted on the jamb. The mechanism of the surface-mounted deadbolt can be controlled from the inside with a thumb-turn or a key.

To install the lock, you must use the hole saw to drill a hole through the door. The cylinder will be mounted in this cavity. Next, drill four smaller holes 3/4-inch deep with a 1/8-inch drill bit. Those are pilot holes for the lock mounting screws. The cylinder is held in place with a reinforcing plate. The lock case is then slipped onto the cylinder drive bar and screwed into place.

This lock is easy to install because all the holes are drilled into the face of the door, and mortising is not required. Obviously, it's important to get the holes in the right place, but that is not difficult; instructions and a paper template usually are provided with the lock.

The lock does not come with a cylinder guard, but you can buy one at a locksmith's or hardware store. The cylinder guard is a hardened steel plate with a clearance hole for the key. To mount it, place it over the cylinder and bolt it in place with four carriage bolts. ⊕

Animal Pest Control

Many homeowners are finding that such animals as deer, raccoons, squirrels, and rabbits are invading their yards, gardens, and sometimes even their homes. These animals have adapted to the human environment and now include it as part of their territory. In doing so, they eat flowers, shrubs, and vegetables and damage trees and property. What can the homeowner do?

MANY ANIMALS HAVE ADAPTED TO THE HUMAN ENVIRONMENT.

Erecting fences is the most effective way to restrict the animal invaders. Unfortunately, it is also the most expensive method of control. If you decide to go that route, consult with your local agricultural station to obtain information on what type of fence works best to keep out the animals in your area.

Not all fences need to be of steel or wood. Thorny bushes, such as holly, Japanese barberry or hawthorr

can be an effective barrier against deer. If rabbits are nibbling in your vegetable garden, try planting a perimeter of marigold plants. They have a strong, pungent odor, which repels rabbits. The two common species of marigold are the African and French marigold. The African variety has the stronger smell and seems to be more effective against rabbits.

Marigolds and vegetables attract slugs, land mollusks closely related to snails but without the shells. You can stop these nocturnal predators with beer. Bury a few jars up to their necks in the soil around your garden; then fill them with beer. Cheap domestic beer will be effective, unless you want to impress the neighbors — in that case,

MARIGOLDS KEEP RABBITS AWAY.

ANIMAL PEST CONTROL

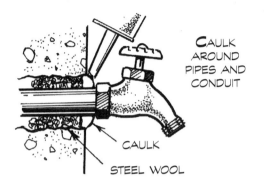

CAULK AROUND PIPES AND CONDUIT

CAULK

STEEL WOOL

use imported beer. The beer lures the slugs into the jars, where they drown.

In protecting your property, consider your house as well as your yard. During the winter an attic, basement, or even the cavities in the walls can seem cozy and inviting to a wild animal. Now is the time to take preventive measures, before any animal moves in.

Cut back all branches and tree limbs that might allow squirrels and raccoons access to the roof or chimney. Then walk around the house and look for any holes or openings that might provide entrances for critters. The chimney, exhaust vents — including the dryer vent — and gaps around water pipes are all common targets.

Put mesh screening over the chimney and all exhaust vents. Push steel wool into the gaps around water lines, then fill them with caulk. The steel wool is important because mice will often eat through the caulking but not the steel wool.

Don't forget your pet's private door. Your dog or cat may find it convenient to come or go on his own terms, but raccoons or squirrels soon discover the availability of this ready-made door and use it to enter the home. If that happens, you will have to seal up the door.

Most animals invade your property in search of food. If you offer them a "free lunch," they will return — often with relatives — to claim your yard as part of their territory. If there is nothing to eat, however, they will search elsewhere. So don't feed the wild animals. As obvious as this rule is, it is astonishing how many people break it. They think that all animals are cute and can be tamed easily; but once wild animals lose their fear of humans, they literally can eat their way into your home.

Even without handouts animals can find ample food around the average home. Raccoons, for example, are notoriously adept at raiding garbage cans.

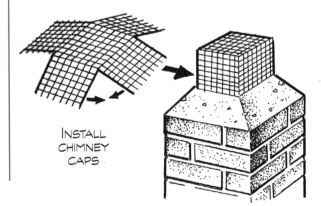

INSTALL CHIMNEY CAPS

ANIMAL PEST CONTROL

To keep them and other animal predators out, fit your trash cans with tight-fitting lids or attach springs to keep the lids secure. Even that may not be

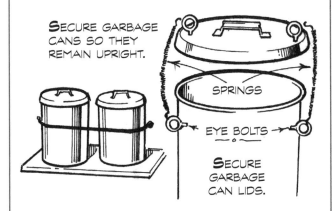

SECURE GARBAGE CANS SO THEY REMAIN UPRIGHT.

SPRINGS

EYE BOLTS →

SECURE GARBAGE CAN LIDS.

enough, because raccoons frequently push the cans over to dislodge the lids. To thwart this maneuver, chain the cans into an upright position or, better still, place them in an enclosure. You also can sprinkle cayenne pepper, which acts as a repellent, around the cans.

If all those tactics fail, you can make your garbage more repulsive by spraying it with a commercial repellent like ROPEL. While that makes trash, and indeed all food, foul-tasting, it does not harm the animal and is environmentally safe.

If deer come to nibble on your flowers and trees, you might consider planting something deer won't eat: barberry, English ivy, daffodils, irises and thorny bushes like holly. Avoid planting tulips, fruit trees, strawberry plants, azaleas, and yew.

Finally, consider making your property less hospitable to wild animals. Get a dog or a cat. Cats can be effective in keeping squirrels and mice at bay, but for larger animal invaders you will need a dog — a large one. Most animals learn that a small dog is all bark and poses no threat.

You also can spray your yard with repellents. Commercial preparations, such as Big Game Repellent, Deer Away, Magic Circle, and Hinder, are available at most garden or farm supply stores. If, however, you can't find them, you can concoct your own deer repellent by mixing 20 raw eggs into one gallon of water. For raccoon repellent mix one

FENCES ARE THE BEST DEER DETERRENT.

BAMBI GO HOME

cup of children's shampoo with one cup of ammonia. Garden supply stores also sell dried-blood fertilizer, which can be effective as an animal repellent.

Those repellents are environmentally safe, but they taste bad and smell worse — to animals. The odor is too weak to bother humans. Spray the repellents on ground vegetation, on tall bushes, and on trees. Remember that deer can reach as high as 6 feet. After a heavy rainstorm you will have to spray again. After a few weeks you may have to do it again, but with a different repellent, because animals can adjust to a scent.

Some manufacturers make devices that emit high-frequency sounds, inaudible to humans and "most pets." These transmitters are designed to chase away rodents, insects, and sometimes larger animals. Most tests show that these devices are only marginally effective at best.

However, one sound can chase raccoons away — rock and roll music. Heavy metal is most effective. Place a speaker near the raccoon lair and turn on the music. Usually, the raccoons will retreat. However, there is a downside to this strategy. Some homeowners report that while the music does indeed chase the raccoons away, it also attracts teenagers from around the neighborhood.

One word of caution: Never attempt to confront or handle a wild animal. They can scratch and bite and inflict vicious wounds. Some animals, especially raccoons, can be rabid. Many carry ticks and lice. If you encounter a wild animal, give it a wide berth and consult a professional pest-control expert. ⊕

HOUSEHOLD HELPS • FILES

APPLYING A THIN COAT OF CHALK TO THE FILE WILL HELP REDUCE CLOGGING AND MAKE IT EASIER TO CLEAN THE FILE.

USE A SMALL TRIANGULAR FILE TO MAKE NOTCHES IN YOUR KEYS SO YOU CAN IDENTIFY THEM IN THE DARK.

FRONT DOOR KEY HAS ONE NOTCH.

BACK DOOR KEY HAS TWO NOTCHES.

Bird Pests

Most people like birds. They like to watch them, and they like to feed them. Sometimes, however, the nesting habits and behavioral patterns of some birds can turn them into pests. Some birds may build nests in your vents, gutters, or eaves, while others can damage your cedar shingles by pecking holes in them.

What can you do when birds become pests? First, it's important to understand what you cannot do to eliminate problem birds. Federal and state laws protect all wild birds, except English sparrows, pigeons, and starlings. The laws strictly prohibit individuals from killing, trapping, or tampering with the nests of protected species without special permits. That leaves you with only three options: You can erect barriers and guards on and around your home, you can scare the birds away, or you can tempt them to move to a more remote part of your property.

Before taking any action, try to identify the bird and analyze what's attracting it to your environment. That may be obvious, but sometimes a bird problem may arise for no apparent reason. You can get expert advice by calling your U.S. Fish and Wildlife Service Regional Office, your state wildlife officer and county Cooperative Extension agent.

Understand that birds are not stupid creatures, and utilizing only one method to solve your problem may not be enough. Birds learn quickly and are able to adapt to changing conditions, so a seemingly effective solution may work only for a short time. In the final analysis your battle against bird pests may turn into a full campaign incorporating a variety of tactics.

Ornithologists estimate that there are about 650 species of birds in North America. Fortunately, only a few of them cause the homeowner problems. Pigeons can be a major problem for the city dweller. They build nests on balconies, terraces, and on ledges around windows. Some people try to frighten the pigeons by mounting plastic replicas of owls, a natural enemy of the pigeon, nearby. The pigeons quickly learn that the stationary figure is no threat, and they often adopt the fake owl as a perch. The owl figure can be made more lifelike and a little more threatening if it is suspended by a thin wire and allowed to swing in the breeze.

Since motion usually frightens birds away, you can try mounting flags on rails or tying ribbons to posts. That may be enough to scare the pigeons. Noise also can be an effective weapon against pigeon infestation. The noise doesn't have to be particularly loud or grating; sometimes hanging wind chimes will work.

There are some bird repellents on the market. A few are available as sprays or powders, but they generally come in paste form that can be spread on ledges or railings. If you use this stuff, it's essential to cover all likely perches, or else the pigeons will collect on the untreated places. Bird repellent is nontoxic, but it can stain painted surfaces, so protect the surface with masking tape first.

Probably the most effective strategy is to deny birds access to your property. That may require hanging netting around the balcony and stringing a type of bird-deterrent barbed wire, called Nixalite, on ledges. Admittedly, those methods are not visually attractive, but

❋

STARLINGS PRESENT PROBLEMS BECAUSE THEY BUILD NESTS IN GUTTERS, VENTS, AND OTHER OPENINGS. SOMETIMES THE BIRDS CAN BE FRIGHTENED OFF BY ATTACHING FLAGS OR RIBBONS NEAR THE NESTING SITES. A BETTER SOLUTION INVOLVES SEALING ALL CRACKS AND COVERING VENTS WITH HEAVY-DUTY SCREENING.

NO VACANCY

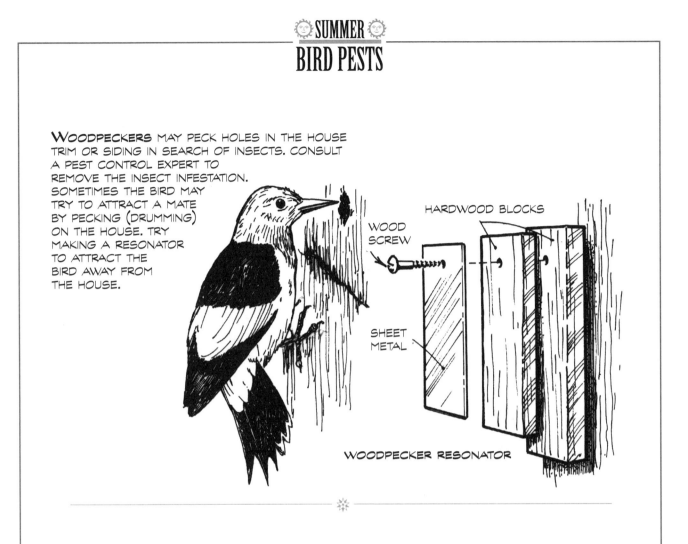

WOODPECKERS MAY PECK HOLES IN THE HOUSE TRIM OR SIDING IN SEARCH OF INSECTS. CONSULT A PEST CONTROL EXPERT TO REMOVE THE INSECT INFESTATION. SOMETIMES THE BIRD MAY TRY TO ATTRACT A MATE BY PECKING (DRUMMING) ON THE HOUSE. TRY MAKING A RESONATOR TO ATTRACT THE BIRD AWAY FROM THE HOUSE.

HARDWOOD BLOCKS

WOOD SCREW

SHEET METAL

WOODPECKER RESONATOR

then neither are pigeon nests or droppings.

Suburbanites may not be troubled so much by pigeons as by starlings, house sparrows, or barn swallows. Usually starlings are the biggest problem because they aggressively build their nests in any nook or cranny around the house. Here again it's best to discourage the birds before they build their nests. Walk around the outside of the house and seal up any holes. Do not rely on caulk alone as a plug; birds can easily peck through it. Instead, force coarse steel wool into the holes and cover them with wood or metal. Next put heavy-duty screening on all gutters and vents.

You also can try to make another part of your property more enticing by putting up bird houses or feeders. They may tempt the birds to take up residence away from your house.

If the birds already have built a nest you usually can scare them away with load noises or bright lights. Since starlings are not protected by federal or state law you can legally remove the nest; however, it's still a good idea to check with local authorities first. If you do decide to clean out a bird site, be sure to wear rubber gloves and a respirator to protect yourself from the mites or diseases that some birds carry.

Woodpeckers can present two problems for the homeowner. During the mating season, males try to attract a mate by "drumming." Usually, they pick a resonant dead tree to peck, but occasionally they turn to the house. Here they make noise by pecking on the gutters, a TV antenna, or metal siding. The bird can make a lot of noise, but it doesn't cause any damage. You can deaden the noise by temporarily wrapping the antenna with padding or stuffing the gutter with insulation. Obviously, you cannot pad large sections of siding. You can try building a resonator (see accompanying illustration) and positioning it nearby, not on the house.

A more serious problem occurs when the woodpecker picks your house as a source of food. He will drill holes into the wood siding or trim in search of insects. You can, of course, chase the bird away, but it's possible that the woodpecker knows something that you don't. You probably have insects crawling under your siding, and you should consult with a pest control expert to find the extent of the problem. When you remove the infestation, the bird will look for food elsewhere. ⊕

HOUSEHOLD HELPS • FURNITURE

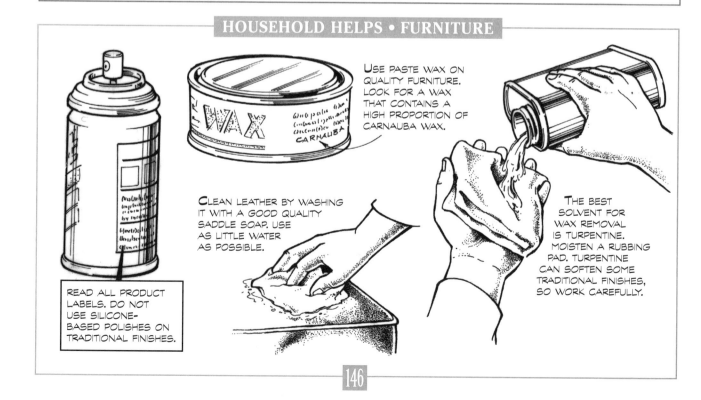

USE PASTE WAX ON QUALITY FURNITURE. LOOK FOR A WAX THAT CONTAINS A HIGH PROPORTION OF CARNAUBA WAX.

CLEAN LEATHER BY WASHING IT WITH A GOOD QUALITY SADDLE SOAP. USE AS LITTLE WATER AS POSSIBLE.

THE BEST SOLVENT FOR WAX REMOVAL IS TURPENTINE. MOISTEN A RUBBING PAD. TURPENTINE CAN SOFTEN SOME TRADITIONAL FINISHES, SO WORK CAREFULLY.

READ ALL PRODUCT LABELS. DO NOT USE SILICONE-BASED POLISHES ON TRADITIONAL FINISHES.

Outdoor Work

Summer is the time when many home-owners tackle outdoor projects. While the warm temperatures and bright sunshine make it convenient and even enjoyable for outdoor work, too much of a good thing can be dangerous. Overexposure to the summer sun can result in severe sunburn and heat exhaustion.

Doing strenuous work outdoors on a hot, humid day can quickly take its toll on your body. In addition to the heat absorbed from the sun, your muscles will generate heat as they flex, causing your body temperature to rise higher. Too much heat will shut down your body's thermoregulation mechanism and induce heatstroke unless it can be released in some way.

Unfortunately, most people don't realize they are overdoing it until it is too late, but you can take a number of precautions to protect yourself from the hazards of heat and sun. First, it's important to condition yourself to the rigors of outdoor work in the summer sun. It takes about 15 days for the average person to get acclimated to the hot weather. Don't launch into a long, stren-uous project on the first hot, humid day of summer; instead start with smaller jobs for brief periods early in the season and work up to larger tasks.

It is also important to wear the right clothes. It's tempting to wear shorts and a T-shirt, but long pants and a long-sleeved shirt will protect your arms and

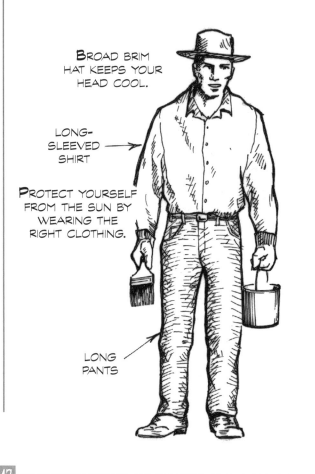

BROAD BRIM HAT KEEPS YOUR HEAD COOL.

LONG-SLEEVED SHIRT →

PROTECT YOURSELF FROM THE SUN BY WEARING THE RIGHT CLOTHING.

LONG PANTS

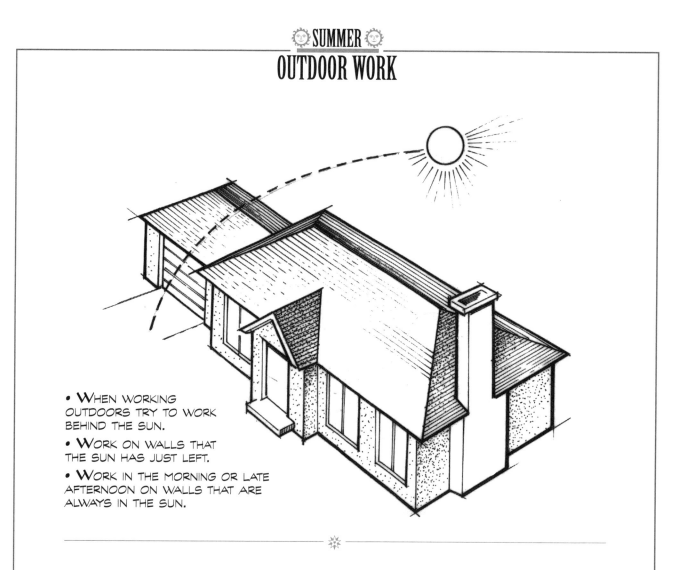

- WHEN WORKING OUTDOORS TRY TO WORK BEHIND THE SUN.
- WORK ON WALLS THAT THE SUN HAS JUST LEFT.
- WORK IN THE MORNING OR LATE AFTERNOON ON WALLS THAT ARE ALWAYS IN THE SUN.

legs from the sun's intense rays. A wide-brimmed hat is essential because it can protect your face and neck from the sun. It can help you in another way. The head is the body's heat regulator. More than 50 percent of the body's temperature is absorbed or dissipated through the head. The hat can shield your head from the sun and keep you from soaking up too much heat.

Cotton fabrics are usually cooler than synthetics because they allow more air to circulate between the fibers. Some synthetics, however, have a "wicking" action that pulls perspiration away from your body and keeps you cool.

Dark fabrics block the sun's rays better than light ones, but they also absorb more heat. So it's better to wear light-colored clothes and apply a sunscreen. That is essential if you a wearing thin fabrics because the sun can penetrate through them. Apply a good sunscreen with a sun protection factor (SPF) of 15 or higher, at least 30 minutes before you start working outdoors. Apply more every two hours. Along with its skin-pro-

tection properties, sunscreen also can cool the skin as it evaporates.

Dehydration, or the loss of body fluid, is another danger because it can cause heat exhaustion as well as heat stroke. Heat exhaustion starts with extreme thirst and progresses into nausea, dizziness, vomiting, headaches, and heat cramps. If it is not checked, it will lead to heat stroke.

The way to avoid dehydration is by drinking extra liquid, about 16 ounces, two hours before starting work. Then continue to drink as you feel thirsty. While water is fine, a sports drink or fruit juice is better because they replace natural body salts and help you to retain the fluids you consume. Avoid drinking ice-cold fluids when you are hot. They can "shock" the stomach muscles and cause heat cramps.

Remember to listen to your body. Know the symptoms of heat exhaustion and heat stroke and be ready to quit working if they arise. If possible, enlist the aid of a buddy to help you with your work. That will make the workload lighter, and you will be able to monitor each other for the warning signs of heat exhaustion. Often the other person can be a better judge of your condition then you are. He can stop you before you overwork yourself.

Schedule your project so that you do most of the work in the morning when it is cool. Start in the early morning and work till noon. As the day begins to heat up, pause for a long lunch and take an additional rest. This break will allow you to get out of the sun and cool off. Resume in the late afternoon. With some jobs, such as exterior painting, you may be able to work "behind the sun." Start on a side of the house that the sun has left. Continue around behind the sun as the day progresses.

Even with all those precautions, on hot days you may have to lower your expectations and do less work than originally planned. You cannot accomplish as much because the body's heart rate is elevated on a hot day, so fatigue is apt to occur sooner than you might expect. When the temperature and humidity climb to high levels, it may be better to put off your projects and wait for cooler days. ⊕

FALL INSPECTION

FALL is a transition from the hot days of summer to the cold days of winter. The early part of the season should be devoted to putting away the tools and furniture used during the summer months. After that, while the weather is still mild, work outdoors in the yard and on the exterior of the house. When the temperature drops, move indoors and prepare the heating system for the cold days ahead.

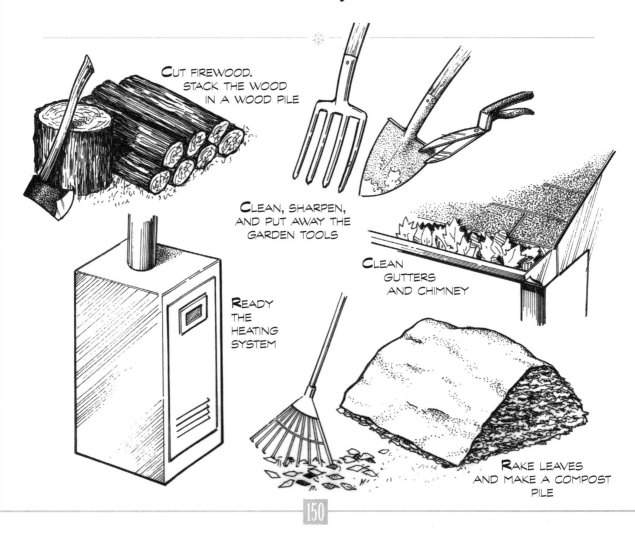

CUT FIREWOOD. STACK THE WOOD IN A WOOD PILE

CLEAN, SHARPEN, AND PUT AWAY THE GARDEN TOOLS

CLEAN GUTTERS AND CHIMNEY

READY THE HEATING SYSTEM

RAKE LEAVES AND MAKE A COMPOST PILE

In many ways the fall schedule is like the spring plan in reverse. You'll be **cleaning and putting away the garden tools and patio furniture** and **recovering the air conditioner**. It's tempting to hang your tools on the rack and forget about them, but now is really the time to **sharpen them and spray them with a light coat of oil** so that they will be rust resistant and ready for springtime chores.

 It's also a good idea to **inspect the rain gutters** again to see if they've collected any leaves. With the cold weather approaching, you may want to start a fire in the fireplace. Before you do, **inspect the chimney** again to be sure that squirrels or other rodents haven't built a nest there.

Check your heating system early in the fall so that it's ready in the event of a sudden frost. Also **make a thorough inspection outside, examining the insulation, weatherstripping, caulking, and window glazing**. Remember to **shut off the supply water to all outdoor faucets**.

Obviously, fall is also the time to **rake and gather leaves**, so allot some time for the chore. If you're a gardener, you can use the leaves to **make a compost pile**.

Finally, if you have a wood-burning stove or fireplace, you'll want to **lay in a stack of firewood**.

Early fall is the time when severe thunderstorms hit many parts of the United States. Such storms usually discharge awesome bolts of lightning that can kill people and destroy property. Every homeowner should take the time to consider the risk of lightning damage and **decide whether or not lightning protection is worth installing** on the house.

Thunderstorms can cause another problem for homeowners. Excessive amounts of rainwater can seep into the basement of the house and cause damage. Severe water problems may require **installing waterproof membranes and drainage systems**. Usually, however, the problem can be prevented by making sure that the **grounds around the house are graded properly** to ensure all rain runoff is directed away from the house. That is a job that is best tackled in the early fall while the weather is still warm.

Fireplaces

A recent survey of homeowners revealed that there are over 35 million fireplaces in homes throughout the United States, and each year homeowners light more than 1 billion fires in those fireplaces.

Those statistics may not surprise most readers, because they picture a crackling fire in the living-room fireplace as the ideal setting for cozy comfort on a cold winter night. Fireplaces may be romantic and cozy, but they are not efficient. Ninety percent of the heat created in the fireplace escapes up the chimney. The fire also pulls additional air — five to 10 times the amount required for combustion — from the room.

Can anything be done to improve the efficiency of the average home fireplace? Yes, it is possible to make modifications by adding inserts. A wood-burning insert fits in the fireplace and uses the existing chimney — fitted with a flexible metal liner — to exhaust smoke and combustion gases. A faceplate with metal or glass doors fits across the fireplace opening and encloses the fire. The heart of the unit is a heat exchanger that pulls in cool air from the room, warms it, and blows it back. Controls allow the user to adjust the level of air going directly into the firebox and thus regulate the intensity of the fire.

Another type of insert is an enclosed, gas-fired unit. It is sealed completely, so fresh air for the fire is drawn in through a chimney tube while combustion gases are expelled through a parallel tube. It also has a heat exchanger to circulate warm air into the living room. The unit does not burn wood, however; the fire comes from ignited natural gas that burns around artificial logs.

Even though the inserts are efficient as heating units, they do detract from the charm of the fireplace; in effect, they convert the fireplace into a stove.

- **MATCHES OR LIGHTER**
- **NEWSPAPERS**
- **KINDLING**
- **LOGS**

In addition, modifications can be expensive and may not be worth the cost and bother if you use the fireplace only occasionally. However, you can do some things to make your fireplace a little more efficient without additional expenditures.

Adding glass doors to the face of the fireplace can help to conserve room heat at night after the fire has died down. The doors, however, should be kept open when the fire is burning; otherwise, the closed doors will prevent heat from radiating into the room.

Whenever possible, burn hot, blazing fires, not low, smoldering ones. Hot fires burn the wood gases more completely and heat the fireplace bricks so that they reflect more heat into the room. Most people have raised grates in their fireplace, but the old-fashioned andirons are better because they allow the burning logs to fall onto the hot bed of coals and burn more efficiently.

Inspect and clean the fireplace and chimney every year. Ideally you should do this in the spring, so if you discover damage, such as cracked flue tiles, there will be plenty of time for repair work. Look into the chimney again in the fall to make certain that squirrels, raccoons or birds haven't made a nest in it. Installing a chimney cap is a good way of preventing unwanted intruders from nesting in the flue.

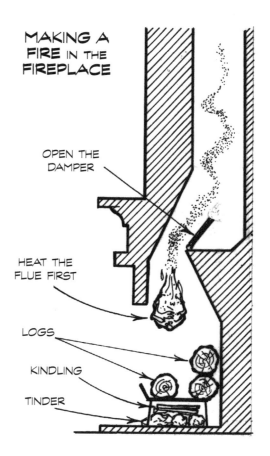

MAKING A FIRE IN THE FIREPLACE

OPEN THE DAMPER

HEAT THE FLUE FIRST

LOGS

KINDLING

TINDER

Take the time to inspect the damper carefully. The damper is the hinged metal plate that swings to close the flue opening. Dampers in new fireplaces are made to fit tightly so they close to keep cold air from coming down the chimney into the house. Over time a damper may rust and deteriorate so it no longer makes an effective barrier against the cold air. You should replace a defective damper. Also consider installing a chimney-top damper. It will help to cut heat loss when you are not using your fire-place.

When you are ready to make a fire, start with a bed of four or five crumbled newspaper balls. Lay finger-thick kindling in a grid pattern on top of the newspaper. The fire will require oxygen as it burns so keep the newspaper and kindling layers loose, allowing the air to circulate. Finally, place three logs across the andirons. It may be tempting to start with only one log and add others as each one is burned. But a full fire with three logs burns more efficiently and produces more heat per log.

Before starting the fire, make sure the damper is open fully, and heat the air in the flue to create a stronger draft. To heat the air in the chimney, hold a burning torch made of rolled-up newspaper directly under the damper. Use the torch to light the newspaper bed below the logs. Once the fire is roaring, close the damper as far as it will go without restricting the flow of smoke up the chimney. ⊕

HOUSEHOLD HELPS • SAWING

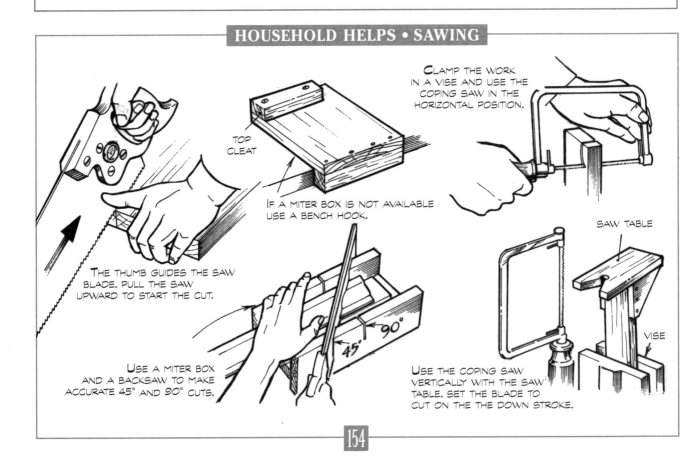

THE THUMB GUIDES THE SAW BLADE. PULL THE SAW UPWARD TO START THE CUT.

TOP CLEAT

IF A MITER BOX IS NOT AVAILABLE USE A BENCH HOOK.

CLAMP THE WORK IN A VISE AND USE THE COPING SAW IN THE HORIZONTAL POSITION.

SAW TABLE

VISE

USE A MITER BOX AND A BACKSAW TO MAKE ACCURATE 45° AND 90° CUTS.

45° 90°

USE THE COPING SAW VERTICALLY WITH THE SAW TABLE. SET THE BLADE TO CUT ON THE THE DOWN STROKE.

Firewood

Many cost-conscious homeowners are aware that using an energy-efficient fireplace or wood stove can cut heating bills. It is not always necessary to keep the fireplace or stove working all of the time, only on especially cold days. The main drawback to those heaters is that you must lay in a supply of firewood. You can either buy wood or gather your own.

Buying firewood can be a little confusing, because it is sold in a standard unit of measure called a cord. A cord measures 4 feet wide by 4 feet high by 8 feet long. Homeowners who use their fireplace infrequently may require less than a full cord. To accommodate those customers, dealers sell fractions — for example one-half or one-quarter of a full cord.

Some dealers also sell firewood in "face cords." A face cord is made up of logs that are cut to more manageable lengths — you really can't fit a 4-foot log in the average fireplace. So the cord may be 2 feet or 1 foot wide instead of the traditional 4-foot width. Unfortunately, not all dealers sell their cords in convenient stacks. They simply may show you a pile of wood and explain that it is a full cord. If you have any doubts about the quantity of wood you are about to purchase, you should stack the wood and measure it so that you can make accurate price comparisons.

Whenever possible, purchase "seasoned wood," wood that has been cut, stacked, and allowed to dry out or "cure." Fresh-cut wood has a high moisture content, which makes it difficult to burn. Ideally, firewood should stand for a year before it is used.

However, good, seasoned firewood often is sold at a premium price and may be unobtainable during the fall and winter. It's best to purchase extra firewood early in the season and store it for next year. Some of your fires may be

TOOL BOX

■ DROPCLOTHS, TARPAULIN, OR OTHER COVERING MATERIAL

■ SPACER LOGS

tough to light and maintain this year, but next year you will reap the fruits of your labors when you use the stored firewood.

If you are unsure if the wood is seasoned or not, examine it. Fresh-cut wood is pale yellow in color, while seasoned wood is dull gray; the logs usually have wide cracks running through them. After you buy the wood and have it delivered, you are faced with the problem of proper storage.

Large quantities of wood should be stacked outdoors and away from the house to allow the outdoor air and sunlight to season the logs. Choose the location carefully. The wood pile should be located far enough away from the house so that prevailing winds can circulate around and through the logs. It also should be away from dense brush and standing water, and it should face south to get the maximum benefits of the sun.

Another problem to consider is wildlife. Woodpiles make fine habitats for mice and other rodents, which, in turn, will attract snakes. If you want to avoid turning your woodpile into "the Wild Kingdom," build a wooden platform 18 inches high and stack the logs on it.

Even without the platform, the wood should not rest directly on the ground. Lay down two logs 4 inches in diameter or similar-sized lumber directly on the ground and stack the firewood across them. Place the firewood bark up and leave space between each log for air circulation.

As the pile rises you will notice that the logs on each end tend to roll off. You can use one of several different methods to hold them in place. For example, on alternate layers you can stack the end logs so that they are at right angles to the layer below. Those crisscrossed logs will lock the others in place.

You also can drive vertical stakes into the ground at either end of the pile. The stakes will function like bookends and keep the logs in the pile from rolling off. You can situate the wood pile between two trees. The trees will serve the same purpose as the vertical stakes. The only drawback to the tree method is that the shade from the trees will block the sun's rays, preventing the logs from drying.

It is essential to keep outdoor firewood covered, or else rain and snow will retard the seasoning process. You can use old boards, metal roofing, or heavy plastic sheeting to cover the top of the wood pile. Leave the sides open, however, to allow air to circulate between the logs.

For that to be cost effective, however, the homeowner must gather, cut, split, and stack his own firewood.

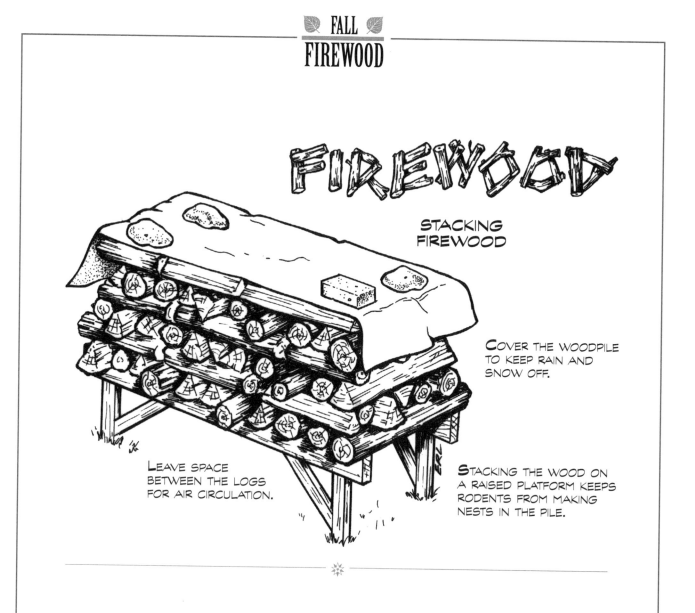

FIREWOOD

STACKING FIREWOOD

COVER THE WOODPILE TO KEEP RAIN AND SNOW OFF.

LEAVE SPACE BETWEEN THE LOGS FOR AIR CIRCULATION.

STACKING THE WOOD ON A RAISED PLATFORM KEEPS RODENTS FROM MAKING NESTS IN THE PILE.

Remember that any wood you cut now will be green wood and as such is not ready for the fireplace yet. If you don't have a stack of cured wood, you may have to buy some. But in the meantime you can start working on next year's wood pile.

Where can you find firewood? Obviously, if you own wooded land you may be able to find enough wood for your needs. Many state and federal agencies have programs that allow private citizens the opportunity to cut a limited amount of wood for a reasonable fee in government forests. To find out more about such programs, contact your local state forestry department or the U.S. Forest Service. Sometimes an owner of private, wooded land will allow you to cut some of his trees for a small fee. Before venturing onto any private or public lands, however, be sure to obtain permission.

You will encounter two problems when you try to remove wood from a forest. First, in order to get the wood, you'll have to fell standing trees. In theory that can be simple enough, but getting the tree to fall where you want it can be difficult. The ideal way to learn how to cut down a tree is to talk with an experienced forester or logger. Listen and ask questions so that you understand the techniques and safety precautions required; then start with smaller trees, about 6 inches in diameter, before tackling a large one.

In addition to knowing how to fell a tree, you should know which ones to cut. Most people assume that it's best to remove all the dead or dying trees — which loggers call "snags" — first. However, that is not always a good idea. Dead trees often have internal hollows. As they are being cut, they can break apart and drop heavy chunks of wood. In addition, snags can be an important link in the forest's ecological chain because they offer shelter to many insects, birds, and mammals.

The best trees to cut are live hardwoods, such as ash, beech, locust, hickory, maple and oak. Avoid such softwoods as cedar, fir, pine, and spruce: They have high resin contents that can leave creosote deposits in your flue. If you have problems with tree identification or questions concerning the environmental impact of your work, contact the U.S. Forest Service for advice.

If you decide not to tackle standing trees, you can try to collect cut logs and limbs. Highway construction crews, power companies, tree surgeons, and land developers frequently cut trees during the course of their work. Often you can have any logs that you can cart away. Another place to gather cut logs is the local dump or landfill. Con-

THE SAWBUCK
SAWBUCK WIDTH SHOULD BE TWICE THE LENGTH OF YOUR FIREWOOD.

2x4s NAILED TOGETHER

CLEATS 1x6 PINE 4 REQ'D

6d COMMON NAILS

WIDTH

WAIST HIGH

RUNG 1x3 PINE 2 REQUIRED

8d COMMON NAILS

tractors often dispose of logs that they remove from a building site. Beware, however, of taking wood that has been buried under a mound of garbage. It may have absorbed detergents or chemicals that will later give off noxious odors when burned.

When you get the logs and limbs home, you'll have to cut them to length. First, measure the width of your fireplace or stove's fire box so that you'll know how long to cut each piece.

Cutting logs usually is done on a sawhorse — called a "sawbuck" — and the cutting operation is called "bucking." The sawbuck holds the wood at a convenient height so that sawing is less tedious. If you don't have a sawbuck, you can make one out of 2 x 4s and scrap lumber.

Bucking logs is easier with a chain saw. Before using the saw, inspect the chain to see that the teeth are sharp and the chain tension is correct. Next, fill the fuel tank with the proper mixture of gas and oil. Obviously, this is not necessary if you own an electric chain saw. Consult your owner's manual for the correct fuel-to-oil ratio. Mix the fuel in a safe container and fill the tank at least 10 feet away from your work area.

When you're ready to start the saw, position it on level ground and stabilize it by holding the left grip with your left hand while anchoring the right handle

STARTING A CHAIN SAW

CHAIN MUST BE CLEAR OF SNAGS.

1. PLACE FOOT ON REAR HANDLE.
2. GRIP FRONT HANDLE.
3. PULL STARTER CORD UP.

with your right foot. Start the saw by pulling the starting cord straight up through its guide. Remember to don safety gear before bucking the logs.

Even with the sawbuck, the logs may roll or wander during the cutting operation, so you may want to enlist the aid of a helper to steady the logs. However, the helper also should wear safety gear and should be instructed to maintain a safe distance from the sawyer while the saw is running.

After the logs have been cut into lengths, called "rounds," they must be split. Split wood cures more rapidly than unsplit rounds. You can split the wood with an ax or a heavier splitting maul, also called a wood-splitter's hammer. Set the log on a solid wooden base or chopping block. Grip the ax with both hands, raise it above the log, and aim for the far side of the log. Allow the ax to fall into the log. Repeat with successive swings. With each swing aim closer to yourself. After a few strokes the log should split.

If you find it difficult to use an ax or a maul, then buy two 6- or 8-pound steel wedges. You can use a sledge hammer to drive them into the log. When using any striking tool, remember to wear goggles and heavy duty gloves. ⊕

WOOD SPLITTING TOOLS

AX

SPLITTING MAUL

WEDGES

SLEDGE HAMMER

CHOPPING BLOCK

Choosing and Using a Chain Saw

Homeowners who use wood stoves as a heat source know that they can save money if they gather and cut their own firewood. Cutting wood is a lot of work, but one tool that can make the job easier is a chain saw. However, many weekend woodcutters are afraid to use a chain saw because it seems like a dangerous tool. Undoubtedly, any tool that can slice through a 10-inch log quickly poses a risk to a careless or unskilled user.

In an effort to make those tools safer and more accessible to the average do-it-yourselfer, manufacturers have introduced safety features that reduce some of the hazards. Antikick nose guards, quick-stop brakes, vibration dampers, and wraparound handguards are important safeguards that buyers should look for when purchasing a chain saw.

When the chain saw blade, particularly the nose, hits an obstruction, motor torque can cause the saw to arc backward toward the operator. Known as kickback, it accounts for almost one-third of all chain saw accidents. Antikick nose guards, quick-stop brakes, and wrap-around handguards can help to reduce the hazard. Quick-stop brakes also can be used to lock the chain should a problem arise or if you have to set the saw down momentarily.

Powerful chain saw motors are prone to vibration, which can be exacerbated when the chain starts cutting into a log. Excessive vibration can cause fatigue and numbness. Prolonged exposure can cause traumatic vasospastic disease (TVD), an occupa-

TOOL BOX

- CHAIN SAW
- FACESHIELD
- HEAVY-DUTY GLOVES
- EAR PROTECTION
- WORK BOOTS
- SHARPENING GUIDE
- WIRE BRUSH
- FILE
- FILE GUIDE

tional disability of professional loggers. TVD probably is not a concern for the weekend woodcutter, but fatigue and numbness should be. Vibration dampers are therefore a desirable safety feature on a chain saw.

Safety features reduce the hazards of using a chain saw, but they never can be substitutes for the knowledge and skill of an alert operator. So when purchasing a chain saw, look for a dealer who will take the time and effort to demonstrate the proper use of the tool. After purchasing a chain saw, sit down and carefully read the owner's manual. Usually, it will provide instructions for safe and efficient operation of the saw.

SELECTING A CHAIN SAW: Before buying a chain saw, take the time to consider the available models and balance the features offered against your needs. Price probably will be a consideration, and it can be a rough indication of quality. Lower-priced models often are of light-weight construction and are suitable for only occasional use. If you intend to do a lot of wood cutting, then invest in a heavy-duty saw.

Chain saws are available with various cutting bar lengths, the cutting chain being mounted on the bar. For most weekend woodcutters a saw with a cutting bar between

12 inches and 20 inches will meet their needs; anything exceeding 25 inches will be too difficult to handle.

The best way to evaluate a potential purchase is to borrow it for a weekend test. If that is not possible, try to rent a comparable model. Again, arrange for adequate instruction before you take the saw home. When testing a saw, first consider its weight and balance. Make sure that all controls are simple to operate and accessible to the control hand.

Inspect the motor housing; it should have no sharp corners or protruding parts that could snag on clothing or brush. All moving parts, linkages, oil lines, and rotating parts — except, of course, the chain — should be enclosed.

On gasoline-powered saws the muffler should be enclosed in a protective

GASOLINE SAW

HANDLE

PULL-CORD

HANDLE

BAR

SAW CHAIN

CHOOSING AND USING A CHAIN SAW

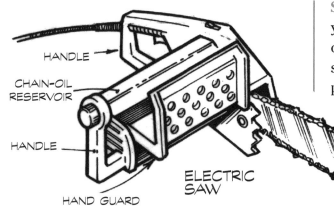

HANDLE

CHAIN-OIL
RESERVOIR

HANDLE

HAND GUARD

ELECTRIC
SAW

SAFETY GEAR: Besides the chain saw, you'll also need safety gear. During operation, the chain saw throws up sawdust, dirt, and occasionally metal particles; so safety goggles are essential. A full-face shield is even better.

Chain saws easily can create noise levels exceeding 100 decibels, so ear protection is necessary. While earplugs can be an effective noise barrier, most people find that the more expensive earmuff protectors are easier to don and offer a better fit.

Your safety gear should include a pair of sturdy work gloves. Besides cushioning your hands from motor vibration, they can protect you from blisters, splinters, and motor burns. Invest in a pair of high-quality leather gloves with double palms if possible. Some logging supply catalogs offer

shield, and the exhaust ducts should direct smoke and exhaust gases away from your face.

Electric chain saws also are available and they can be a good choice for limited woodcutting chores. Electric chain saws are lightweight and easy to handle and are generally less noisy than the gasoline-powered saws. If you intend to purchase an electric model, buy one that is double insulated.

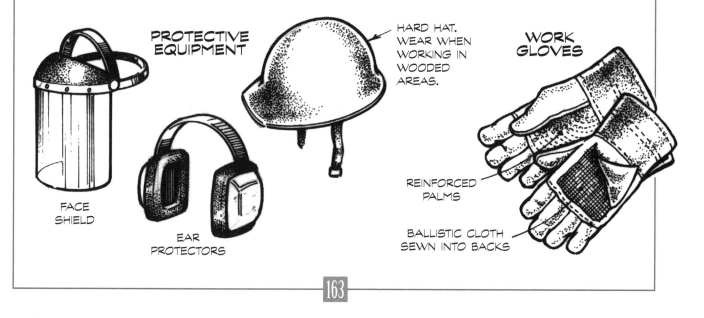

PROTECTIVE
EQUIPMENT

HARD HAT.
WEAR WHEN
WORKING IN
WOODED
AREAS.

WORK
GLOVES

FACE
SHIELD

EAR
PROTECTORS

REINFORCED
PALMS

BALLISTIC CLOTH
SEWN INTO BACKS

CHOOSING AND USING A CHAIN SAW

heavy-duty woodcutter's gloves with ballistic fabric — the same synthetic fabric found in bullet-proof vests — sewn into the backs. These gloves are expensive (some cost more than $100), but they can protect your hands from chain saw lacerations.

Don't forget your feet: Wear heavy-duty work boots. Sturdy boots with steel caps can protect you from chain saw cuts and from falling log ends.

In addition to the saw and safety gear, you should invest in a sharpening guide. A good quality sharpening guide can be purchased for less than $30. It might seem to the reader that having the chain saw sharpened at the beginning of the season would suffice, but that is not the case. Trees and logs often are covered with dirt and grit, which can take the edge off the sharp sawteeth quickly. Brushing the wood with a stiff wire brush can help. But even so, the sawteeth can lose their edge after a day of cutting. Professional loggers usually carry a small file and periodically touch up the chain.

You can buy a file guide that will help to maintain the proper angle and depth when you sharpen the chain. You also can invest in a model that chucks into your portable electric drill. ⊕

HOUSEHOLD HELPS • NAILS & SCREWS

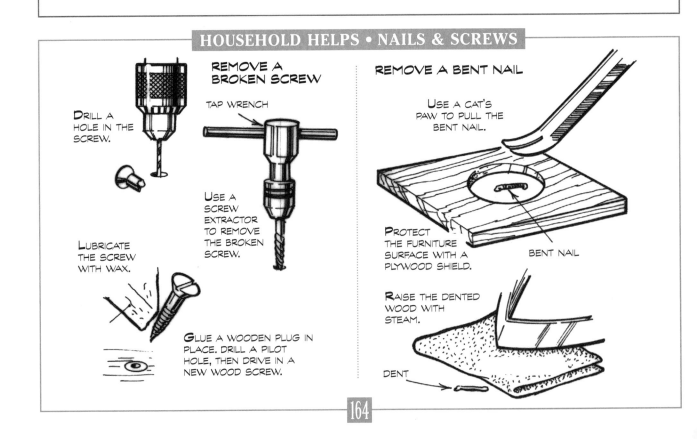

REMOVE A BROKEN SCREW

DRILL A HOLE IN THE SCREW.

TAP WRENCH

USE A SCREW EXTRACTOR TO REMOVE THE BROKEN SCREW.

LUBRICATE THE SCREW WITH WAX.

GLUE A WOODEN PLUG IN PLACE. DRILL A PILOT HOLE, THEN DRIVE IN A NEW WOOD SCREW.

REMOVE A BENT NAIL

USE A CAT'S PAW TO PULL THE BENT NAIL.

PROTECT THE FURNITURE SURFACE WITH A PLYWOOD SHIELD.

BENT NAIL

RAISE THE DENTED WOOD WITH STEAM.

DENT

Using a Felling Ax

You already should have enough firewood on hand for this year, but you'll have to gather more for next year. If you have to cut a large quantity of wood, you'll need a chain saw. But for smaller quantities you can get by with a felling ax, also called an American ax, a square ax, or a Yankee ax. Even if you own a chain saw, a felling ax can be useful for trimming branches from newly cut trees and for cutting the occasional log to size.

Tool historians tell us that the ax is an ancient tool — probably the oldest of all the woodworking tools. During the Stone Age the earliest axes were sharp, hand-held stones. Later primitive toolmakers lashed the stone head, or celt, onto a wooden handle.

During the Bronze Age, metal replaced stone heads, but curiously the method of attaching them to the handle remained the same. In many parts of the world, particularly Western Europe, the technique of casting an ax head with a shaft hole for the handle was unknown. By the Iron Age, however, smiths realized that a superior ax could be made if the handle was wedged into

TOOL BOX

- **FELLING AX**
- **MEDIUM-COARSE FILE**
- **SHARPENING STONE**

a cast head socket. By the Middle Ages the ax was the carpenter's most important and useful tool.

Today the plane, chisel, and saw have replaced the ax in the woodworking shop, but the ax is still useful for cutting firewood. In the Middle Ages, smiths and toolmakers made a variety of axes to fit the type of work being done and the local wood available. Today only two models are available: the felling ax and the double-bit ax.

The double-blade — also called a double-bit — ax is essentially two axes in one. It has two cutting edges and a straight, symmetrical handle. If one blade dulls, the ax can be flipped over and cutting can continue with the other blade. The double edge is handy if you cut a combination of hard and soft woods. For cutting soft woods the cutting edge should have a narrow acute angle, but it would dull quickly on hard woods. Here a wider, cutting angle is needed.

The novice woodcutter will find that the felling ax is easier and safer to handle. The weight is concentrated in the thick, short head, with only one cutting blade; the handle, generally made of hickory or ash — although now some axes are available with head and handle made of a single piece of forged steel — is easy to hold and guide because it has a gentle curve with a carved end, called the "fawn foot."

When selecting an ax, look for one with a 36-inch handle and a head weight of 3 to 3 1/2 pounds. Anything heavier than that will cause muscle fatigue, and it is difficult to deliver enough power with a lighter ax. Look for a tempered steel blade of medium hardness. A blade forged of hard steel will be more likely to chip, while a soft blade will dull quickly if you hit a hard knot. If you're forced to choose between a hard-tempered and a soft-tempered edge, choose the soft one and carry a sharpening stone.

Obviously, your ax will cut better if it has a sharp edge, but unlike most cutting tools, the blade should not have straight sides, called V-ground, or concave sides, called hollow-ground. Instead the sides should curve away from the edge, called a cleaver grind. The convex contour keeps the ax from getting stuck in the wood after each stroke.

SHARPENING AN AX: To sharpen a dull ax, first clamp the ax head, blade up, in a vise. Use a flat, medium-coarse file, 8 to 10 inches long, and stroke the blade with slight, rocking motions. Always lift the file away from the blade on return strokes. File one side; then turn the ax around and do the other side. Finish sharpening the blade by honing the edge with a hand-held sharpening stone. Work the stone in circular motions across the edge.

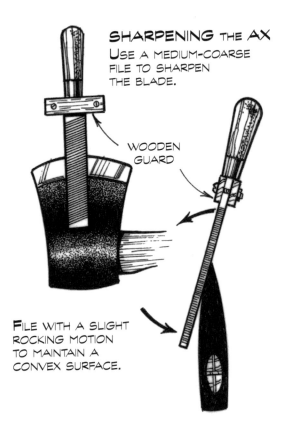

SHARPENING THE AX
USE A MEDIUM-COARSE FILE TO SHARPEN THE BLADE.

WOODEN GUARD

FILE WITH A SLIGHT ROCKING MOTION TO MAINTAIN A CONVEX SURFACE.

USING A FELLING AX

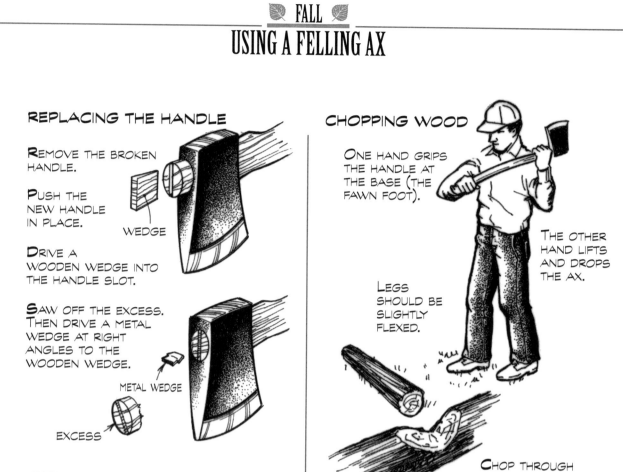

REPLACING THE HANDLE

REMOVE THE BROKEN HANDLE.

PUSH THE NEW HANDLE IN PLACE.

WEDGE

DRIVE A WOODEN WEDGE INTO THE HANDLE SLOT.

SAW OFF THE EXCESS. THEN DRIVE A METAL WEDGE AT RIGHT ANGLES TO THE WOODEN WEDGE.

METAL WEDGE

EXCESS

CHOPPING WOOD

ONE HAND GRIPS THE HANDLE AT THE BASE (THE FAWN FOOT).

THE OTHER HAND LIFTS AND DROPS THE AX.

LEGS SHOULD BE SLIGHTLY FLEXED.

CHOP THROUGH THE LOG BY MAKING A LARGE V-CUT.

REPLACING AN AX HANDLE: Most ax handles will last a lifetime, but occasionally you may have to replace one. First, remove the old handle by knocking it out of the hole — commonly called the "eye" — in the ax head. Use a metal punch or a narrow chisel. Before inserting the new handle, saw a slot across the top end. Push the end firmly into the eye to ensure a tight fit, and drive a wooden wedge — usually these are provided with the new handle — into the sawed slot. Saw off any excess so the wood is flush with the head. Finally, drive one or two metal wedges at right angles to the wooden wedge. The metal wedges also should be provided with the new handle.

USING AN AX: Using a felling ax requires two hands. Grip the handle at the fawn foot with one hand, which will remain there during the swing. The other hand will slide from the head to the foot to lift and then swing the ax. It should strike the wood at an angle, first from one side and then the other, making a large V-shaped cut.

Before using the ax make sure that the area is free of anything that might obstruct your swing. Stand firmly on both feet with your legs slightly flexed and keep your eyes on the log being cut. ⊕

Sharpening Tools

Everyone has some cutting tools around the house. Knives and scissors are in the kitchen; chisels, planes, and saws are in the workshop. Those tools will cut better and be safer to use if the cutting edge is sharp when you use them. Sharpening tools is not a difficult skill to learn. It consists of wearing away some of the metal to form an acute angle on the cutting edge. Essentially, that is an abrasive cutting process utilizing either abrasive papers, stones, files, or strops to remove the metal. It consists of two distinct stages. The first is grinding, which involves wearing away the metal to reduce the main thickness of the blade. Honing, the second stage, wears away discrete amounts of metal to give the blade a fine edge.

For occasional sharpening jobs you can use coated abrasives. Abrasive papers are sandpapers with aluminum oxide — emery — or silicon-carbide grains bonded to a paper or cloth backing. They are inexpensive and come in a variety of grits from coarse to fine. If you use abrasive papers to sharpen your tools, place them on a flat surface

TOOL BOX

- **ABRASIVE PAPERS**
- **BENCH STONES**
- **OIL OR WATER**
- **LEATHER STROP**

and use a lubricant, such as oil or water. The lubricant serves two purposes: It controls the cutting action — that is, how much metal is worn away — and it floats the worn metal particles away so that they don't clog the abrasive.

SHARPENING STONES: Most people find that bench stones are better than papers because they last longer and are easier to hold in place. Bench stones are rectangular blocks of abrasive material. They are either man-made or quarried from natural stone. Besides the well-known oilstone, waterstones and diamond stones also are available.

Oilstones are available as natural stone, aluminum oxide, or silicon carbide composition stones. Natural oilstones are quarried in the state of

Arkansas and frequently are called Arkansas stones. They are graded as hard (fine) and soft (coarse). The soft stone cuts faster but leaves a rough cutting edge. It's necessary then to hone the cutting edge with a hard stone. Man-made oilstones, such as aluminum-oxide and silicon carbide, are cheaper than natural stones, but they leave a coarser edge. Here again it's necessary to polish the tool's cutting edge with a hard, natural stone.

As the name implies, oilstones require oil as a lubricant. Natural stones are porous and quickly soak up the oil lubricant; therefore, manufactur-

ers recommend that you immerse the stone in a pan of oil for a few hours before use. That is not necessary with man-made stones.

What's the best kind of oil to use? Some manufacturers offer a special oil, which is available at fine woodworking shops and through mail-order. But most craftsmen use motor oil or machine oil for sharpening tasks. In general, the thicker the oil, the slower the cutting action. It's possible to customize the viscosity of your cutting oil by thinning it with kerosene. The cutting oil will collect the metal particles as they are removed. They can collect in the stone, so wipe away the oil frequently and recharge the stone with fresh oil.

Many woodworkers do not like oilstones. They feel that the oil collects on their tools and stains and contaminates their projects. They prefer to use waterstones. Since water is less viscous than oil, the stones cut faster than oilstones. Waterstones are also available in natural or man-made compositions. Man-made stones are designated in grit sizes, ranging from 100 (coarse) to 8,000 (ultra-fine). Before using a man-made waterstone, soak it in water for about 10 minutes. That is not necessary with natural waterstones. Keep the stone wet during the sharpening operation. It's possible to create a very sharp and polished edge on a tool

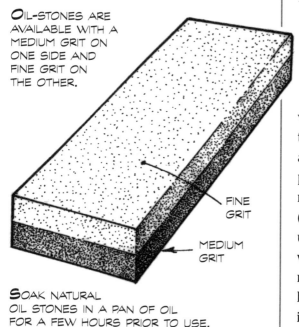

OIL-STONES ARE AVAILABLE WITH A MEDIUM GRIT ON ONE SIDE AND FINE GRIT ON THE OTHER.

FINE GRIT

MEDIUM GRIT

SOAK NATURAL OIL STONES IN A PAN OF OIL FOR A FEW HOURS PRIOR TO USE.

by starting with a coarse stone and progressing to an ultrafine one. Waterstones have a fast cutting action, but they also wear down quickly. Usually, wear creates an uneven or "dished" stone surface. Therefore, it's frequently necessary to flatten or "true" the stone's surface by grinding it on a piece of medium-grit silicon carbide abrasive paper. Lubricate the paper with water and support it on a piece of glass or metal.

THE SURFACE OF A STONE CAN BECOME WORN OR "DISHED" WITH FREQUENT USE. FLATTEN THE STONE BY GRINDING IT ON A PIECE OF MEDIUM-GRIT SILICON CARBIDE PAPER.

LUBRICATE THE PAPER WITH WATER.

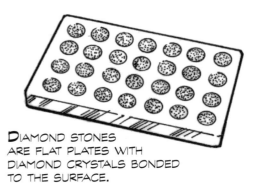

DIAMOND STONES ARE FLAT PLATES WITH DIAMOND CRYSTALS BONDED TO THE SURFACE.

Diamond "stones" are not really stones at all; they're flat steel plates with microscopic diamond crystals bonded to them. They are also called diamond plates or honing blocks. Because the diamond particles are incredibly hard, the stone's surface receives little wear and remains virtually flat and true indefinitely. They require no lubricant although it's a good idea to add a little water periodically to wash away accumulations of metal particles. Diamond honing blocks are manufactured in grit sizes from 600 (coarse) to 1,200 (fine).

Benchstones are positioned on the workbench. The tool to be sharpened is then stroked across the surface of the immobile stone. For some tools, such as axes, handsaws, and garden tools, it's easier to lock the tool in the vise and dress the edge with a hand-held stone or a file. Hand-held stones are called slipstones. They are available in the same materials as benchstones. They are also available in a variety of sizes and shapes to fit the contours of any possible cutting edge. Files come in a variety of cuts and shapes, although small triangular and flat files are probably the most useful.

After grinding and honing with a stone, you can produce a razor-sharp edge on a tool by stropping. Most people are familiar with the leather strop used by a barber to sharpen a straight razor. Similar strops of cowhide or composition material are available for the workshop.

TOOL BLADE INSPECTION & SHARPENING TECHNIQUES: Before attempting to sharpen any tool, first examine it for signs of rust, pitting, and pitch and resin deposits. Remove rust deposits with fine steel wool. Pitting can be removed by grinding the blade on a coarse benchstone. Pitch and resin deposits can be removed with a variety of solvents, such as a commercial tool cleaner, an oven cleaner, turpentine, or paint thinner. When using any solvent, read the directions carefully and take adequate safety precautions.

At this point the reader may wonder why it's necessary to remove rust and pitch deposits before sharpening. Surely those blemishes will come off during the sharpening process. They will, but they also will collect on the

benchstone, clogging its surface and causing it to glaze over.

Before attempting to sharpen any tool, look carefully at the blade to determine the cutting angle. Most cutting tools have two bevels or angles on the blade. The primary angle is wider and less acute than the secondary angle.

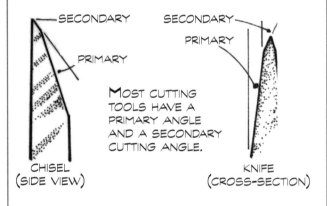

SECONDARY — PRIMARY — CHISEL (SIDE VIEW)

SECONDARY — PRIMARY — KNIFE (CROSS-SECTION)

MOST CUTTING TOOLS HAVE A PRIMARY ANGLE AND A SECONDARY CUTTING ANGLE.

Near the edge of the blade is the narrower, secondary angle. In most cases you'll only have to hone the secondary angle. Tools that are excessively dull or pitted probably will have to have the primary angle reground. The secret to obtaining a sharp cutting edge is maintaining the correct blade angle during the sharpening process.

If you've never sharpened a tool before, it's best to start with either a chisel or a knife. Those tools have simple, straight cutting edges and being hand tools, they are easy to control. Sharpen small knives, such as pocket knives or paring knives, on a bench-stone. Charge the stone with a few drops of light-weight honing or machine oil; use water if you're working with a waterstone. Grip the knife by the handle and place the blade at the correct angle on the stone. Draw the knife toward you while simultaneously moving it laterally across the stone. Flip the knife over and make another pass; this time push the knife away from you. Make the same number of strokes on each side of the blade and try to maintain the same angle and pressure on both sides of the blade. If you simply are honing the edge, you can start with a medium grit stone and then progress to a fine grit.

You can sharpen larger knives on a benchstone, but many people find it easier to use a hand-held slipstone or a metal honing rod. It takes a bit of practice to maintain the proper honing angle because both hands are in the air and you don't have a workbench for support. If you are right-handed, hold the stone with your left hand and grip the knife handle with your right. Place the knife at the proper angle on the stone just above your left hand. Now stroke the knife toward the end of the stone in an arc so that the entire edge of the knife is honed. Flip the knife over and repeat the stroke from the same starting point. For safety always stroke the knife away from your left hand.

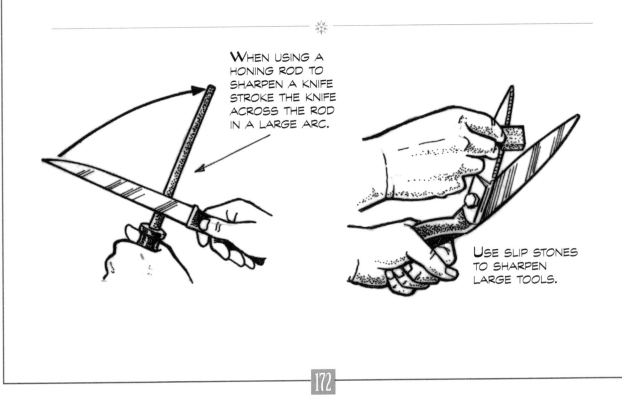

WHEN USING A HONING ROD TO SHARPEN A KNIFE STROKE THE KNIFE ACROSS THE ROD IN A LARGE ARC.

USE SLIP STONES TO SHARPEN LARGE TOOLS.

The ultimate cutting edge can be achieved by stroking the blade across a leather or composition strop. It usually is charged with an abrasive rouge or polishing compound. Most beginners find it easier to place the blade on the strop and use a draw stoke.

It's often difficult to maintain the proper bevel when you are sharpening a chisel. Fortunately, you can use tools called honing guides, which hold the chisel at a preset angle while you're drawing it across a stone. The primary

DRESS THE BACK OF A CHISEL. THIS WILL REMOVE BURRS AND SCRATCHES.

With chisels it's also important to hone and polish the back of the tool. Dressing the back removes any burrs resulting from honing the cutting bevels. To dress the back of a chisel, place it flat on a fine-grit stone and use small, circular strokes. The ideal back should be well polished and free of burrs and scratches.

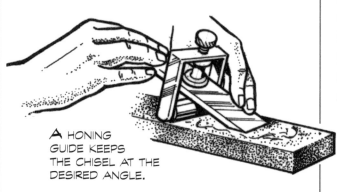

A HONING GUIDE KEEPS THE CHISEL AT THE DESIRED ANGLE.

Whether or not you strop the cutting edge of your chisel depends largely on the type of work you do. General woodworking does not require a razor edge, so stropping is not necessary. Stropping, however, is essential for woodcarving chisels.

bevel on general-purpose woodworking chisels is between 25 and 30 degrees. The secondary bevel is wider, between 40 and 50 degrees, and it is so narrow, one-sixteenth inch or less, that many beginners are not even aware of it. That is the true cutting edge of the chisel, and it should be honed carefully.

Unlike knives and chisels, scissors have only one cutting bevel. To sharpen scissors, place the blade on a bench-stone at the proper angle. Use a draw stroke with a slight sideward movement to dress the entire blade. Repeat the operation with the opposite blade.

With garden shears it's easier to sharpen the cutting edges with a hand-held slipstone. Clamp the tool in a vise and make a continuous stroke along the full length of the blade with the stone. ⊕

USE A SLIP STONE TO SHARPEN LARGE GARDEN TOOLS.

SCISSORS HAVE ONLY ONE CUTTING ANGLE. PLACE THE BLADE ON THE STONE AND USE A DRAW STROKE.

HOUSEHOLD HELPS • HAMMERS

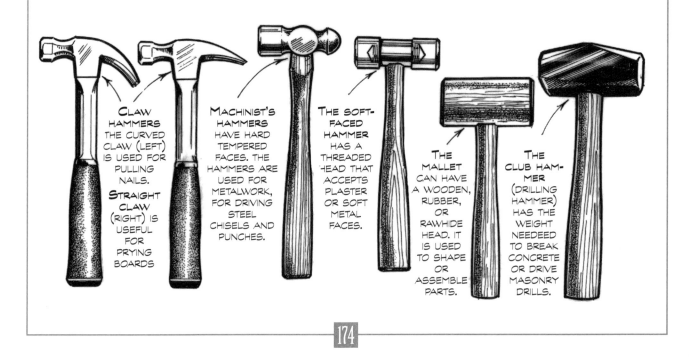

CLAW HAMMERS THE CURVED CLAW (LEFT) IS USED FOR PULLING NAILS. STRAIGHT CLAW (RIGHT) IS USEFUL FOR PRYING BOARDS

MACHINIST'S HAMMERS HAVE HARD TEMPERED FACES. THE HAMMERS ARE USED FOR METALWORK, FOR DRIVING STEEL CHISELS AND PUNCHES.

THE SOFT-FACED HAMMER HAS A THREADED HEAD THAT ACCEPTS PLASTER OR SOFT METAL FACES.

THE MALLET CAN HAVE A WOODEN, RUBBER, OR RAWHIDE HEAD. IT IS USED TO SHAPE OR ASSEMBLE PARTS.

THE CLUB HAMMER (DRILLING HAMMER) HAS THE WEIGHT NEEDEED TO BREAK CONCRETE OR DRIVE MASONRY DRILLS.

Clearing Away Leaves

Fall is the time of year when the leaves turn bright colors. Soon they fall from the trees and what was once beautiful, becomes a chore for many homeowners. Somehow the homeowner has to gather all the dead leaves and dispose of them. What is the best way to do that?

If you have a small yard with few trees, raking up the leaves may be the best method. Raking is good exercise; it's also safe and quiet, but it's work. If you have a large yard with many trees, you might try using a power blower instead. The power blower can blow the leaves into piles, which can be picked up. Some blowers also have a vacuum-and-shred feature that takes the work out of bagging the leaves. Before investing in a power blower, however, check with local ordinances. Power blowers can be noisy, and many towns have restrictions governing their use; some communities ban them entirely.

Two type of power blowers are available to the homeowner: gasoline-powered models and electric models. Many, but not all, gasoline-powered blowers are much noisier than the electric ones, so it's a good idea to wear ear protectors when you are using them. Even so, a noisy gas-powered blower can destroy the serenity of any locality and make you unpopular with your neighbors.

Larger gas-powered blowers offer a backpack feature. With that model the user straps the motor on his back; his hands are now free to control and

BACK-PACK BLOWERS HAVE LARGE, POWERFUL MOTORS. BE SURE TO WEAR EAR PROTECTION.

direct the blower nozzle. Many lawn-care professionals use backpack blowers because they like the large, powerful motors. However, backpack blowers don't have a vacuum feature, and unless you have a very big yard, you probably won't need the extrapowerful motor.

Some homeowners and professionals shun electric-powered blowers because the early models had small motors, which couldn't handle big jobs. But that has changed, and the newest models feature more powerful motors capable of handling big jobs.

It's often difficult to choose a powerblower because the horsepower, engine size, or nozzle air speed are not accurate indicators of the machine's effectiveness. The best way to judge a blower is to borrow or rent one and try it out. In general, look for a model with a comfortable, well-positioned handle. It should have an engine shutoff switch that's easy to reach and operate. Gas-powered blowers should have a throttle

ELECTRIC BLOWERS SHOULD BE DOUBLE INSULATED.

NOZZELS WITH RECTANGULAR ORIFICES ARE LESS EFFICIENT THAN ROUND OPENINGS.

control that allows you to preset two or more positions. Electric blowers should have variable speed settings. Tests show that blower nozzles with round orifices are more efficient than those with rectangular openings.

If you don't like raking or can't handle a power blower, you have other options. You could use your lawn mower to gather the leaves, shred them, and blow them through the discharge chute into the grass catcher. If that does not appeal to you, you can always hire someone else to gather the leaves for you, but of course, it can be expensive. ⊕

TOOL BOX

- **RAKE**
- **POWER BLOWER**
- **LAWN MOWER WITH LEAF GATHERING ATTACHMENT**

Composting

Once you've collected the leaves, you're faced with the problem of disposing of them. You could bag them and leave the bag on the curb for the sanitation department. You also could compost the leaves. Composting is an eco-friendly alternative that produces nutrient-rich humus for your garden.

A compost pile can be built in many ways. The simplest is to dump the leaves and other organic matter into a pile and wait for aerobic bacteria to attack and decompose it. Given enough time, sometimes a year or more, the pile will be reduced to humus. A better solution is to build a structured pile that provides the right conditions for aerobic bacteria.

The bacteria require air and moisture to thrive. A good compost pile should provide both. Start by clearing an area about 3 feet square in the corner of your yard. The size can vary depending upon the quantity of leaves. First loosen up the soil with a rake then lay down a base of thick twigs, branches, or brush. That layer will trap some air at the bottom of the pile. Ideally, you should start the first layer of the com-

TOOL BOX

- **ACTIVATORS**
- **TARPAULIN OR CARPET**

post pile with "green" material, this includes grass clippings, dead flowers, or vegetable peels, but it may be too late in the season to collect any. So start layering the leaves, or "brown" material, onto a twig base. You also can add straw, wood chips, sawdust, and shredded newspaper to the pile. As you gradually build up the pile, stop to sprinkle some water on the layers. The object is to make the pile moist but not sopping wet.

Do not throw meat, bones, or dairy products onto the pile. That material doesn't decompose well, and it attracts animals.

The bacteria will start to work on your pile almost immediately, but the decomposition process will be slow. You can "jump-start" the process by adding animal manure to the pile as you're layering it. The manure contains the essential nitrogen that the bacteria

need to break down the material in the pile. You should include about one shovelful for every 6 inches of compost. If you live near a farm or a riding academy, you easily can obtain enough manure to meet your needs. If not, you can purchase commercial "activators," compost starters, or blood meal at gardening supply centers.

In a few weeks the bacteria will start to break down the organic mater-ial, and the pile will start to heat up. Remember to check the pile periodically to be sure that it is still moist. It's a good idea to cover the pile with a tarp or an old carpet. The covering will contain the heat throughout the pile and ensure that all the material is decomposed. Occasionally, mix the pile with a shovel or a pitchfork; by spring you should have rich humus for your garden. ⊕

THE COMPOST PILE

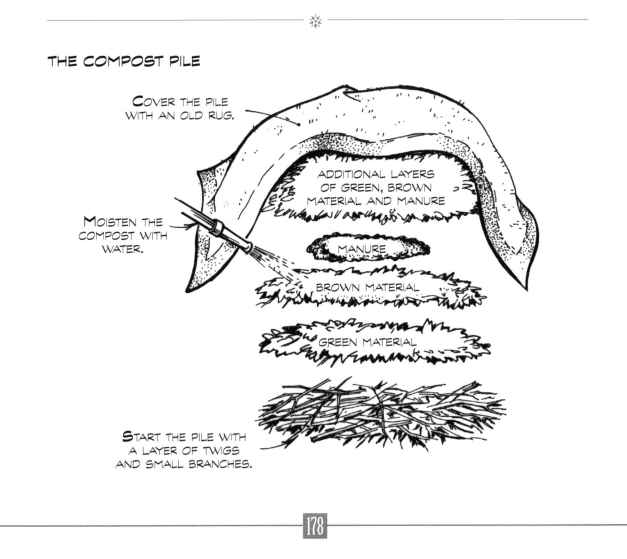

COVER THE PILE WITH AN OLD RUG.

ADDITIONAL LAYERS OF GREEN, BROWN MATERIAL AND MANURE

MOISTEN THE COMPOST WITH WATER.

MANURE

BROWN MATERIAL

GREEN MATERIAL

START THE PILE WITH A LAYER OF TWIGS AND SMALL BRANCHES.

Maintaining the Home-Heating System

It's important for the homeowner to understand his heating system so that he can keep it maintained properly. Heating systems often are characterized by the medium they use to transmit heat from the furnace to the living quarters. Systems that heat and move air throughout the house are called forced-air heating systems. Hydronic systems use either hot water or steam to conduct heat.

Forced-Air Heating

With a forced-air system, the central heating unit — it may be an oil burner or a gas furnace — heats air, which moves through a duct system around the house. Early air systems relied on the principle of convection to move air about. The hot air was allowed to rise through the ducts while the heavier cold air dropped down through return ducts to the furnace.

Modern air systems have an electric fan, technically known as a "centrifugal blower," to propel the air through the ducts. The addition of the blower in the system allowed designers to reduce the size of the ducts and still move a large quantity of air. Well-designed systems have supply ducts for the hot air and return ducts for the cold air.

Obviously, a forced-air system will not be able to deliver heat if the central heating unit is not up to par. Therefore, you should call in a professional service technician to clean the burners and combustion chamber periodically and tune up the unit.

TOOL BOX

- ■ PUTTY KNIFE
- ■ LIGHT-WEIGHT MACHINE OIL
- ■ VACUUM
- ■ NEW DRIVE BELT
- ■ WRENCH
- ■ SCREWDRIVER
- ■ RAG AND CLEANING FLUID
- ■ ALUMINUM-FACED DUCT TAPE
- ■ FIBERGLASS INSULATION

HOME-HEATING SYSTEM

Once the furnace has been serviced, you can attend to the air system. Start with the blower fan. First, shut down the system. Your service manual can tell you how to do so, or you can ask your service technician. Inside the air handler, the large metal cabinet connected to the furnace, is the blower fan. It is a large, cylindrical drum with curved blades, frequently referred to as a "squirrel cage."

Often the blades are caked with dust and dirt. If they are, scrape them clean with a putty knife. Next lubricate the blower bearings with a few drops of light-weight machine oil. Then remove any dust and dirt around the unit with a vacuum.

An electric motor drives the blower. Most motors have sealed bearings, so lubrication is not required. However, you may have an older-style motor with an oil reservoir. If so, fill it with a few drops of lightweight oil. Check with your manual for oil specifications.

Not all motors are connected directly to the fan; many are coupled to it with a drive belt. Inspect the belt and replace it, if it is worn or cracked. If the drive belt should break, it won't shut down the system; but the blower will not push the hot air through the ducts. It's a good idea to keep a spare belt on hand in case that happens.

Near the blower fan is an air filter. It is designed to capture air-borne parti-

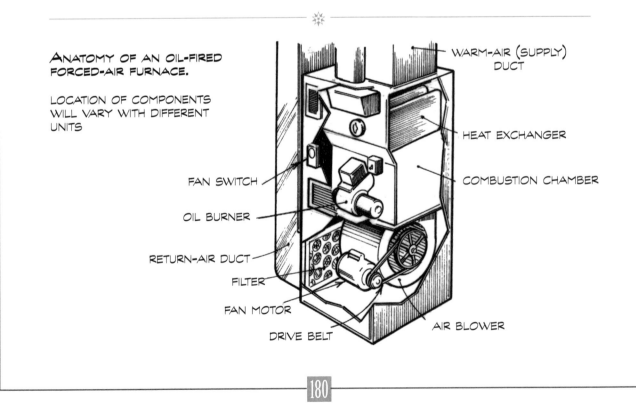

ANATOMY OF AN OIL-FIRED FORCED-AIR FURNACE.

LOCATION OF COMPONENTS WILL VARY WITH DIFFERENT UNITS

WARM-AIR (SUPPLY) DUCT
HEAT EXCHANGER
COMBUSTION CHAMBER
FAN SWITCH
OIL BURNER
RETURN-AIR DUCT
FILTER
FAN MOTOR
DRIVE BELT
AIR BLOWER

cles, such as dust or bacteria. It may be made of woven fiberglass or steel mesh. Fiberglass filters are enclosed in a cardboard frame; they are disposable and should be replaced whenever they get dirty. The steel-mesh filters can be washed and reinstalled.

Mounted somewhere on the outside of the air-handler cabinet is the fan switch. The switch is designed to sense the temperature of the air inside the furnace. When the air is warm enough, it turns the blower on. Conversely, it senses when the air temperature in the furnace drops below a comfortable level and it shuts off the blower.

The switch has a high level, the "on" setting, and a low level, the "off" setting. Most service technicians set the high level at 135 degrees F and the low at 100 degrees F. That range ensures that your home almost always will be warm. With a little experimentation you still may be able to keep the same comfort index and also reduce your fuel bills slightly. For example, you can move the high-level setting down to 110 degrees and the low to 90 degrees. If you find that this leaves your home a little on the cool side, you can nudge the setting up a few degrees.

DUCT MAINTENANCE: It might seem that the ducts are relatively maintenance free; after all, they have no moving parts. Nevertheless, there are some concerns the homeowner should address. The ductwork often develops air leaks around seams and joints. Leaks often can occur when the duct tape around the seams deteriorates from the heat, humidity, and air pressure.

Unfortunately, the leaks are sometimes difficult to detect because the ducts run through inaccessible routes, such as the attic or crawl space. The best way to evaluate the efficiency of a heating duct system is to have a heating specialist run a flow hood or blower door test on the ductwork. Both tests are effective in determining the amount of leakage in the system and in pinpointing where the leaks are. Then he will seal them with patching mastic.

The costs for the tests vary between $250 to $500, depending upon the size of the heating system in a house. The biggest problem that the homeowner may encounter, however, is finding a qualified technician to perform the tests, which were developed and standardized only within the last few years. Consequently, few heating specialists are even aware of them, much less trained to implement them.

Still the homeowner should inspect as much of the duct system as possible. Pay particular attention to the seams around the return-air plenum, all joints where branch ducts connect to the main line, and the junction point where a duct is attached to a room outlet.

If you find a loose duct connection, first clean it with a rag dipped in non-flammable cleaning fluid; then close the gap by installing sheet-metal screws through the duct flanges. Finally, seal the joint with aluminum-faced duct tape. Do not use the familiar cloth-backed duct tape for sealing seams and joints. It deteriorates quickly when exposed to heat, and many local codes prohibit its use on heating ducts. Another way to seal duct seams is with 3-inch-wide fiberglass scrim tape. Wrap the seam with the tape and then paint over it with a water-based duct sealant, which is available at air-conditioning supply outlets.

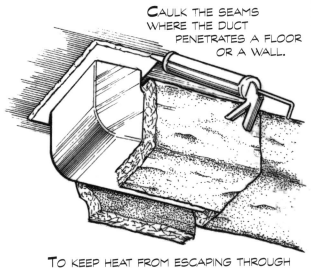

To keep heat from escaping through supply duct walls, wrap the ducts with insulation.

Another thing you can do is make sure that the ducts that run through uninsulated areas are wrapped in fiberglass insulation. That will help to minimize conductive heat loss through the duct walls.

People sometimes complain that they feel cold even though warm air is coming out of the heating registers. That can happen because the incoming air, moving across a person's skin, creates a "wind-chill" effect. One way to correct this is by installing the supply registers with diffusers or deflectors, which moderate or redirect the incoming air.

All heating systems tend to dry the air, but the problem seems more acute with forced air. The best way to correct the problem is by installing a humidifier. It is important to clean it periodically to prevent contamination from airborne bacteria.

Hot-Water Heating

Many homeowners in the Northeast are surprised to hear that two-thirds of the homes in the United States are heated with forced air. This is not the case in the Northeast, where most homes use either steam or hot-water heat. Heating systems that use water or steam are grouped together in the category of "hydronic heating."

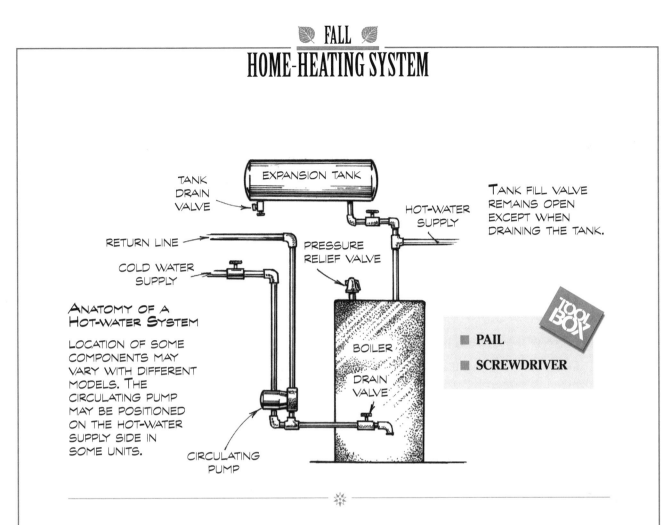

TANK
DRAIN
VALVE

EXPANSION TANK

TANK FILL VALVE
REMAINS OPEN
EXCEPT WHEN
DRAINING THE TANK.

HOT-WATER
SUPPLY

RETURN LINE

COLD WATER
SUPPLY

PRESSURE
RELIEF VALVE

ANATOMY OF A HOT-WATER SYSTEM

LOCATION OF SOME
COMPONENTS MAY
VARY WITH DIFFERENT
MODELS. THE
CIRCULATING PUMP
MAY BE POSITIONED
ON THE HOT-WATER
SUPPLY SIDE IN
SOME UNITS.

BOILER

DRAIN
VALVE

CIRCULATING
PUMP

TOOL BOX

■ **PAIL**

■ **SCREWDRIVER**

Hot-water systems have some advantages over forced-air heating. Generally, hot-water systems run quieter than forced-air systems — although that is not true of a steam system, which can be noisy.

Hot-water heating provides radiant heat, which many people find more comfortable than forced hot air. Hot-water systems take up less room because the water circulates in small-diameter pipes. In contrast, the forced-air system relies on large-diameter ducts to move the air around.

Hot-water systems do have their problems, however. For example, they are usually more expensive to install than forced air, and they are not easily adapted for air conditioning or cooling. Water leaks are rare, but should one occur, it can result in serious damage.

The heart of the hot-water system is the central boiler. The water in the boiler is heated by gas, oil, or, in some older systems, by coal or wood. The hot water circulates through pipes to radiators or heating panels that radiate the heat into the rooms.

Early hot-water systems relied on gravity to circulate the water. As the water heated, it expanded and pushed into the radiators, where it relinquished

its heat. After giving up the heat, the water dropped down to the boiler. One drawback to the gravity system was that it took time for the water to expand sufficiently to circulate. In an effort to make the system more responsive, hydronic designers added a circulating pump to move the water through the system.

In addition to the boiler, pipes, radiators, and circulating pump, hot-water systems also have an expansion tank, which is simply a metal container filled with water and air. It allows the water in the system to expand or condense without rupturing the pipes or fittings in the network.

HOT-WATER SYSTEM MAINTENANCE: The annual maintenance routine for a hot-water heating system should start with a furnace tune-up by a professional service technician. The technician should inspect and clean the combustion chamber, and the fuel nozzle. He also should run a combustion test.

The furnace tune-up is a job for a professional, but every homeowner can do a number of simple maintenance tasks. Water systems often accumulate sludge in the form of mineral deposits and rust. If the sludge is allowed to collect, it can hamper the water circulation and eventually damage the system. To remove the sludge, simply drain a buck-

et or two of water from the boiler. First, turn off the burner; then close the water inlet valve to the boiler. Now position a bucket under the boiler drain valve.

The water in the boiler will be hot, so to avoid getting burned, it's best to wait an hour or two before opening the drain valve. Drain the water until it runs clear; then close the drain valve, open the supply valve and turn on the furnace. Newer systems should be drained once a year, but older systems collect sludge more readily. With such a system it may be necessary to drain the water monthly.

If you have an old hot-water system that never has been drained, then drawing a few buckets of water may not be enough. You may need to call in a professional to flush out the system. A "professional flush" is done with chemical additives and extremely hot water. It will clean out heavy deposits of sludge and restore the operating efficiency to your old boiler.

After draining the boiler, check the expansion tank. Depending upon the age of your system, you may have either one of two types. Newer systems have a diaphragm tank. That type of tank is sealed, so it's not necessary to drain it. Older systems have tanks that should be flushed out yearly. You easily can recognize this type of tank because it has two valves: a shutoff valve going into the furnace and a drain valve on the bottom of the tank.

To drain the tank, first close the shutoff valve. Position a bucket under the drain; then open the valve. The water should flow out, but if it doesn't, it may be necessary to open the vacuum-breaker plug on the drain valve — although it should be noted that not all tanks have that plug. You can open the plug with an adjustable wrench. After the tank has been drained, close the drain valve and vacuum-breaker plug and open the shutoff valve. If all that seems like a lot of trouble, you might want to consult a heating technician about replacing your old expansion tank with a newer diaphragm model.

Next, you should bleed the radiators. Air frequently becomes trapped inside, and it can prevent the hot water from entering the radiators. Bleeding releases the trapped air. To bleed a radiator, first position a pan under the bleed valve. Then open the valve. Depending upon the type of bleed valve, you can use either a screwdriver or a radiator key — which is available at hardware stores or plumbing supply stores — to open the valve. At first air will come out of the valve, then water. At that point close the valve. You should bleed each radiator once or twice each year.

Draining water and bleeding the radiators are simple tasks that are within the abilities of the average homeowner, but they can help to keep a hot-water heating system working efficiently.

Steam Heating

Steam heating is the hydronic heating system that uses steam to carry the heat from the furnace into the rest of the house. The steam is generated in a boiler in the basement. It expands and rises through pipes into radiators throughout the house. Each radiator is equipped with an air valve, which is mounted on the side of the radiator, and allows the cool air trapped in the radiator to escape so that the steam can enter. The heat from the hot steam closes the valve and traps the steam.

As the steam releases its heat, it condenses into water that flows back to the boiler. In a one-pipe system, the water returns to the boiler in the same pipe that carries the steam. In a two-pipe system, the water travels through a different pipe to return to the boiler. The two-pipe system is a loop design that utilizes a supply pipe and a return pipe.

Around 1841, Joseph Nason and James Jones Walworth designed some of the earliest steam-heating systems

for home use. The average homeowner was reluctant to have a steam boiler in his house because industrial boiler explosions were frequent. Nason and Walworth designed a safe boiler for home use. Their system proved to be so safe that in 1855, the U.S. government contracted them to install a steam-heating system in the White House.

Steam heating is not so popular as it once was. Newer homes usually have either hot-water heating or forced air. Still, people who live in older homes find that a steam system can provide comfortable, dependable heat. Like all heating systems, the steam-heating system must be maintained properly if it is to remain efficient and dependable.

STEAM SYSTEM MAINTENANCE: The maintenance schedule should start with a furnace tune-up by a qualified service technician. Oil burners should be inspected and cleaned yearly. Gas-fired burners generally burn cleaner than oil burners, so a tune-up is needed only every other year.

Because steam systems have a mixture of steam, water, and air flowing through the pipes, rust and sediment quickly collect in the pipes and boiler. You easily can remove the sediment by draining a bucket of water from the system. The drain valve usually is located at the base of the furnace. During the winter months you should do that weekly.

Before draining any water, first check the sight glass to make sure that water is in the boiler. The sight glass usually is mounted on the outside of the burner/boiler cabinet. With some older systems you may have to open the cabinet to read the sight glass, which should be half full. As you drain water from the system, the water level will drop. If the furnace is running, it may shut down, but that is nothing to get alarmed about. A low-water cutoff valve near the boiler automatically shuts off the furnace if the water level drops. That safety feature protects the boiler from burning out. If, however, the sight glass reads low and the furnace does not shut off automatically, then you should have a service technician check out the cutoff valve.

Whenever the water drops below the halfway mark on the sight glass, it will be necessary to add more water. Some units have an automatic refill control, which adds water to the boiler. With other units it's necessary to open a supply valve manually to add the makeup water.

If you have to fill the boiler manually, be careful not to add water too quickly. A sudden influx of cold water into a hot boiler can cause it to crack. Check the sight glass. If there is some

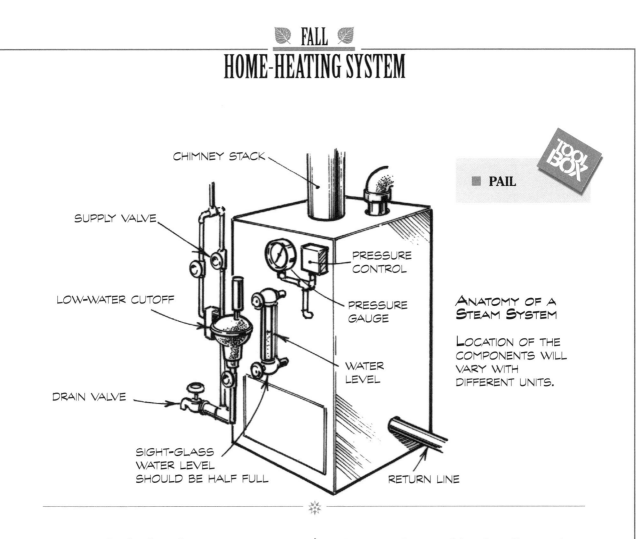

CHIMNEY STACK

SUPPLY VALVE

LOW-WATER CUTOFF

DRAIN VALVE

SIGHT-GLASS
WATER LEVEL
SHOULD BE HALF FULL

PRESSURE
CONTROL

PRESSURE
GAUGE

WATER
LEVEL

RETURN LINE

TOOL BOX

■ PAIL

ANATOMY OF A
STEAM SYSTEM

LOCATION OF THE
COMPONENTS WILL
VARY WITH
DIFFERENT UNITS.

water in the boiler, then you can open the supply valve slightly and let the cold water trickle in. Bringing the water up to the proper level may take 10 or 15 minutes, but it will save you from a costly repair bill. If there's no water in the boiler, you'll have to wait a few hours for the boiler to cool before adding water.

You should check the sight-glass level weekly and add water if the level drops. Sometimes, however, the level may start to rise for no apparent reason. This may be a symptom of a serious problem, such as a leak in the system, or it may be something relatively minor, such as a bit of sediment in a supply valve. If the water level is allowed to rise, it may flood the system and trickle through the radiator air valves.

It's easy to lower the water level: Simply open the drain valve and allow the excess water to escape. However, you should check the sight glass daily to make sure that the water level doesn't start to rise again. If it does, call in a service technician to inspect the system.

Perhaps the most vexing problem with a steam-heating system is the noise. When the steam is coming up, the pipes start to bang. Technicians

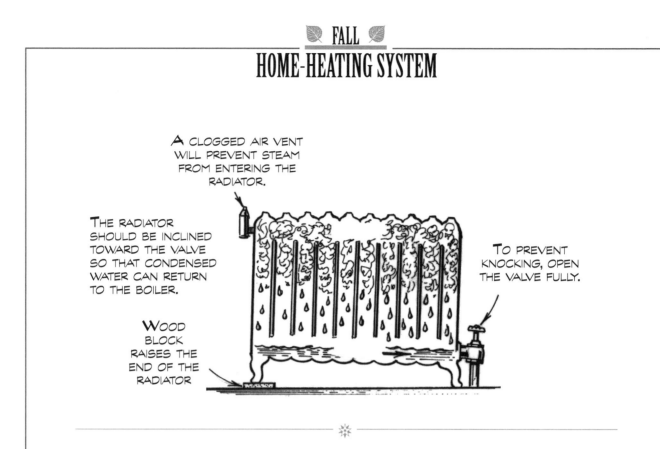

A CLOGGED AIR VENT WILL PREVENT STEAM FROM ENTERING THE RADIATOR.

THE RADIATOR SHOULD BE INCLINED TOWARD THE VALVE SO THAT CONDENSED WATER CAN RETURN TO THE BOILER.

TO PREVENT KNOCKING, OPEN THE VALVE FULLY.

WOOD BLOCK RAISES THE END OF THE RADIATOR

refer to that effect as "water hammer." It happens when the cool, condensed water gets trapped in the radiators or pipes. As the hot steam enters the chambers, it meets the cool water, quickly condenses, and creates a vacuum. The water rushes to fill the vacuum, and it slams into the pipes.

The best way to prevent water hammer is to ensure that the return pipes are inclined toward the boiler. In a one-pipe system, radiators should be tilted toward the valve end so that water is allowed to drain out. In a two-pipe system, radiators have a special steam trap near the return pipe. If the radiator bangs, then the steam trap may be at fault.

Finally, it's important to open radiator valves fully. A partially opened valve will allow the steam to enter, but it will also trap the condensed water and create a water hammer.

Radiators

A radiator is a device used for dispersing the heat generated in the furnace to other parts of the house. The heat may be transmitted from the furnace to the radiator with either steam or hot water.

Most radiators use a combination of convection and radiation to heat their surroundings. With convection the heat is transferred from the radiator directly to the surrounding air. People and objects are warmed by the heated air. Radiation warms the people and

objects directly without noticeably heating the air in between.

Modern radiators have slim, sleek lines and may be made out of aluminum, copper, or even high-temperature plastic. Most of the units are mounted in unobtrusive, out-of-the-way places near the baseboard. They function well in that location provided that the homeowner doesn't restrict surrounding airflow by moving furniture or carpets too near the radiator.

RADIATOR MAINTENANCE: The radiators require little maintenance. Occasionally, trapped air may prevent a hot-water radiator from filling up completely, and the radiator never will get hot enough to heat the room. When

- **LEVEL**
- **RADIATOR KEY OR SCREWDRIVER**
- **BRUSH AND PAINT**

that happens, it's a simple matter to bleed the air out of the unit. Place a pan under the radiator bleed valve and open it with a radiator key, which is available at hardware stores or plumbing supply stores for less than a dollar. Allow the valve to remain open until all the air escapes and only water flows out; then close the valve.

Steam radiators do not require bleeding. The trapped air will be forced out through the air vent — the small metal cylinder on the side of each radiator — by the incoming steam. Occasionally, the vent's escape port may become clogged with hard-water scale deposits. When that happens, the trapped air will remain in the radiator and will keep the hot steam out. Sometimes you can open the port by sticking a straightened paper clip into the hole.

If that doesn't work, close the steam supply valve at the base of the radiator; then remove the vent by turning it counterclockwise. Place it in a pan of white vinegar and boil it for about a half hour. Do not use an aluminum pan for

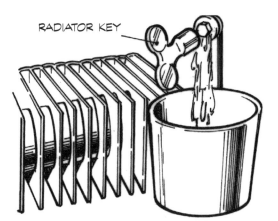

RADIATOR KEY

BLEED THE TRAPPED AIR FROM A HOT WATER RADIATOR BY OPENING THE VALVE. CLOSE IT WHEN WATER FLOWS FROM THE VALVE.

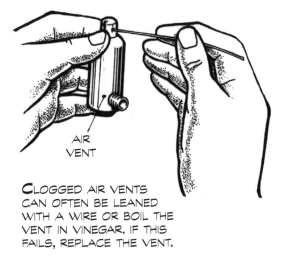

CLOGGED AIR VENTS CAN OFTEN BE LEANED WITH A WIRE OR BOIL THE VENT IN VINEGAR. IF THIS FAILS, REPLACE THE VENT.

the task; the vinegar will discolor it. If the vinegar boil fails to clear the vent, replace it.

Older homes are likely to have old-fashioned cast-iron radiators instead of baseboard units. In an ideal layout the radiators should be in position directly under the windows, come up to the sill, and span the width of the window. For maximum convective efficiency, there should be about 2 1/2 inches of clearance between the unit and the wall.

Even with proper air circulation some of the heat dispersed from the radiator will be wasted on the back wall. An easy way to redirect the heat back into the room is with a piece of foil-faced foam insulation board. Cut the board to size with a sharp utility knife and place it behind the wall, foil side out.

METHODS OF CONNECTING RADIATOR SECTIONS: Designers of commercial and residential heating systems frequently needed radiators in a variety of widths. Manufacturers hit upon the idea of casting radiators in sections, and then linking the sections together into one unit. Consequently, it was relatively easy to make radiators to custom widths by joining any number of sections together.

Two methods for connecting the sections used short lengths of pipe. One technique used threaded pipe, called nipples. The nipples were unusual in that one end had left-hand threads, while the other had right-hand threads. Turning the nipple caused the threads to tighten and pull the radiator sections together. Threaded nipples no longer are being manufactured today, so it is almost impossible to modify old radiators assembled with that technique.

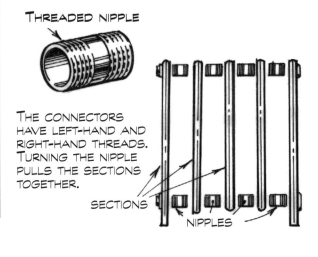

THREADED NIPPLE

THE CONNECTORS HAVE LEFT-HAND AND RIGHT-HAND THREADS. TURNING THE NIPPLE PULLS THE SECTIONS TOGETHER.

SECTIONS

NIPPLES

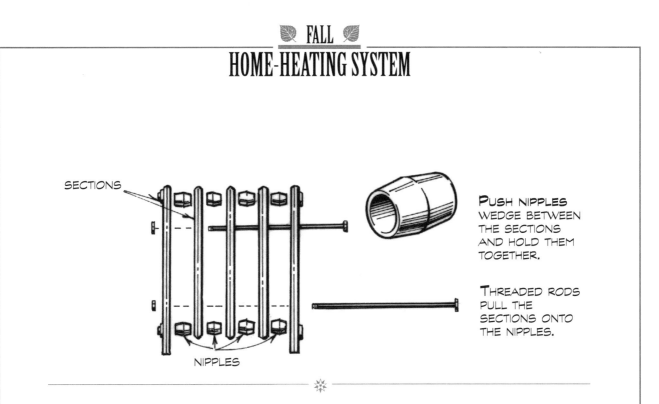

SECTIONS

PUSH NIPPLES WEDGE BETWEEN THE SECTIONS AND HOLD THEM TOGETHER.

THREADED RODS PULL THE SECTIONS ONTO THE NIPPLES.

NIPPLES

The other joining technique also used pipe couplings called push nipples. Those connectors were not threaded; instead they tapered toward the ends, forming a sort of double wedge. To assemble a radiator, manufacturers inserted push nipples between each section and then squeezed them together by tightening a threaded rod that ran through the entire radiator. Push nipples still are manufactured by the Oneida County Boiler Works in Utica, N.Y.

With new push nipples it is possible to modify the width of an old cast-iron radiator by unbolting the connecting rods and prying the sections apart. That, however, can be difficult because the sections are likely to be locked together with accumulations of heated rust and corrosion. Separating them will require hard work and a lot of penetrating oil.

Rebuilding a radiator is not a concern for most homeowners, but repainting one is. While most people make the mistake of repainting a radiator with aluminum paint, it is not a good choice because the reflective surface of the paint can reduce the heat radiation by as much as 20 percent. Actually, tests show that light beige, with a matte finish, is the best color to paint a radiator.

If your radiators already are coated with aluminum paint, you don't need to scrape it off. Simply repaint them with another color. The new top coat will allow the radiator to radiate the maximum amount of heat. Likewise, heating efficiency is not to be reduced by multiple layers of paint.

You may, however, want to remove accumulations of paint that obscure ornate surface decoration on a beautiful, old radiator. Here the focus is on

esthetics, not function. The best way to expose the bare metal is by sandblasting the radiator, but first you'll have to disconnect the radiator and lug it to a sandblasting facility.

It's best to use two wrenches to uncouple the fittings — one to hold the pipe and the other to loosen the connecting nut. Also bear in mind that cast-iron radiators are extremely heavy. Enlist the aid of a friend and use a dolly or hand truck to move the piece.

Supplemental Heaters

Every year more than 50,000 fires are reported to fire departments. Ninety percent of those fires occur in one- and two-family houses, and more than 4,000 people die in such home fires. Twenty-two percent of the residential fires were caused by careless use of supplemental room heaters, such as wood- or coal-burning stoves, kerosene heaters, and electrical heaters. In addition to causing fires, supplemental heaters also can pose other safety hazards in the form of air pollution or electric shock.

Consumers themselves install about 70 percent of all wood- and coal-burning stoves. Most of those stoves are installed incorrectly without regard to the building or safety codes.

Incorrect installation is one of the leading causes of wood or coal stove fires.

WOOD AND COAL STOVES: Wood and coal stoves should stand on a noncombustible floor protector that extends 18 inches beyond the stove on all sides. The protector will shield the floor from the stove's heat and lessen the danger of a floor fire. In addition, stove manufacturers and building codes require stoves to be positioned away from combustible walls; this distance may vary with specific stoves.

Do not use your wood stove to burn trash; that could cause the stove to overheat. Avoid using gasoline or other flammable liquids to light the stove. They could explode or overheat the stove. Not all stoves can handle a coal fire, so check the manufacturer's specifications before adding coal to your stove.

Even a wood-burning stove that's correctly installed must be maintained. Creosote buildup is inevitable with wood burning, and too much creosote in the flue can cause chimney fires. Creosote deposits also reduce the size of the chimney vent and force toxic gases back into the room. The chimney should be inspected and cleaned annually by a professional chimney sweep.

Chimney fires also can occur above fireplaces also. Fire extinguishers for-

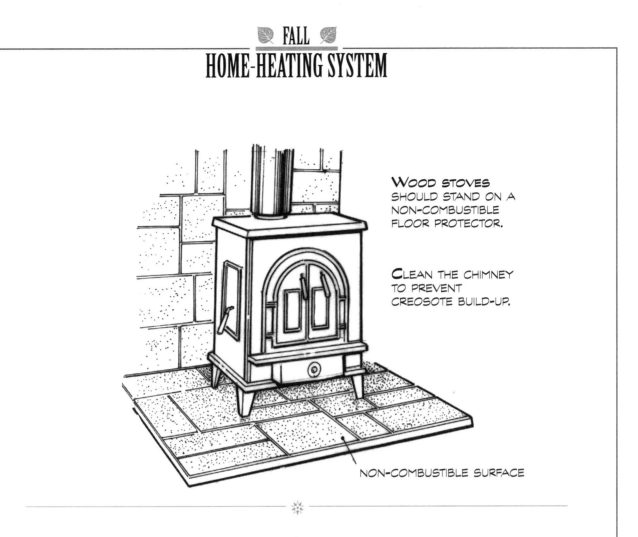

WOOD STOVES SHOULD STAND ON A NON-COMBUSTIBLE FLOOR PROTECTOR.

CLEAN THE CHIMNEY TO PREVENT CREOSOTE BUILD-UP.

NON-COMBUSTIBLE SURFACE

mulated for chimney fires are available at home centers and hardware stores. They cannot always extinguish intense chimney fires, but they can slow the spread of the fire and give you extra time to call the fire department.

KEROSENE HEATERS: Many codes prohibit the use of kerosene heaters in the home, so check with the local fire marshal before using one. If you decide to heat a room with a kerosene heater use only 1-K — also known as K1 — a highly refined white kerosene, as a fuel. Kerosene is graded according to the sulfur content. Grades other than 1-K

contain more sulfur and generate increased sulfur dioxide emissions. You cannot always tell 1-K by looking at it. Some white kerosenes that appear clear and deceptively pure have high sulfur levels.

Do not mix gasoline with the kerosene; that could cause an explosion. Store the kerosene outdoors in tightly sealed metal containers and always refuel it outdoors where accidental spills will be less hazardous. Never attempt to add fuel to the heater while it is operating.

Kerosene heaters usually are not vented, so it is essential to provide adequate air circulation, such as a slightly open window, while the heater is operating. Most people are afraid of losing valuable heat, so they keep all windows tightly closed. But that only increases indoor air pollution problems. Turn the unit off when everyone retires for the evening and never allow the heater to operate unattended.

Position the heater so that it's at least 3 feet away from any combustibles, such as furniture or curtains. It should also be placed out of doorways and traffic areas so that it cannot be knocked over or trap people in case of fire. Should the heater flare up, activate the manual shutoff switch and call the fire department. Do not attempt to move the heater; it could allow the fuel to leak and increase the height of the flames.

ELECTRIC HEATERS: The U.S. Consumer Product Safety Commission estimates that about half the deaths and about one-third of the injuries resulting from electric heater fires occurred at night when family members were asleep and the heater was left unattended. Most of those fires were caused when combustible materials, such as bedding, drapes, or furniture, caught fire. Heaters should be situated at least 3 feet away from all combustible mate-

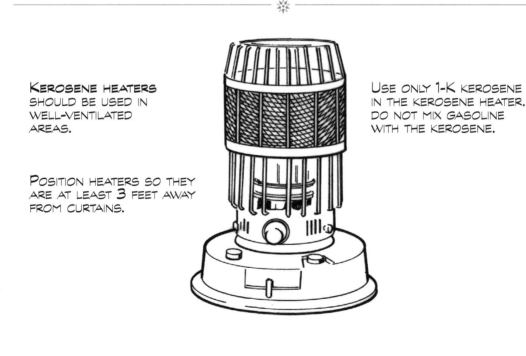

KEROSENE HEATERS SHOULD BE USED IN WELL-VENTILATED AREAS.

POSITION HEATERS SO THEY ARE AT LEAST 3 FEET AWAY FROM CURTAINS.

USE ONLY 1-K KEROSENE IN THE KEROSENE HEATER. DO NOT MIX GASOLINE WITH THE KEROSENE.

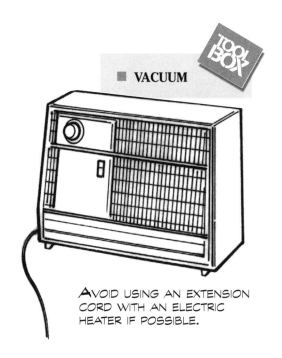

■ VACUUM

Avoid using an extension cord with an electric heater if possible.

rials. Do not place the heaters where towels or clothing could fall on the appliance and trigger a fire.

After taking the heater out of summer storage, vacuum the heating element to remove any dust or debris that might catch fire. Examine the cord carefully. Make sure the plug connection is secure and the insulation sound. Plug the heater in, wait about 15 minutes, and then feel the cord. It should be cool, not hot. If it is hot, replace it.

Replacing an electrical cord seems like a straightforward job, but the replacement must be a HPN heater cord with the correct amperage rating, so it's best to leave the job to a professional.

When the heaters are hooked up to an outlet with a light extension cord, high current flows can cause it to overheat and generate a fire. Avoid using extension cords unless absolutely necessary. If you must use one, make sure that it has a power rating equal to that of the heater itself. Keep the cord stretched out and do not bury it under rugs or carpets.

In addition to presenting a fire hazard, heaters pose the possible threat of electric shock. That can happen if the heating element contacts the metal housing and energizes it. Anyone touching the appliance will receive a nasty jolt. The problem is exacerbated in the bathroom, where a bather, still dripping from the shower, easily can become an electrical conductor. It's best to heat the bathroom before bathing and then unplug the heater before stepping into the shower. ⊕

Lightning Protection

The destructive power of lightning is awesome. Since prehistoric times man has looked for ways to protect himself against that power and wrath from above. During the Middle Ages people put pieces of trees destroyed by lightning under their beds in an effort to ward off lightning bolts. They believed that lightning never strikes the same place twice and that the tree shards might provide some measure of protection.

In 1753, Benjamin Franklin included an article titled, "How to Secure Houses, &c. from Lightning" in an issue of *Poor Richard's Almanack*. In the article he described the use of lightning rods, their placement, and his belief in their ability to protect a house and its occupants from lightning.

It is estimated that more than a thousand readers of the Almanack recognized the value of the lightning rod and outfitted their homes with the new

How Lightning Can Strike Your Home

1. A tree struck by lightning can send a side flash into the house. Install rods on trees.

2. Lightning can strike the house directly. Rods with connectors can intercept the charge.

3. Lightning can strike the T.V. antenna. Antenna should be grounded and have an arrester.

4. Lightning strike to the utility pole can send an induced surge into the house. Surge arresters can intercept the induced surges.

devices. Still, many people remained skeptical about their value. The first successful test of the lightning rod came in 1760, when a house owned by Mr. West of Philadelphia and fitted with Franklin's lightning rods sustained a direct hit from lightning. Three inches were burned off the tip of the rod, but the house was unharmed.

Franklin's rods began to appear on rooftops of homes, barns, and buildings throughout the colonies. The design of modern lightning rods is essentially the same as Franklin's original design, and they continue to be installed today as an effective way to protect property from the damage and destruction caused by lightning.

But are lightning rods a good idea for every home? Some people maintain that the average home does not really need the protection of lightning rods. Generally, they accept the ability of the lightning rod to protect a building. However, they also consider the cost of installing a lightning-rod system, which can range anywhere from $500 to $1,500, depending upon the size of the building and its location. But, they say, the chances of that building getting hit by lightning are slim. Therefore, if the protection gained from the system might never be needed, is it really worth the cost of installation?

TOOL BOX

NO TOOLS REQUIRED. ALL INSPECTION AND INSTALLATION SHOULD BE DONE BY PROFESSIONALS.

Of course, every argument has two sides, and both sides can offer impressive statistics and expert opinion to buttress their arguments. In the end the individual homeowner must sift through the data and decide for himself if he really wants to spend the money to protect his home against a catastrophe that may not occur. Besides statistics and opinion, the homeowner should consider a few other factors when making that decision.

Homes of historic value or those with landmark status would benefit from lightning-rod protection because repairing damage to those structures is often difficult or impossible. The cost of installation, therefore, is minimal compared with the possible loss of an architectural treasure.

Homes that are taller than surrounding structures stand a greater chance of being hit by lightning than do the lower buildings. Isolated homes on high, exposed ground are in a more hazardous location than those nestled in valleys or situated on low, flat land. Tall trees in the vicinity of a home can

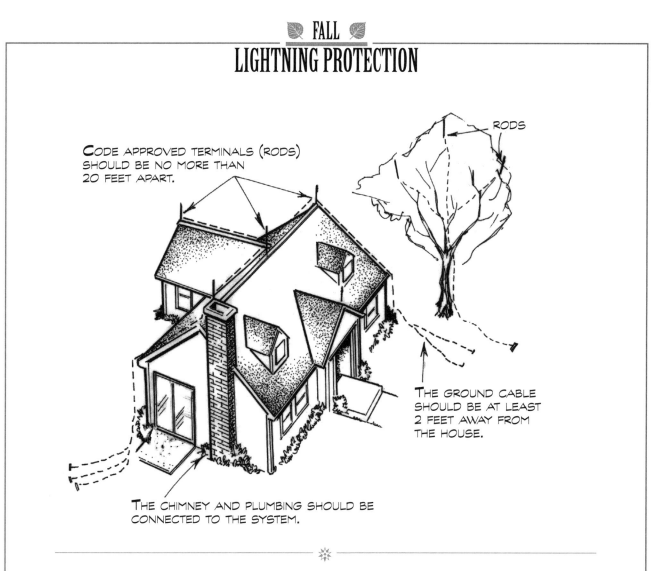

CODE APPROVED TERMINALS (RODS) SHOULD BE NO MORE THAN 20 FEET APART.

RODS

THE GROUND CABLE SHOULD BE AT LEAST 2 FEET AWAY FROM THE HOUSE.

THE CHIMNEY AND PLUMBING SHOULD BE CONNECTED TO THE SYSTEM.

attract lightning, causing them to explode and send debris flying in all directions.

Climate and latitude are other factors to consider. Warm southerly locations have more thunderstorms — and consequently more lightning — than do colder northern areas. Thus, the danger from lightning is greater in Florida than in Maine. The New York area averages about 31 thunderstorms a year.

If you do decide to install a lightning-rod system, here are some guidelines to ensure that it is installed correctly. The contractor installing the system should be certified by the Lighting Protection Institute (3365 North Arlington Heights Road, Arlington Heights, Ill. 60004).

The terminals, or rods, should be code approved and placed no more than 20 feet apart. The rods should be attached by braided copper, aluminum, or galvanized steel wire to ground connections that are positioned at diagonally opposite corners of the house. The ground cable should be at least 2 feet away from the foundation and penetrate 8 feet into the ground. Penetration depth can vary with soil conductivity. The chimney and plumbing — including the vent stack and the water pipes — also should be connected to the system. If metal flues and gutters are within 6 feet of the system, they should be connected.

You also should be aware of the possibility that lightning current may enter the house as power surges through incoming electrical service lines. The surges can damage appliances and household electrical components. To prevent that from happening, you can have surge arresters installed by a licensed electrician or by a representative from the utility company. In addition, many experts recommend protecting home computers, televisions, and audio equipment with individual surge protectors.

Many homeowners wrongly assume that their television antennas can protect the house from lightning. In fact, unless the antenna is properly installed, it may invite trouble by attracting lightning strokes. The television antenna should have a good ground connection and an arrester at the antenna lead-in. Without the ground connection, any surge of electricity from a lightning bolt can jump from the antenna to a better-grounded conductor, such as water pipes in the walls of the house. That can cause a fire. However, even a properly grounded television antenna does not afford adequate lightning protection for the average home.

Trees often have been called "nature's natural lightning rods" because they readily attract lightning. It seems that poplar, silver fir, oak, and spruce trees attract more lightning bolts than do other trees, but soil conductivity and location can make good lightning rods of other trees. Trees within 10 feet of the house should be fitted with terminals and flexible ground connectors to protect them and your home. ⊕

Caulking

Caulking is a necessary part of home maintenance. It seals the many cracks and gaps in the wood, metal, and masonry around the house. Unplugged, those crevasses allow cold air and moisture to penetrate into the walls, causing heat loss and damage.

Perhaps the most difficult part of the caulking job is choosing the right caulk. Generally, caulking is sold in disposable cardboard cartridges that fit into standard, ratchet-driven "guns." Cartridge prices range anywhere from $2 to $25. While cost is always a consideration, other factors are more important.

A good caulk should be sticky so that it adheres to different surfaces. It should be flexible so that it can adjust to the expansion and contraction of gaps. It should be durable so that it resists the ravages of weather and does not have to be replaced frequently. It should be easy to clean up. Paintability also may be a factor; not all caulks can be painted. Those that can, usually require a drying or curing time before paint application.

Caulks are grouped into five categories based upon their composition.

Oil-based caulks were the first caulks marketed. They are the least expensive and also the least durable. They are paintable but do not weather well, becoming brittle with exposure to the elements. Consequently, they are not a good choice for exterior use.

Butyl rubber caulks were introduced shortly after World War II and are still quite popular. They are sticky and adhere well to many surfaces, including masonry and metals; are an excellent choice where moisture or standing water is a problem; and require a lengthy curing time — about a week — before you can paint them. Cleanup requires solvents or mineral spirits.

Latex is an inexpensive caulk that is easy to apply and cleans up with soap and water. It cures quickly and can be painted; adheres well to wood and masonry, but not to metal, unless it is primed first; and does not weather well. Therefore, it is best used for interiors.

Acrylic latex caulk has all the advantages of plain latex caulk with the added plus of exterior durability. It is a good choice for exterior use.

Finally, you may want to consider silicone caulks. These will stick to almost any surface. They are extremely durable and offer a long service life — some manufacturers claim they can last for 20 years or more. Most cannot be painted, but they do come in colors as well as a clear formula. Cleanup requires mineral spirits or solvents. On the downside, they are expensive. Some brands cost as much as $20 a cartridge.

When purchasing caulk, read the label carefully. It will tell you if the caulk is suitable for a particular surface, whether it is paintable, the curing time, and the recommended application temperature. Most caulks require an ambient temperature of 40 degrees F or higher.

Once you've purchased the caulk, applying it is fairly easy. Most caulking guns have the same design; they have a long plunger rod with a series of notches on one side. The trigger mechanism engages the notches and drives the plunger forward, pressing it against the inside of the cartridge. The caulk is forced through the nozzle, forming a "bead."

LOADING THE CAULKING GUN: Before loading the gun, cut off the tip of the cartridge nozzle. The nozzle is tapered, which allows you to shape the width of the bead. If you cut close to the

LOADING THE CAULKING GUN

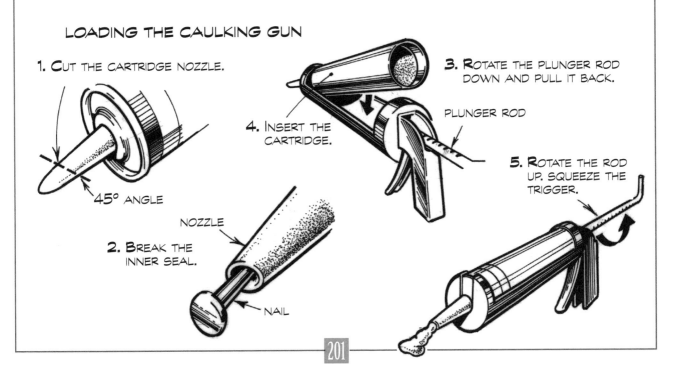

1. CUT THE CARTRIDGE NOZZLE.

45° ANGLE

2. BREAK THE INNER SEAL.

NOZZLE

NAIL

3. ROTATE THE PLUNGER ROD DOWN AND PULL IT BACK.

PLUNGER ROD

4. INSERT THE CARTRIDGE.

5. ROTATE THE ROD UP. SQUEEZE THE TRIGGER.

tip, the bead will be narrow; a higher cut will make a wider bead. Inside the nozzle is a foil seal. Puncture it with a sharp nail or stiff wire.

To load the gun, rotate the plunger rod so that the notches face up and then pull it all the way back. Drop the cartridge into the gun and reverse the rod. Squeeze the trigger enough to bring the plunger into contact with the cartridge but not enough to force the caulk out.

APPLYING A BEAD OF CAULK: Before applying a bead of caulk to any crack or joint, clean the joint by removing any dirt, debris, or old caulk. Caulking compound will not adhere to dirty surfaces. Deep gaps should be filled first with a foam backer rod, which is essentially a flexible dowel of foam insulation. This is more economical than trying to fill the gap with caulking compound.

Now you are ready to draw the "bead." You can choose between two basic beading techniques: the "push" method and the "pull" method.

To push a bead, hold the gun at a 60-degree angle and squeeze the trigger. As the caulk emerges, move the gun forward, away from you. The bead will be formed behind the gun. This method tends to push more caulk into the cracks — as opposed to the push method — but it makes an uneven bead.

The pull method is exactly the opposite. Hold the gun at a 45-degree angle and start squeezing the trigger. As

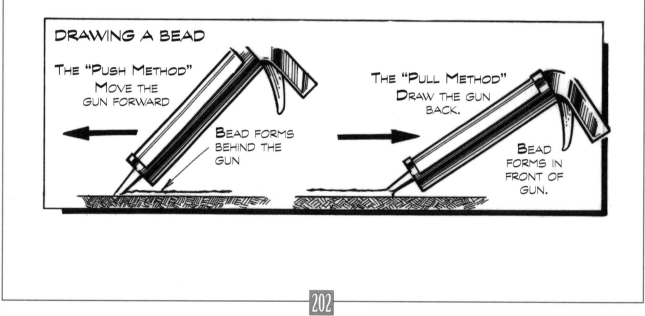

DRAWING A BEAD

THE "PUSH METHOD"
MOVE THE
GUN FORWARD

BEAD FORMS
BEHIND THE
GUN

THE "PULL METHOD"
DRAW THE GUN
BACK.

BEAD
FORMS IN
FRONT OF
GUN.

the bead forms, draw the gun toward you. This method tends to stretch the bead out, making it thinner but smoother.

THE PERFECT BEAD

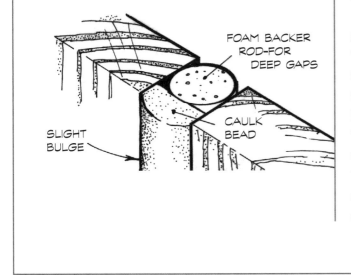

FOAM BACKER ROD-FOR DEEP GAPS

CAULK BEAD

SLIGHT BULGE

Whichever method you choose, you may want to practice first. Pick an inconspicuous, less-observed part of the house and practice on the joints in that area. As you acquire the knack for drawing a good bead, you can move to the more prominent sections.

Most people want to touchup or smooth out a bead with their finger. That, however, creates a concave bead that is not so elastic nor as water resistant as a convex bead. A good caulk bead should bulge slightly at the center. When you are caulking, it is a good idea to keep nearby a clean cloth and a bucket of soapy water — or a container of solvent depending upon the type of caulk — for quick clean-up. ⊕

HOUSEHOLD HELPS • PAINTING

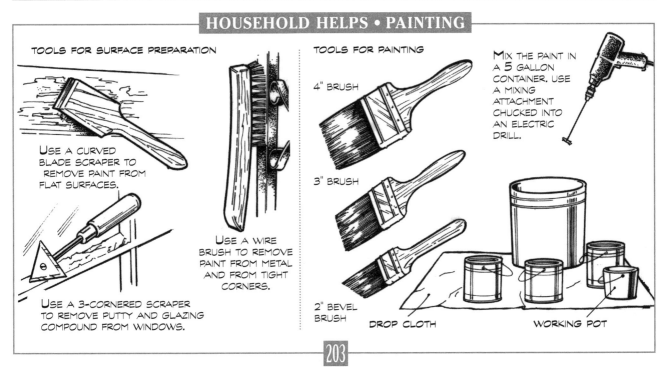

TOOLS FOR SURFACE PREPARATION

USE A CURVED BLADE SCRAPER TO REMOVE PAINT FROM FLAT SURFACES.

USE A 3-CORNERED SCRAPER TO REMOVE PUTTY AND GLAZING COMPOUND FROM WINDOWS.

USE A WIRE BRUSH TO REMOVE PAINT FROM METAL AND FROM TIGHT CORNERS.

TOOLS FOR PAINTING

4" BRUSH

3" BRUSH

2" BEVEL BRUSH

DROP CLOTH

MIX THE PAINT IN A 5 GALLON CONTAINER. USE A MIXING ATTACHMENT CHUCKED INTO AN ELECTRIC DRILL.

WORKING POT

Insulation Inspection

Within the last 30 years, insulation and caulking have become major concerns for homeowners and builders. Before the energy crunch of the '70s, homeowners found that fuel was inexpensive and the cost of keeping the home warm was low compared with the cost of installing insulation. But that situation changed. Builders and homeowners installed insulation in attics, walls, and under floors in an effort to make homes more energy efficient. Even so, many homes, including some of those built within the last few years, are not insulated properly.

How can you be sure that your home has enough insulation? First, you have to determine how much insulation, if any, you have. To do so, you'll have make a visual inspection of the building from top to bottom. Your home may have several forms of insulation: batts or blankets of fiberglass or mineral wool; loose fill of either rock wool, cellulose, or glass fiber; rigid foam boards; or foam, which expands and hardens after being injected into a cavity.

In addition to verifying the presence of insulation, try to measure its thickness whenever possible. Match the measurements to the figures on the accompanying chart to calculate for your home, the approximate R-value — the ability of the insulation to resist heat flow. The higher the R-value, the more efficient the insulation. The U.S. Department of Energy has suggested R-values for homes in various regions of the United States. Compare your R-values with those in the chart at right. In addition, you can call your local building inspector for insulation recommendations in your area.

Your inspection should start in the attic. Look between the joists for insulating materials; they may be in the form of insulation batts or loose fill. If you have insulation here, now is a good time to inspect its condition. Even

- **FLASHLIGHT**
- **GLOVES AND LONG-SLEEVE SHIRT**
- **DRILL WITH BITS**

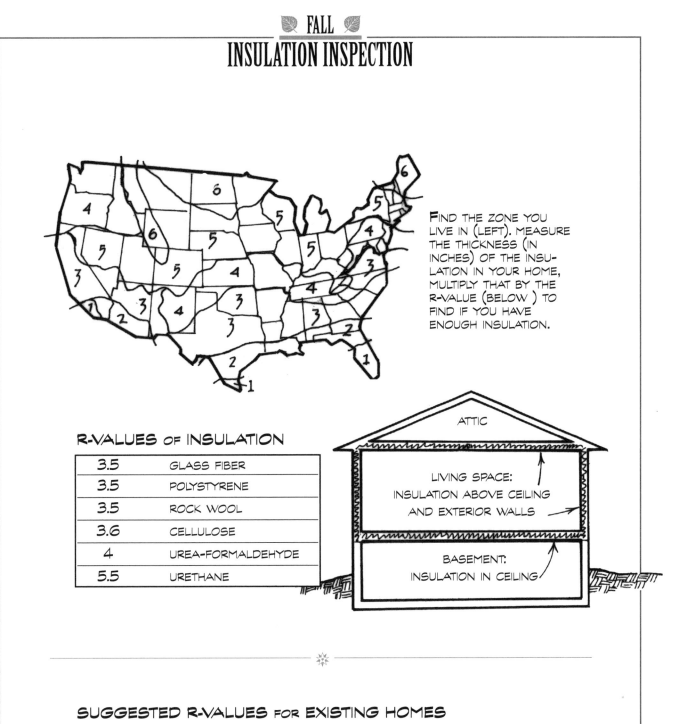

FIND THE ZONE YOU LIVE IN (LEFT). MEASURE THE THICKNESS (IN INCHES) OF THE INSULATION IN YOUR HOME, MULTIPLY THAT BY THE R-VALUE (BELOW) TO FIND IF YOU HAVE ENOUGH INSULATION.

R-VALUES OF INSULATION

3.5	GLASS FIBER
3.5	POLYSTYRENE
3.5	ROCK WOOL
3.6	CELLULOSE
4	UREA-FORMALDEHYDE
5.5	URETHANE

ATTIC

LIVING SPACE:
INSULATION ABOVE CEILING
AND EXTERIOR WALLS

BASEMENT:
INSULATION IN CEILING

SUGGESTED R-VALUES FOR EXISTING HOMES

INSULATION ZONE	1	2	3	4	5	6
FLOORS	–	–	19	19	19	19
EXTERIOR WALLS	11	11	11	11	11	11
ATTICS (GAS OR OIL HEATING)	19	30	30	38	38	49
ATTICS (ELECTRIC HEATING)	30	30	38	38	49	49

though most insulation is quite durable, a number of things still can degrade its value. Leaks in the roof or moisture from condensation can mat it, making it useless. Make sure that it's not compressed or compacted anywhere — usually the result of faulty installation. If you have loose fill, make sure that invading rodents are not nesting in it.

After the attic you'll want to examine the house walls. Naturally, you need only to check the outside walls. Evaluating the insulation in the walls is difficult because it's sealed behind the wallboard. You can verify the presence of insulation, but may not be able to measure the thickness. But that is not really a problem, because in most cases the insulation will be fiberglass batts, blown-in loose fill, or expanded foam. You can assume then, that it is approximately the size of the wall cavity, i.e., 3 1/2-inches thick.

Sometimes you can get a peek at the insulation by removing the cover plate on a switch or outlet and looking into the stud area. Don't forget to turn the power off first. You also can try drilling a small inspection hole in the wall. If you use that method, be careful not to drill past the wallboard into the insulation. After you've looked through the hole, you can patch it with an all-purpose joint compound.

Next, go into the basement. If it is unfinished, the inspection will be easy. Simply look up between the floor joists to determine if there are fiberglass batts. Not all homes have underfloor insulation, but it is essential if the basement connects directly to the garage or has an outside access door. Many building codes require that underfloor insulation be covered with gypsum wallboard. So if your ceiling has wallboard, it's safe to assume that it has insulation.

Look at the basement walls. Insulation is not really necessary if the basement is not used for living quarters or any activity, but a finished basement should be insulated. If it already has finished walls, use the same wall-inspection techniques described above to detect the insulation. Before leaving the basement, inspect the air ducts, pipes, and electrical wires. The ducts and pipes should be wrapped, and openings around incoming pipes and electrical wires should be plugged with insulation.

If you have a crawl space, check it. The crawl space may have insulation blankets spread between the joists. Some sort of moisture barrier also should be on the ground. It usually consists of 6-mil polyethylene film laid over the exposed soil.

After your inspection you can calculate the average R-value for your house

and compare it with the local code specifications or the U.S. Department of Energy recommendations. If that seems like a lot of effort, you can simplify matters by calling in a professional energy auditor, who will assess your home and make cost-effective suggestions — for a fee. Look in the yellow pages or call your utility company for the names of energy auditors.

Some energy auditors are able to perform an infrared scan on your house, which can be helpful even for homeowners with state-of-the-art insulation. The scan technician, or thermographer, uses a special heat-sensitive camera that measures slight differences in temperature. The scan is best done at night or on a cool day when there is a 30-degree temperature difference between the inside and the outside of the house. A good scan can reveal areas where heat is leaking out through the insulation barrier, and it can pinpoint the weak spots in your home insulation. To locate a thermographer, look in the yellow pages under "Infrared Inspection Services" or contact The Infraspection Institute, 33 Juniper Ridge, Shelburne, Vt. 05482. Scan rates vary from $75 to $250.

Your inspection may show that your home is well insulated; but if not, then you're faced with the problem of choosing the right insulation materials and installing them properly. ⊕

HOUSEHOLD HELPS • GLUING

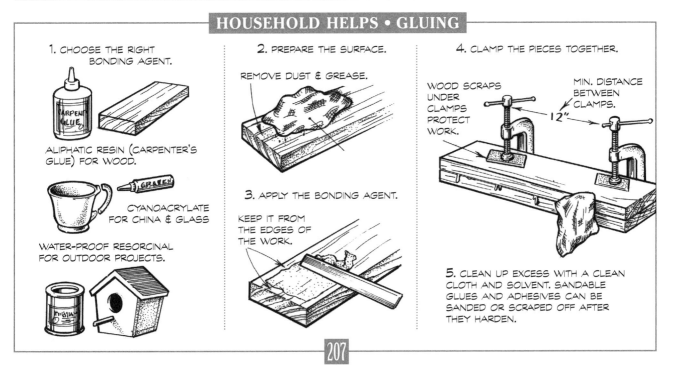

1. CHOOSE THE RIGHT BONDING AGENT.

ALIPHATIC RESIN (CARPENTER'S GLUE) FOR WOOD.

CYANOACRYLATE FOR CHINA & GLASS

WATER-PROOF RESORCINAL FOR OUTDOOR PROJECTS.

2. PREPARE THE SURFACE.

REMOVE DUST & GREASE.

3. APPLY THE BONDING AGENT.

KEEP IT FROM THE EDGES OF THE WORK.

4. CLAMP THE PIECES TOGETHER.

WOOD SCRAPS UNDER CLAMPS PROTECT WORK.

MIN. DISTANCE BETWEEN CLAMPS. 12"

5. CLEAN UP EXCESS WITH A CLEAN CLOTH AND SOLVENT. SANDABLE GLUES AND ADHESIVES CAN BE SANDED OR SCRAPED OFF AFTER THEY HARDEN.

Installing Insulation

Choosing home insulation is not a complicated task once you are aware of the materials available and have some understanding of the way they are put together to provide insulation. Insulating materials can be grouped into three categories: materials made from living or natural resources, materials made from mineral resources, and materials made from chemical synthesis.

Materials made from living resources include cellulose, made from recycled paper; wood-wool; and cotton fiber, a recent addition to the list of insulation materials. Those organic materials are less expensive than the mineral or chemical products, but they are more susceptible to damage from moisture and insect or rodent infestation. In addition, they are flammable and should not be used unless they've been treated with a fire-retardant chemical, such as boric acid or aluminum sulfite powder.

Common mineral products are mineral wool, often known by the trade name Rock-wool; expanded mica, also known as vermiculite or perlite; and

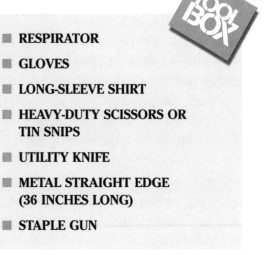

- RESPIRATOR
- GLOVES
- LONG-SLEEVE SHIRT
- HEAVY-DUTY SCISSORS OR TIN SNIPS
- UTILITY KNIFE
- METAL STRAIGHT EDGE (36 INCHES LONG)
- STAPLE GUN

glass fiber, a common trade name is Fiberglas. Those materials are a little more expensive than the organics, but they are relatively nonflammable.

Products of chemical synthesis that have excellent insulation properties are Polystyrene, also called Styrofoam; polyurethane, also called urethane; urea formaldehyde; urea-tripolymer; and isocyanurate. Unfortunately, these products have some serious drawbacks. Polystyrene, polyurethane, urea formaldehyde, and isocyanurate are all flammable and give off toxic fumes when burning. For that reason urea formaldehyde has been banned by the

U.S. Consumer Product Safety Commission, and urethane is banned by some local building codes.

Urea-tripolymer has a low fire-hazard rating, but some environmentalists are concerned that it could release formaldehyde gas into the house over time. They also point out that all those plastic materials might damage the earth's ozone layer by releasing chlorofluorocarbons, or CFCs, into the atmosphere. Manufacturers point out that at present there has not been enough research to substantiate those claims.

Not all chemical synthetics have such problems. A relatively new foam, whose trade name is Air-Krete, is an environmentally safe product that will not burn. It can be injected into closed wall cavities, but that is not a job for the do-it-yourselfer since it has to be formulated carefully on the job site.

Chemical synthetics have a slightly higher R-value — the ability of the material to resist heat flow — than either the natural or mineral products. However, besides the material, structure and form are also important. Insulation material is designed to trap air in a network of minute, closed pockets. The trapped air is really the insulator, because it blocks heat losses that normally occur from convection.

Insulation designers use two different methods to trap air: a cluster of fibers in the form of loose fill or batt insulation or tiny bubbles in the form of rigid or injected foam.

BLANKET & BATT INSULATION: Glass fiber, mineral wool, and cotton fiber can be spun into blankets or batts. Blankets are rolls of fiber, 16 or 24 inches wide and up to 64 feet long. Thicknesses are usually 3, 6, and 9 inches; although thinner, 1-inch rolls are available for sill insulation and pipe wrap. Batts are sim-

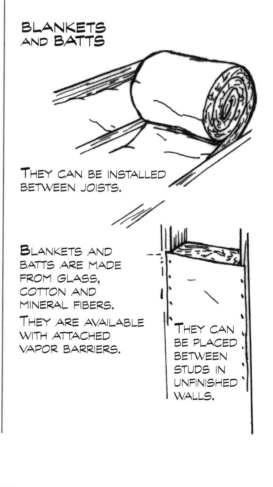

BLANKETS AND BATTS

THEY CAN BE INSTALLED BETWEEN JOISTS.

BLANKETS AND BATTS ARE MADE FROM GLASS, COTTON AND MINERAL FIBERS. THEY ARE AVAILABLE WITH ATTACHED VAPOR BARRIERS.

THEY CAN BE PLACED BETWEEN STUDS IN UNFINISHED WALLS.

ply blankets cut into manageable lengths of 4 or 8 feet.

Some people experience allergic reactions to glass fiber. It's best then to put on a respirator, goggles, and gloves and wear long sleeves when you are working with it.

LOOSE-FILL INSULATION: Mineral wool, expanded mica, glass fiber, cellulose, wood-wool, and cotton fibers are used for loose-fill particles. Those particles are not compressed or spun into any fixed shape. Instead, the loose material,

LOOSE-FILL
ROCK-WOOL
MICA

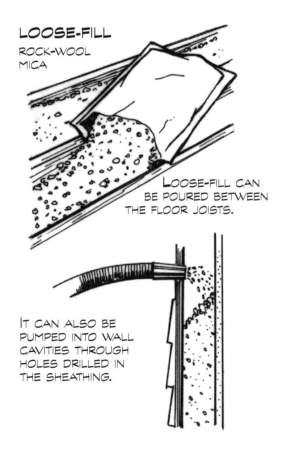

LOOSE-FILL CAN BE POURED BETWEEN THE FLOOR JOISTS.

IT CAN ALSO BE PUMPED INTO WALL CAVITIES THROUGH HOLES DRILLED IN THE SHEATHING.

RIGID BOARDS

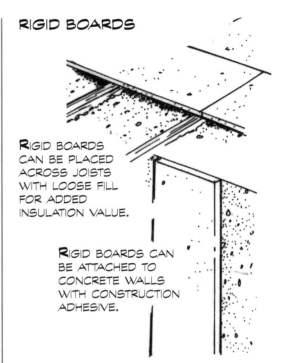

RIGID BOARDS CAN BE PLACED ACROSS JOISTS WITH LOOSE FILL FOR ADDED INSULATION VALUE.

RIGID BOARDS CAN BE ATTACHED TO CONCRETE WALLS WITH CONSTRUCTION ADHESIVE.

available in large bags, is poured into spaces between joists or pumped into wall cavities. Loose fill tends to settle with time and become more compact. More loose fill must then be added to compensate for the loss in insulation value. Do-it-yourselfers can easily pour loose fill in the gaps between joists. Pumping it into wall cavities requires more skill, because the air pressure and blower speed of the pump can affect the way the material settles in place.

RIGID BOARD: Polystyrene, urethane, and glass fiber can be compressed or molded into rigid boards. They are available in 8-foot lengths and widths of 16, 24, and 48 inches. Polystyrene and urethane have excellent insulation properties, but they are flammable and should be covered with gypsum wallboard. Those plastic boards are not waterproof, and excessive moisture can penetrate and cause them to lose up to half their R-value.

An extruded form of polystyrene, which is commonly called "blueboard" for its color, and glass fiber boards are impermeable to moisture.

FOAM INSULATION: Foam in the form of urea formaldehyde, urethane, and Air-Krete can be pumped from tanks into the wall cavities. As the foam cures, it shrinks and loses some of its insulating effectiveness. The shrinkage will be minimal, less than 5 percent, if the foam is formulated correctly and injected when the ambient temperature is moderate — ideally between 50 and 80 degrees. Obviously, that is a job for a professional contractor.

Insulation can help to cut heat losses in a house, but it also can create additional problems when it traps the moisture-laden air. When that air hits the cold sheathing on the other side of the insulation, the moisture condenses and collects in the framing cavities, which can result in ruined insulation and wood rot. An effective way to pre-

vent this is by installing a vapor barrier. Some forms of insulation, such as blankets, batts, and rigid panels, are available with vapor barriers. For loose fill you can install 4-mil or 6-mil polyethylene sheeting before pouring. The insulation should be installed so that it faces the heated space. When you are blowing insulation into a closed wall cavity, you cannot fit a vapor barrier in place. Here you can paint the interior wall with two coats of oil or alkyd-base paint. While it is not so good as a plastic barrier, it is still effective in stopping the moisture from penetrating through the wall. ⊕

FOAM

FOAM CAN BE PUMPED FROM TANKS INTO WALL CAVITIES. THE FOAM MUST BE CORRECTLY FORMULATED AND INJECTED.

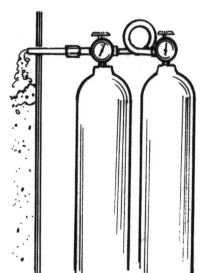

Wet Basements

A wet basement can be a source of frustration and aggravation for any homeowner. Sometimes the condition is subtle and appears as dampness; other times obvious signs like puddles or leaks are present. The best way to minimize the wet-basement problem is with a good foundation. The exterior of the foundation should be waterproofed with a coating of asphalt sealer and a barrier of 6-mil black polyethylene film. Waterproofing isn't enough, however; a good drain field consisting of a drain pipe in a gravel bed may be required to carry ground water away from the foundation. Many new homes have waterproof barriers and drain fields included as part of the construction process.

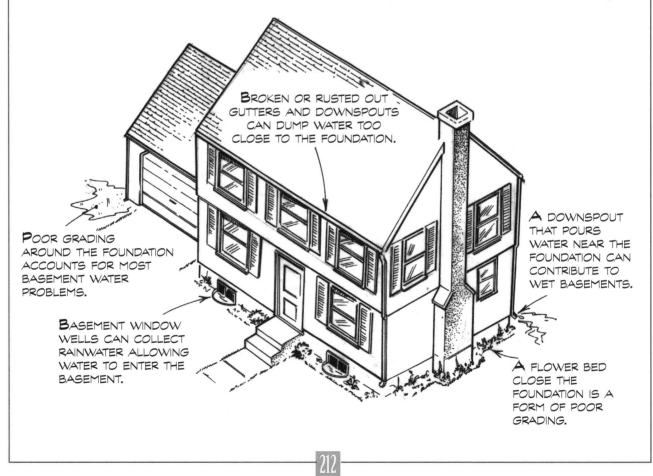

BROKEN OR RUSTED OUT GUTTERS AND DOWNSPOUTS CAN DUMP WATER TOO CLOSE TO THE FOUNDATION.

A DOWNSPOUT THAT POURS WATER NEAR THE FOUNDATION CAN CONTRIBUTE TO WET BASEMENTS.

POOR GRADING AROUND THE FOUNDATION ACCOUNTS FOR MOST BASEMENT WATER PROBLEMS.

BASEMENT WINDOW WELLS CAN COLLECT RAINWATER ALLOWING WATER TO ENTER THE BASEMENT.

A FLOWER BED CLOSE THE FOUNDATION IS A FORM OF POOR GRADING.

TOOL BOX

- **SHOVEL AND RAKE**
- **WIRE BRUSH**
- **TROWEL**
- **WORKGLOVES**

Older homes usually do not have those features. If you have severe water problems, it may be necessary to dig up the ground around the foundation to provide a waterproof barrier and a drain field. Obviously, that is a job for a professional contractor. Beware of the contractor who offers to waterproof the outside of the foundation without digging. That method consists of inserting a hose into the ground and forcing a claylike material into the soil. The process does not work.

Before putting the time and money into waterproofing your foundation, you can do a few things that may keep water out of your basement. Rainwater causes most leaks and moisture problems. As water penetrates the soil around the house, it eventually builds up enough hydrostatic pressure to force its way through the foundation. Even the best foundation walls with water-resistant coatings will give way to that pressure. The first thing that every homeowner should do is make sure that the ground around their house is graded properly so that rainwater is drawn away from the foundation. The ground should slope down and away from the house 1/2 inch per foot. The slope should run for at least 6 feet and ideally for 10 feet.

That will work if your house is on level ground, but suppose your house is situated at the base of a hill? Water cascading down the slope ultimately will find its way into your basement. In that case you can't very well level the hill. The solution is to install a French drain — a gravel-filled, U-shaped ditch that surrounds the house. The base of the ditch is parallel to the hill and the arms extend around the house. Rocks placed at the ends of the arms divert water and prevent it from eroding the nearby soil. The depth and width of the ditch will vary depending upon the severity of the water problem.

In addition to the rainwater falling directly on the ground, the groundwater problem is exacerbated by the addition of runoff water. Runoff water is the rainwater that flows off the roof through the gutters and downspouts and collects around the foundation. It is essential to make sure that the gutters channel this runoff water to the downspouts. Check the gutters to make sure that they are free of leaves and debris. Repair breaks and replace rusted-out sections. Inspect the downspouts and clear them of any obstructions. Next, it's important to make sure that the downspout pours the runoff water away from the house. The easiest way to do that is to place concrete splash blocks under the downspouts. A better solution involves attaching a rolled vinyl hose to each downspout. As the rainwater comes through the down-spout, it forces the hose to unroll and dump the water some distance from the foundation.

The best solution to the runoff-water problem is to connect all the downspouts to drywells. A drywell is essentially a large hole lined with masonry and filled with rocks. The top is closed with a concrete lid. The dry-

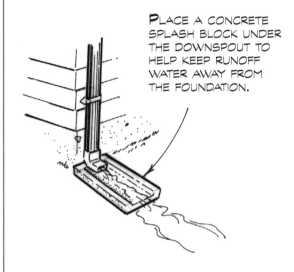

PLACE A CONCRETE SPLASH BLOCK UNDER THE DOWNSPOUT TO HELP KEEP RUNOFF WATER AWAY FROM THE FOUNDATION.

well is buried underground at least 10 feet away from the foundation and con-nected to the downspout with drain tiles.

Many homes have flower beds around the foundation. They may be pretty, but they usually collect more rainwater than does the surrounding ground. The solution is to relocate the flower bed away from the house and replace it with sod or water-thirsty ground cover like pachysandra, vinca minor, or periwinkle.

Rainwater also can enter the base-ment by a more direct route. It can, for example, collect in window wells and enter through the cracks around the windows. Build up the perimeter of the wells with masonry or metal so that it

INSTALL PLASTIC DOMES OVER WINDOW WELLS.

2"

projects 2 inches above grade. The wells should be filled with gravel and, if possible, fitted with a drain that connects to a drywell. Another way to keep rainwater out of the window wells is to fit them with plastic domes, which are available at home centers.

An exterior stairwell leading to a door in the basement can be a potential rainwater collector. The stairwell should have a drain at the foot of the stairs. Inspect the drain periodically to ensure that it is open and free of debris. Also check the curb around the top of the stairwell. It should be high enough to hold back any groundwater that accumulates during a heavy rainstorm.

If you have a metal cellar door, inspect it. Such doors usually have runoff channels that direct rainwater away from the opening. Deformed or bent channels — which can happen if someone walks on the door or drops a heavy weight on it — may not direct the water properly. If possible, bend distorted channels back to position.

After you've corrected all the outside problems, go inside and inspect the walls and floor. Look for cracks and holes. If you find any, remove loose and flaking particles with a wire brush. If the crack is dry, fill it with patching cement. Fill wet cracks with hydraulic cement. ⊕

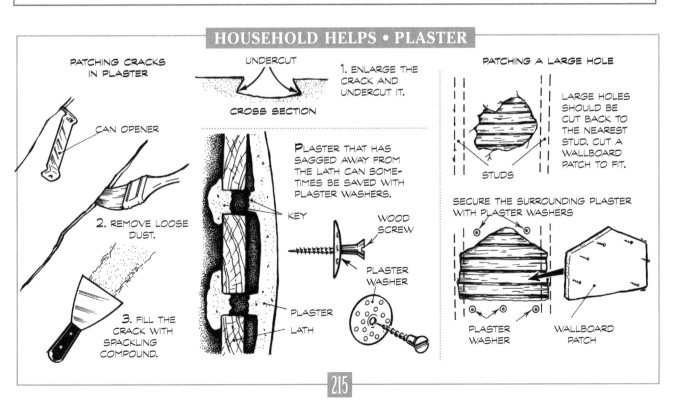

HOUSEHOLD HELPS • PLASTER

PATCHING CRACKS IN PLASTER

CAN OPENER

2. REMOVE LOOSE DUST.

3. FILL THE CRACK WITH SPACKLING COMPOUND.

UNDERCUT

CROSS SECTION

1. ENLARGE THE CRACK AND UNDERCUT IT.

PLASTER THAT HAS SAGGED AWAY FROM THE LATH CAN SOMETIMES BE SAVED WITH PLASTER WASHERS.

KEY

WOOD SCREW

PLASTER WASHER

PLASTER

LATH

PATCHING A LARGE HOLE

LARGE HOLES SHOULD BE CUT BACK TO THE NEAREST STUD. CUT A WALLBOARD PATCH TO FIT.

STUDS

SECURE THE SURROUNDING PLASTER WITH PLASTER WASHERS

PLASTER WASHER

WALLBOARD PATCH

WINTER INSPECTION

DURING the cold months of winter, most maintenance activities will be confined to the indoors. Start by checking the quality of the indoor environment: air, water, and heating. Make sure that all safety devices are in good working order. This is also a good time to make repairs to the interior of the house and plan for any major remodeling or renovation projects in the coming year.

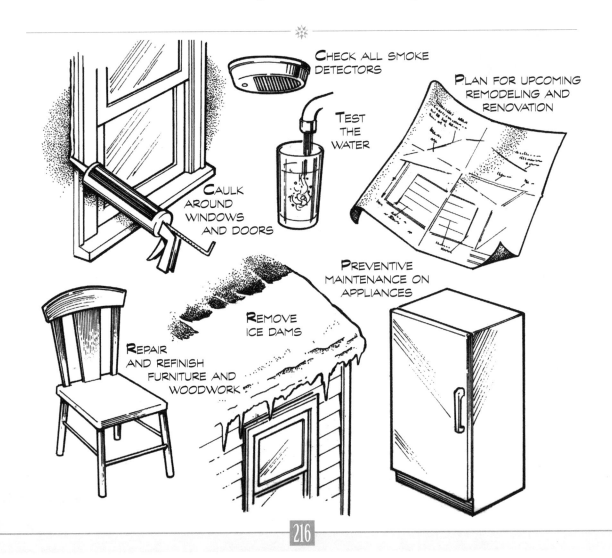

CHECK ALL SMOKE DETECTORS

PLAN FOR UPCOMING REMODELING AND RENOVATION

TEST THE WATER

CAULK AROUND WINDOWS AND DOORS

PREVENTIVE MAINTENANCE ON APPLIANCES

REMOVE ICE DAMS

REPAIR AND REFINISH FURNITURE AND WOODWORK

 During the cold months of winter **check for drafts and air leaks**, and **add caulking and weatherstripping** as needed to make your home comfortable. Inspect all smoke and carbon monoxide detectors and replace the batteries that are old or weak. If you have fire extinguishers, make sure that they are fully charged.

 During the winter months when the house is closed, a serious problem called **backdrafting** can occur when the exhaust gasses from the furnace and fireplace are drawn back into the house. A simple test can determine if you have this problem.

Test for radon and for lead. Both are dangerous elements that can compromise home safety. Have your drinking water tested to ensure that it is free of contaminants.

If you are **planning any major renovations or improvements**, this is a good time to consult with contractors, estimate the materials required, work out financing, and schedule the construction.

 Patch and repair cracks or holes in the walls and ceiling.

Repair floors, doors, stairs, and furniture that may need maintenance.

Plan for an **inspection of the household appliances**, such as the refrigerator, washer, and dryer. Examine the water supply hoses to make sure that they are in good condition and the inline filters at the faucet connection are clear.

 Condensation on windows and wall surfaces can become a problem during the winter months. It may appear as a light coating of frost on a window surface, but in extreme cases the condensation may accumulate as water and cause damage.

 Even if your heating system is in good working order, some parts of the house may never seem warm enough. A number of **heat-saving strategies** will enable you to conserve energy and keep the cold air out.

Bitter-cold temperatures in the winter months can present problems because the water pipes can freeze. Care should be taken to **prevent pipes from freezing** and causing damage.

Winter power failures can pose serious problems. While you have no control over the municipal power supplies, steps can be taken to safeguard your home and family during such emergencies.

Remove snow from around the house to allow safe access and prevent possible damage from ice or leaks.

Backdrafting

Backdrafting is a problem when the air balance in a house is reversed. Lower pressure inside forms a partial vacuum, which sucks air in from the outside. The problem here is that the exhaust gases from the furnace and fireplace are drawn back into the house also. Those gases are toxic; if enough of them are pulled into the living quarters, the home environment can become toxic. What, if anything, can be done to prevent that?

Periodic maintenance inspections of your furnace should keep the unit running properly, but it still may not eliminate the hazards of toxic gases entering your home.

Your furnace, hot-water heater, and fireplace all need air to support combustion. They draw it from the air supply in your house. The air-fuel mixture is burned and converted into heat and noxious gases, one of which is carbon monoxide. These gases are drawn out through the chimney and expelled into the environment.

As the air is burned and expelled, new air must be introduced to replace it. That air comes in through cracks and

■ **CANDLE OR INCENSE STICK**

gaps around the doors, windows, and joints of the house.

Older houses have more cracks and gaps that allow more outside air to enter. In some of those houses all of the air might be exhausted and replaced six times every hour. The air is fresh but also cold and has to be heated six times every hour, resulting in high heating bills.

With the energy crisis of 1973 homeowners looked for ways to cut fuel and heating costs. Architects and builders responded by designing and building tighter houses; insulation was added, and gaps were reduced.

As a result, the air in the newer, tighter houses is replaced twice every hour. Less fresh air comes into the house. Normally, that would be ample air for the needs of the inhabitants and the furnace. However, most modern houses also have appliances that "suck" air. Clothes dryers, range hoods, central vacuuming units, and exhaust fans in the attic, bathrooms, basements, and workshops all have powerful electric fans that pull air from the house and force it outside. Those units can seriously upset the air balance in a house. A modern stove, for example, with a top grill has a down-venting fan that can draw all the air from an average-sized house in less than 25 minutes.

With some, or all of those fans running simultaneously, the air is being pulled out faster than it can enter. That's because modern homes do not have intake fans to replace exhausted air. Replacement air must come from someplace, but where? Like Santa Claus, it comes down the chimney and into the house. It also carries the noxious combustion gases from the furnace or fireplace with it. That reverse airflow is called "backdrafting."

Not all homes have a backdrafting problem, but because of the potential

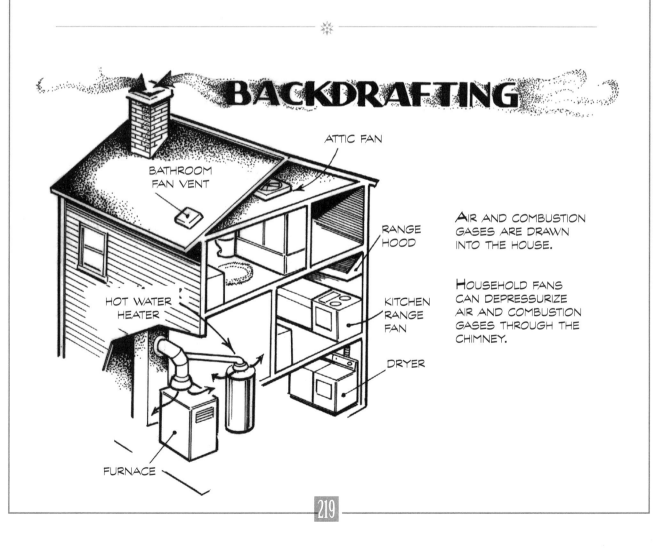

BACKDRAFTING

ATTIC FAN

BATHROOM FAN VENT

RANGE HOOD

HOT WATER HEATER

KITCHEN RANGE FAN

DRYER

FURNACE

AIR AND COMBUSTION GASES ARE DRAWN INTO THE HOUSE.

HOUSEHOLD FANS CAN DEPRESSURIZE AIR AND COMBUSTION GASES THROUGH THE CHIMNEY.

hazards involved, it is important to test for it. Fortunately, the test is neither difficult nor expensive.

TESTING FOR BACKDRAFTING PROBLEMS: First, close all the doors and windows in the house. If you have a fireplace, make sure the damper is fully closed. Next, turn on any exhaust fans and also the clothes dryer. Start the furnace by raising the thermostat and turn-

ing on the hot water heater; opening a hot water faucet should get it going.

Go to the furnace and wait a minute for the flue — the large pipe emerging from the top of the furnace — to heat up. The heated flue should draw all the combustion gases up the chimney. To make the test, hold a lighted match or a smoking incense stick near the draft diverter, the funnel-like collar around the flue pipe. On some furnaces the

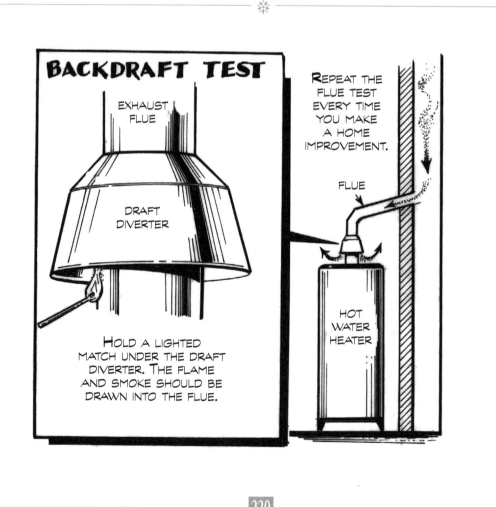

BACKDRAFT TEST

EXHAUST FLUE

DRAFT DIVERTER

HOLD A LIGHTED MATCH UNDER THE DRAFT DIVERTER. THE FLAME AND SMOKE SHOULD BE DRAWN INTO THE FLUE.

REPEAT THE FLUE TEST EVERY TIME YOU MAKE A HOME IMPROVEMENT.

FLUE

HOT WATER HEATER

draft diverter may be a rectangular grill on the front panel. Check the hot-water heater the same way.

If the smoke from the match is drawn into the diverter, then the draft is functioning properly. If the smoke is blown away from the diverter, a back-draft results.

You should repeat the test every time you make a home improvement. Adding insulation, recaulking, changing a window, or installing an exhaust fan are all modifications that can affect the airflow in a house.

Suppose you find that you do have a backdraft problem, what should you do about it? For temporary relief, you can crack open a few windows. That will immediately supply replacement air into the house. It also will defeat the advantages of the weatherstripping and insulation; so consider that a tempo-rary expedient only.

For a more permanent solution you'll want to consult with a heating system professional. He may suggest installing an "induced draft" unit in the flue. That is essentially an electric fan that pulls the combustion gases from the furnace, forcing them outside through the chimney.

While that is an improvement, it may not be enough because the furnace still has to draw air for combustion from the house. A more effective solu-tion involves installing a duct that sup-plies fresh air from outside directly to the furnace. Another duct is installed to expel the combustion gases. That sys-tem is called a "closed" or "sealed" combustion unit. Many building codes now require them in new homes.

Your home also might require addi-tional ducts to bring fresh air into the rest of the house. They should be equipped with heat exchangers to pre-heat the incoming air. Heat exchangers operate with ambient house heat and do not add to the cost of home heating.

Backdrafting also can occur in the fireplace. One way to prevent back-drafting is to install airtight doors. Also inspect the chimney to be sure that it is in good repair and free from obstruc-tions.

Even new homes with the best heat-ing units can experience system mal-functions. That's why it's important to check for backdrafting and to install carbon monoxide detectors. They will alert you to the presence of carbon monoxide should anything go wrong. ⊕

Indoor Air Pollution

F ew people are aware that indoor air can be even more seriously polluted than outdoor air. Indoor air pollution is a serious threat in homes with young children, elderly adults, and chronically ill persons, because those people usually spend long periods of time indoors, and they are more sus-

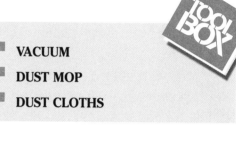

- VACUUM
- DUST MOP
- DUST CLOTHS

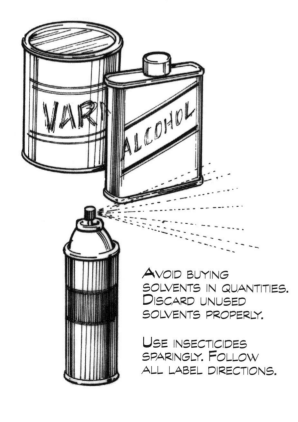

A VOID BUYING SOLVENTS IN QUANTITIES. DISCARD UNUSED SOLVENTS PROPERLY.

USE INSECTICIDES SPARINGLY. FOLLOW ALL LABEL DIRECTIONS.

ceptible to the harmful effects of indoor air pollutants.

Indoor air pollution has many sources, including combustion by-products from gas, oil, kerosene, and wood-burning heaters; environmental tobacco smoke; products for household cleaning and maintenance; organic and biological contaminants; and the outdoors, where such sources as radon originate. Effective strategies for controlling indoor air pollution consist of identifying and eliminating the sources of pollution, improving ventilation and air circulation, and adding air cleaners.

SOURCES OF AIR POLLUTION: How can you tell if you have an air quality problem? Often exposure to bad air results in health problems, such as nose, throat, and eye irritations; headaches; dizziness; and fatigue. If you

INDOOR AIR POLLUTION

experience those symptoms, pay attention to the time and place that they occur. If they fade or disappear when you're away for any length of time, then it's possible that they are brought on by air conditions in the house. Not everyone will experience those symptoms, however. The likelihood of a reaction to air pollutants depends on the sensitivity, age, and general health of the individual.

You can look for other signs when you are evaluating the air quality in your home. Accumulations of moisture and excessive condensation on walls or windows may indicate a lack of air circulation. Stagnant air, stuffiness, and odors are also clues to poor ventilation. Patches of mold or mildew stains are signs of excessive humidity and inadequate air circulation.

Finally, you can check your home for the sources of air pollution. Even though the presence of such sources does not necessarily mean that they are contaminating the air, a careful evaluation of potential pollutants can help you in evaluating the air quality in your home.

Indoor combustion sources include stoves, fireplaces, heaters, and furnaces. They can introduce carbon monoxide, nitrogen dioxide, and particles into the air. Gas stoves will pollute the air if they are improperly adjusted.

A visual check of the burner flames will tell you if you have a problem. Persistent yellow-tipped flames indicate improperly adjusted burners. Ask the gas company to tune the burner so that all the flame tips are blue. In addition the range should be fitted with a hood equipped with an exhaust fan. That should be vented to the outside, if possible, to exhaust airborne contaminates produced by cooking.

Inspect your fireplace periodically for cracks in the flue or chimney that could allow combustion gases to leak back into the house. Examine your wood stove to make sure that the doors

MAKE SURE THAT FURNACES, STOVES, AND FIREPLACES ARE VENTED PROPERLY, AND THAT THEY HAVE AN ADEQUATE SUPPLY OF INTAKE AIR.

are tight fitting and all gaskets are in good shape. Have your furnace and air-handling system inspected annually and adjust or replace all malfunctioning or damaged parts.

Environmental tobacco smoke comes from burning cigar, cigarette, and pipe tobacco. It is a complex mixture of 4,000 compounds, more than 40 of which are strong irritants and are known to cause cancer in humans or laboratory animals. It affects not only the smoker but also all those who inhale it.

AVOID OVER-WATERING PLANTS. TOO MUCH HUMIDITY WILL STIMULATE BIOLOGICAL CONTAMINATES.

The simplest and most effective way to avoid polluting the indoor air with tobacco smoke is to ask all smokers to smoke outdoors. If that is not possible, you will have to install fans to increase the ventilation and air circulation in the house. That, however, is not as easy as it sounds, because mechanical ventilation devices do not remove the smoke so quickly as it builds up. Also running a number of large fans can add to your energy bills.

Household products, such as paints, varnishes, wax, and many cleaning, disinfecting, degreasing, and hobby products contain organic chemicals that can affect human health. Obviously, those products are useful or necessary to maintain your home, so you cannot dispense with them entirely. You can do a number of things to limit exposure to household chemicals.

First, follow the label directions carefully and use the solutions in prescribed amounts and in the proper manner. Read and observe all warnings. If a label advises using the product in a well-ventilated area, go outdoors; indoors, open windows and set up exhaust fans. Buy only as much as you need; and discard partially full containers or old or unneeded chemicals in a safe and environmentally approved manner.

INDOOR AIR POLLUTION

Another common chemical that most people come in contact with is perchloroethylene. That is the chemical most widely used to dry-clean clothes. Studies have shown that it can evaporate into the air from newly dry-cleaned clothes. People wearing dry-cleaned clothes also can breathe low levels of the chemical.

In practice, dry cleaners try to recapture the perchloroethylene from newly cleaned clothes and recycle it back into their cleaning tanks, but not all dry cleaners are able to remove it every time. Do not accept clothes from the cleaner if they have a strong odor of dry-cleaning fluid. Instead, ask the dry cleaner to remove the chemical and properly dry the garment.

Biological contaminants include bacteria, molds, mildew, viruses, dust mites, pollen, and animal dander. Most of those contaminants breed and multiply in warm, moist environments. By keeping the relative humidity levels from 30 percent to 50 percent, you can minimize their effects. Thoroughly dry, or replace, wet carpets or water-damaged materials to keep mold and bacteria from forming. Be sure to refill the water reservoirs in humidifiers daily with fresh water and clean the filter elements according to the manufacturer's directions. Finally, keep your house clean. Dusting and vacuuming regularly will help to reduce the concentrations of dust mites, pollen, and animal dander. ⊕

HOUSEHOLD HELPS • AIR POLLUTION

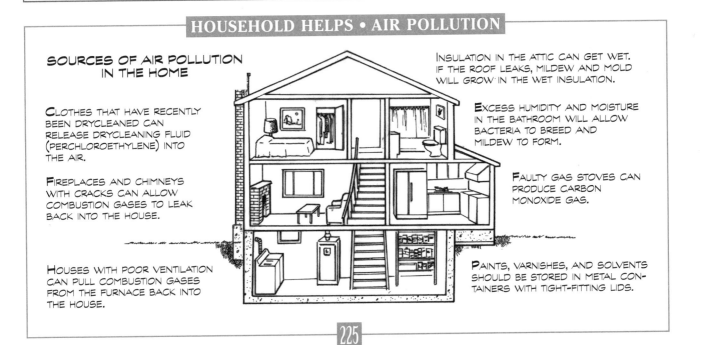

SOURCES OF AIR POLLUTION IN THE HOME

CLOTHES THAT HAVE RECENTLY BEEN DRYCLEANED CAN RELEASE DRYCLEANING FLUID (PERCHLOROETHYLENE) INTO THE AIR.

FIREPLACES AND CHIMNEYS WITH CRACKS CAN ALLOW COMBUSTION GASES TO LEAK BACK INTO THE HOUSE.

HOUSES WITH POOR VENTILATION CAN PULL COMBUSTION GASES FROM THE FURNACE BACK INTO THE HOUSE.

INSULATION IN THE ATTIC CAN GET WET. IF THE ROOF LEAKS, MILDEW AND MOLD WILL GROW IN THE WET INSULATION.

EXCESS HUMIDITY AND MOISTURE IN THE BATHROOM WILL ALLOW BACTERIA TO BREED AND MILDEW TO FORM.

FAULTY GAS STOVES CAN PRODUCE CARBON MONOXIDE GAS.

PAINTS, VARNISHES, AND SOLVENTS SHOULD BE STORED IN METAL CONTAINERS WITH TIGHT-FITTING LIDS.

Radon

Within the last decade a number of articles have appeared on radon. Radon is the invisible gas that seeps into homes and contaminates them with radiation. Where exactly does the gas come from? Why has it suddenly appeared, and how serious is the radon threat?

Radon is a by-product of uranium decay. Uranium is a complex element that is in a constant state of transformation from a heavy, unstable element into a simpler substance. During the transformation process, technically known as the "decay sequence," uranium breaks down into "daughter" elements: thorium, then protactinium, and eventually radium.

Radium is far from stable, and it continues the decay sequence. As it decays, it creates other daughters: radon gas and some radioactive fragments. Those products become airborne where they are easily inhaled into your lungs. Inside the lungs the fragments continue to decay and release radiation in the form of alpha and beta particles.

Uranium and its decay sequence is not a recent phenomenon, but has been going on since the creation of the earth. Nor, for that matter, is radon gas a recent discovery. The German physicist Friedrich Ernst Dorn first identified radon in 1900. Scientists were aware that workers in uranium mines often developed lung cancer as a result of exposure to the natural radiation. They felt, however, that the general population was not exposed, and no threat to public health was presented.

In 1984 Stanley Watras, an engineer at a nuclear power plant in Pennsylvania, set off the radiation detectors at the plant. At first, plant technicians assumed that he became contaminated by some obscure leak somewhere on the job site, but tests and inspections showed that this was not possible. Next, radiation specialists visited the Watras home. They found that radiation levels in the house were 700 times higher than the maximum considered safe for human exposure. Further investigations revealed that the house was situated on rock that contained substantial deposits of low-grade uranium ore.

The problems at the Watras house awakened environmentalists to the possibility that the average homeowner could become contaminated with radioactivity in the privacy of his own home. Soon, health and safety organizations were studying the radon problem to determine if a health threat existed.

The EPA conducted studies of miners exposed to high levels of radiation in uranium mines. From the data collected they extrapolated statistical models that they use to show a relationship between radon exposure and cancer. They estimate that radon is responsible for 7,000 to 30,000 lung cancer deaths each year.

Not everyone agrees with those statistics, however. Many epidemiologists point out that no evidence exists that establishes a strong link between lung cancer and indoor radon exposure. In

To REDUCE THE LEVEL OF RADON SEAL ALL THE CRACKS AND OTHER OPENINGS IN THE FOUNDATION. APPLY A SEALANT TO THE WALLS AND INSTALL A DEPRESSURIZATION SYSTEM.

TOOL BOX

■ TEST DEVICES

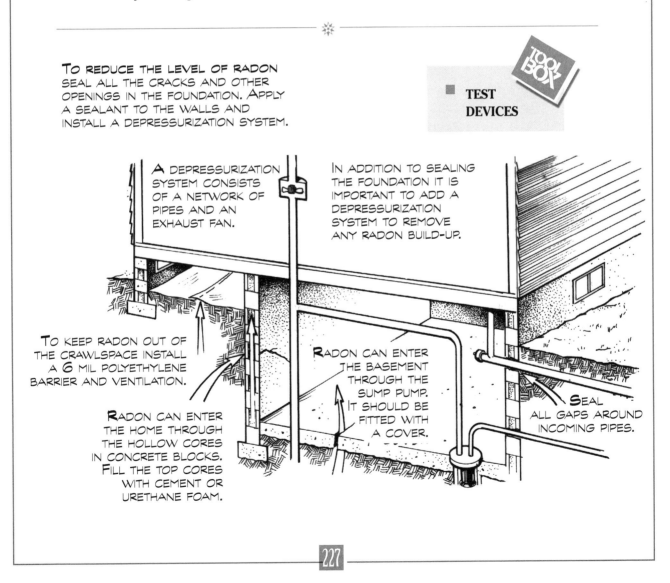

A DEPRESSURIZATION SYSTEM CONSISTS OF A NETWORK OF PIPES AND AN EXHAUST FAN.

IN ADDITION TO SEALING THE FOUNDATION IT IS IMPORTANT TO ADD A DEPRESSURIZATION SYSTEM TO REMOVE ANY RADON BUILD-UP.

TO KEEP RADON OUT OF THE CRAWLSPACE INSTALL A 6 MIL POLYETHYLENE BARRIER AND VENTILATION.

RADON CAN ENTER THE HOME THROUGH THE HOLLOW CORES IN CONCRETE BLOCKS. FILL THE TOP CORES WITH CEMENT OR URETHANE FOAM.

RADON CAN ENTER THE BASEMENT THROUGH THE SUMP PUMP. IT SHOULD BE FITTED WITH A COVER.

SEAL ALL GAPS AROUND INCOMING PIPES.

addition, some scientists feel that the EPA's statistical models are flawed and inaccurate. Studies conducted in Ottawa, Canada, suggest that the radon threat is exaggerated, while studies in Sweden support the EPA's claims.

Representatives for the EPA are aware of the conflicting data, and they are quick to point out that major health organizations, like the Centers for Disease Control, the American Lung Association and the American Medical Association, feel that radon is a real health hazard and is responsible for thousands of lung cancer deaths.

TESTING YOUR HOME FOR RADON:
Adrift in that sea of controversy is the individual homeowner. What should you do to safeguard your home and family? Perhaps the most prudent course of action is to test your home for radon. If the tests show low levels, then the argument becomes academic. On the other hand, you might want to consider radon abatement measures if results reveal high concentrations.

Basically two types of radon-testing devices are available: passive testing devices and active testing devices. Passive devices do not need power to function. Charcoal canisters, alpha-track detectors, and charcoal liquid scintillation devices are passive instruments that are available by mail or at large home centers. The devices are positioned in a suitable location for a specified length of time and then sent to a laboratory for analysis. Active devices function as continuous radon monitors; they require a qualified technician for setup and analysis.

Proper placement of the testing device is an important consideration; otherwise, the test results will be inaccurate. The tester should be placed about 20 inches off the floor in the lowest finished room of the house. This should be a room that receives regular use. Do not place the unit in the kitchen, bathroom, or laundry room.

Some of the testing devices, such as the charcoal canisters, are designed for short-term-testing only. That usually means leaving the canisters in place no longer than four days. It sounds simple and convenient, but a four-day sample is not enough to evaluate the radiation level in your home. Radon concentrations can vary considerably with the seasons. In the winter, for example, when the windows and doors are closed, radon concentrations tend to be high. If you do decide to use a short-term testing device, then plan to make a number of tests throughout the year.

After the test is completed, repackage the device and send it to the laboratory listed on the container. The laboratory will analyze the sample and send you the test results. If the test should show high concentrations of radon, then it's best to call a professional radon tester in to make thorough evaluation. If that evaluation also indicates high levels, then corrective action may be necessary.

Effective radon abatement generally consists of a two-part approach. The first part entails sealing all cracks and openings in the foundation. The second part involves installing fans and ventilators. It is difficult to estimate the cost of those modifications since they depend on the size and construction of the house and also the severity of the radon problem, but the average cost for radon abatement is about $1,500. ⊕

HOUSEHOLD HELPS • HEAVY LIFTING

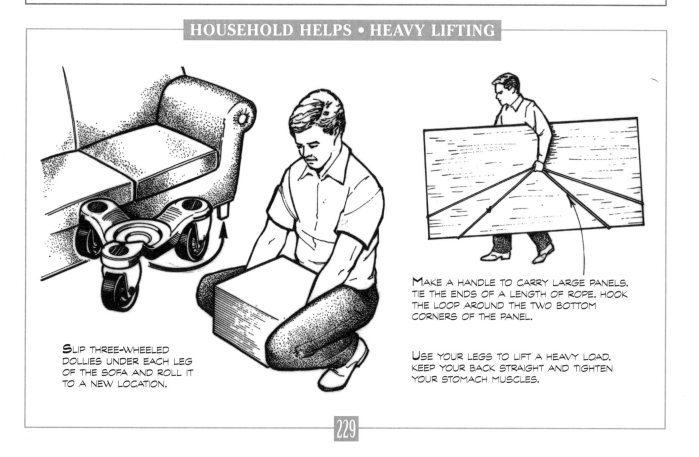

SLIP THREE-WHEELED DOLLIES UNDER EACH LEG OF THE SOFA AND ROLL IT TO A NEW LOCATION.

MAKE A HANDLE TO CARRY LARGE PANELS. TIE THE ENDS OF A LENGTH OF ROPE. HOOK THE LOOP AROUND THE TWO BOTTOM CORNERS OF THE PANEL.

USE YOUR LEGS TO LIFT A HEAVY LOAD. KEEP YOUR BACK STRAIGHT AND TIGHTEN YOUR STOMACH MUSCLES.

Lead

Because lead or lead compounds often were used to sweeten or preserve foods, lead poisoning has been common throughout history. Roman wine merchants added an aromatic liquid, called sapa, to keep their wine from turning into vinegar. Sapa was made by boiling grape juice in lead kettles. The acidic grape juice leached lead from the vessel, turning the sapa into a poison.

During the Middle Ages, lead oxide, called litharge, was added to wine as a sweetener. That caused frequent outbreaks of colic or "wine disease" throughout Europe. Still other beverages became contaminated when they were prepared with lead utensils. Cider often was tainted because the apples were crushed in presses with lead fittings. Rum acquired significant amounts of lead when it was processed in stills fitted with condensers made of lead. Food or beverages also could acquire substantial amounts of lead if they were kept in earthenware vessels with lead glazing — which remains a possibility today.

Lead poisoning also could be contracted in other ways. In the late 18th

TOOL BOX

- KNIFE
- PLASTIC SAMPLE BAGS
- NON-ALCOHOL BABY WIPES
- CLEANING SUPPLIES (PAIL, DETERGENT, AND WASH CLOTHS)

century, litharge was used for wig and face powder. Breathing in the dust was a definite health hazard.

The use of lead or lead products in food, beverages, and cosmetics largely was eliminated by the turn of the 20th century. It was still used until recently in the manufacture of paint, gasoline, and plumbing fixtures. Even though federal regulations have eliminated the inclusion of lead in those products, much of it is still around. For example, many homes built before 1960 contain heavily leaded paint. Some built as recently as 1978 also may have lead paint. Soil by roadways or major highways may yet be contaminated by lead deposits from car or truck fumes. Recent legislation has outlawed the use of lead in paint and gasoline, so new homes are virtually lead free.

Small children face the greatest health risk because they like to chew on the paint chips. Children also have frequent hand-to-mouth contact, so simply placing their hands in paint dust may be enough to introduce significant toxicity into their systems. If you live in an older home and have small children, it is important to examine carefully all the painted surfaces in your house. Look first at the overall condition of paint. Inspect around the edges of all windows and doors and look for paint chips and dust. Even if all paint surfaces are sound, you still may have a problem if you plan to do any remodeling or repairs. Construction work that abrades or cuts into the paint can produce enough dust to contaminate a room.

TESTING FOR LEAD CONTAMINANTS:

How can you be sure that your home and environment is safe and free of lead contamination? If any member of the household shows signs of lead poisoning — appetite loss, stomach pain, extreme fatigue, insomnia, metallic taste in the mouth, joint pain, headaches, or dizziness — he or she should have a blood test. In addition, the EPA recommends testing for all children between the ages of 6 months and

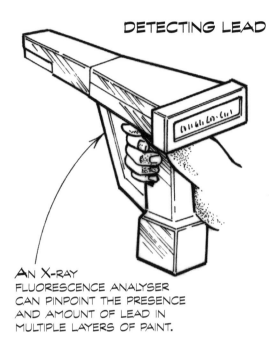

DETECTING LEAD

An X-Ray Fluorescence Analyser can pinpoint the presence and amount of lead in multiple layers of paint.

1 year old, even if they do not display the symptoms. The blood test is a simple one that can be performed by a doctor or at a health center.

It is also a good idea to test your house for lead paint. You can use a home kit for that. The kits are relatively inexpensive, priced from $10 to $30, and are available at hardware stores and home improvement centers. Most kits contain a chemical reagent, sodium rhodizonate, which turns red in the presence of lead. The test is made by scraping the paint surface to expose all layers, and then swabbing the area with the reagent. If you want to test red paint, use a kit with a different reagent, sodium sulfide. It will turn black if lead is present, and the results will be evident on the red paint surface. Those kits also can be used to detect lead on glazed pottery, porcelain, and even old, painted toys. They should not be used to test soil, because different soil compositions can skew the test results.

While the kits provide quick results, independent field studies have not proven their accuracy. A better method is to gather samples of paint chips or scrapings, place them in plastic bags, and send them to an EPA-approved lab for testing. For a list of laboratories that have passed proficiency testing for lead analysis, call the National Lead Information Center at 1-800-424-LEAD. An easy way to gather samples of paint dust is by wiping the surface with a thin, nonalcohol based baby wipe. Enclose it in a plastic bag and send it to the lab.

The testing laboratory will examine the samples using an atomic absorption process, the most accurate procedure available. It then will send you a report that tells you if lead is present and if the amount discovered exceeds EPA guide-

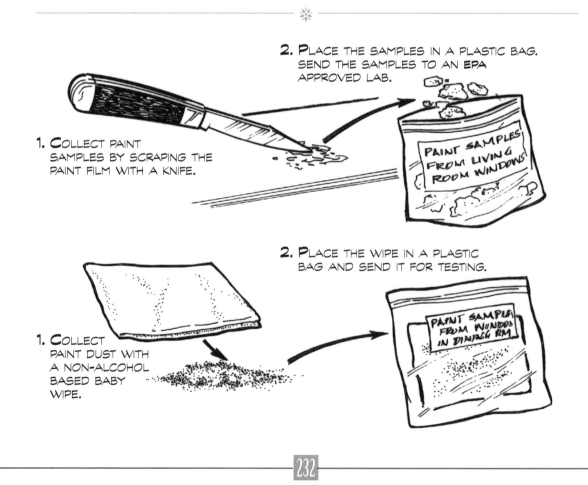

2. PLACE THE SAMPLES IN A PLASTIC BAG. SEND THE SAMPLES TO AN EPA APPROVED LAB.

1. COLLECT PAINT SAMPLES BY SCRAPING THE PAINT FILM WITH A KNIFE.

PAINT SAMPLES FROM LIVING ROOM WINDOWS

2. PLACE THE WIPE IN A PLASTIC BAG AND SEND IT FOR TESTING.

1. COLLECT PAINT DUST WITH A NON-ALCOHOL BASED BABY WIPE.

PAINT SAMPLE FROM WINDOW IN DINING RM

lines. The lab fee and testing time will vary depending upon the individual laboratory.

If the report reveals that your home has high levels of lead, then you are faced with the problem of removing it or containing it. At that point it's best to call in a lead abatement specialist for consultation. Unfortunately, not everyone who claims to know about lead removal is fully qualified to do the job. Contact your local health department or the EPA for a list of certified lead abatement contractors and inspectors. If they reveal the presence of lead, it's important to have a follow-up inspection by a professional.

In most cases the specialist will want to conduct a thorough inspection of your house to determine the extent of the lead. He will take numerous samples of paint and even soil samples outdoors and send them to be analyzed. In addition to the samples, he may use portable testing devices such as an X-ray fluorescence analyzer (XRF). X-ray fluorescence uses a portable analyzer that can pinpoint the presence and amount of lead in all the layers of paint. That type of testing is done in the home without disturbing the layers of paint. After evaluating the test results, the inspector determines the amount and location of lead in the house and assesses the risk to the occupants.

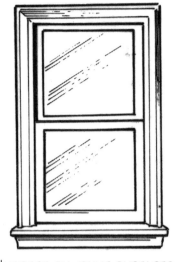

INSPECT ALL PAINT SURFACES. LOOK AROUND THE EDGES OF ALL DOORS AND WINDOWS FOR PAINT DUST.

Even if your home has surfaces coated with lead paint, it may not be hazardous if the paint surface remains undamaged. That, however, is not as simple as it sounds. Windows and doors, for example, often abrade the paint on surrounding moldings whenever they are opened or closed. Other types of molding similarly can be damaged if a piece of furniture rubs against them. That rubbing can break the paint film and pulverize it into fine lead dust that easily can become airborne or come in contact with your hands or mouth.

The only way to control the dust effectively is by washing down painted

REMOVING LEAD

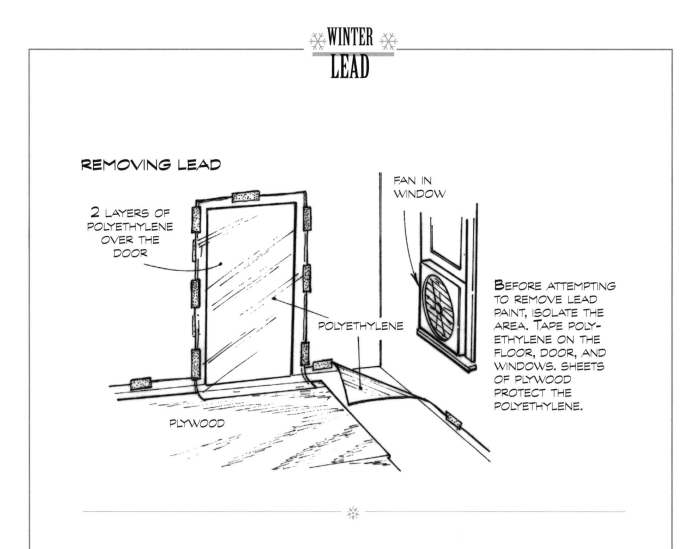

2 LAYERS OF POLYETHYLENE OVER THE DOOR

FAN IN WINDOW

POLYETHYLENE

PLYWOOD

BEFORE ATTEMPTING TO REMOVE LEAD PAINT, ISOLATE THE AREA. TAPE POLYETHYLENE ON THE FLOOR, DOOR, AND WINDOWS. SHEETS OF PLYWOOD PROTECT THE POLYETHYLENE.

surfaces twice a week with a powdered dishwasher detergent. Dishwasher detergents are recommended because they have a high phosphate content. Do not use a multipurpose cleaner for the task. Vacuuming and dusting are not effective and actually may spread the dust around.

LEAD ABATEMENT: Cleaning can deal with the lead problem, but it won't eliminate it. Lead is abated in three ways: removal; replacement; or containment, also called enclosure and encapsulation. Both replacement and removal methods remove the lead hazard from the house.

Removal procedures consist of scraping the paint off or stripping it with a chemical solvent. Sometimes the contractor may remove all pieces of moldings and trim and send them to a paint removal facility. Otherwise paint removal will have to be done on site. This can result in exposure to lead fumes unless proper barriers are erected and containment procedures followed.

The lead abatement team must don protective clothing and seal off the working area with tape and plastic sheeting to isolate the space from the rest of the house. In extreme cases they also will set up temporary industrial showers so that they can wash off any contamination before they leave the work site. At the end of the day the workers must vacuum up any dust with

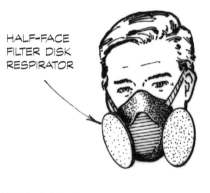

HALF-FACE
FILTER DISK
RESPIRATOR

WEAR A RESPIRATOR APPROVED BY THE NATIONAL INSTITUTE OF SAFETY AND HEALTH FOR PROTECTION AGAINST LEAD DUST.

HALF-FACE
CARTRIDGE
RESPIRATOR

HEPA vacuum cleaners, which have high-efficiency particulate air filters to trap the lead particles. Finally, the area must be wiped down with special liquid cleaners to remove all traces of lead.

Replacement entails carefully removing the moldings and replacing them with new pieces. While that can be expensive, it sometimes can be cost effective if, for example, you replace old windows with modern, energy-efficient ones. Of course, it's not always possible to replace all painted surfaces. That is particularly true of ornate period moldings.

The third method, containment, does not remove the lead, but it seals it behind an elastomeric coating or a surface barrier. It can be an effective solution to the lead problem as long as the barrier remains intact. Any future remodeling jobs, however, can disturb the containment seal, causing the lead problem to resurface. Enclosure is used for walls and ceilings and involves covering the surface with wallboard, wood paneling, or fiberboard. With encapsulation the affected areas are painted with a coating that seals in the lead.

Obviously, lead abatement can be expensive, but it will make the home a much safer place in which to live. ⊕

Water Testing

In Colonial times most people drank milk or cider or, if they could afford it, beer or wine. They avoided drinking water because they believed that it could cause sickness or even death. Actually, they had good reason to distrust the drinking water. Their privies and outhouses were often situated dangerously close to the well or stream, and frequently sewage contaminated the water.

The water situation has improved dramatically since those days. Advances in sanitation engineering and the installation of water treatment plants have reduced significantly the contaminates found in drinking water. In spite of those advances, problems still exist.

About 30 years ago the federal government found that many water systems in the United States were not delivering clean water. In an effort to correct that, Congress passed the Safe Drinking Water Act in 1974. The law required all public water systems using surface water to filter and disinfect it. Under the act the EPA set monitoring standards for 26 substances that could contaminate water. In 1986 Congress directed the agency to add 57 more substances to the list of contaminates.

Water suppliers are required by law to test their water output regularly to make sure that it is up to the standards set by the Safe Drinking Water Act. The results of those tests are available to the public. If you're interested, call the water supply for a copy of the latest test. The number should be on your water bill.

■ **PLASTIC SAMPLE BOTTLES**

Still, some contaminates — certain microbes, for example — are not yet covered by these regulations. In 1993 a microscopic parasite, cryptosporidium, tainted the water supply in Milwaukee and made an estimated 400,000 people sick. Some environmentalists feel that this incident demonstrates the need for increased regulation and monitoring.

Not all homeowners get their water from community water systems. Many homeowners — nearly half of all Americans — draw their water from wells that tap groundwater. The quality of this water is subject only to state and local laws. Those regulations are usually less stringent than federal standards, but that doesn't bother the homeowner who often feels that well water, coming from deep within the ground, is protected by layers of soil and rock. Recently, however, environmentalists have found that pesticides can enter the groundwater and create a potential health hazard.

Studies conducted by various state and federal agencies have found quantities of Dibromochloropropane (DBCP) in California groundwater, Aldicarb in wells on Long Island, and Ethylene Dibromide in Florida drinking water. In fact, the EPA estimates that in at least 23 different states many pesticides may be in some of the groundwater.

Even if your well or local water system supplies clean water, it is still possible that water can become tainted in your own house. Many pipes contain metal that can leach into the water. Lead particles are the major health threat, although copper in significant amounts

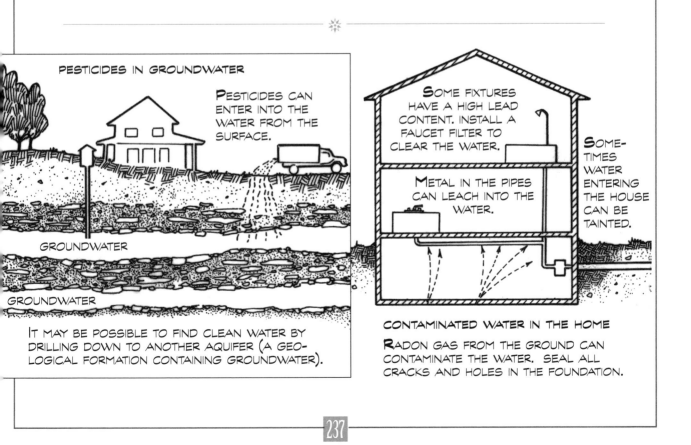

PESTICIDES IN GROUNDWATER

PESTICIDES CAN ENTER INTO THE WATER FROM THE SURFACE.

GROUNDWATER

GROUNDWATER

IT MAY BE POSSIBLE TO FIND CLEAN WATER BY DRILLING DOWN TO ANOTHER AQUIFER (A GEOLOGICAL FORMATION CONTAINING GROUNDWATER).

SOME FIXTURES HAVE A HIGH LEAD CONTENT. INSTALL A FAUCET FILTER TO CLEAR THE WATER.

SOMETIMES WATER ENTERING THE HOUSE CAN BE TAINTED.

METAL IN THE PIPES CAN LEACH INTO THE WATER.

CONTAMINATED WATER IN THE HOME

RADON GAS FROM THE GROUND CAN CONTAMINATE THE WATER. SEAL ALL CRACKS AND HOLES IN THE FOUNDATION.

can also pose problems. Before 1986 lead solder was used routinely to join plumbing pipes. The lead from the solder can leach easily into the water supply. Even homes with plumbing installed after 1986 may have lead problems because some faucets still legally contain as much as 8-percent lead.

WATER TESTING & ANALYSIS: At this point the reader is apt to conclude that today's drinking water is no better than that of Colonial times. Actually, there is no cause for alarm. Much of our drinking water is safe — most of the time. However, the only way to be sure that your drinking water is clean, is to have it analyzed by a state-approved testing laboratory. To find one, look in the yellow pages under "Laboratories — testing" or call the EPA's Safe Drinking Water Hotline at 1-800-426-4791 for a list of certified laboratories in your area.

For a thorough analysis the lab should perform a heavy-metal test, an organic pesticide test, a nitrate test, and a bacteria test. Still, this complex battery may not detect all the contaminates. To help the laboratory, you can alert it to other suspected contaminates. Call your local health department to find out if your area has any specific contamination problems, and, if you use well water, find out which pesticides and fertilizers are used nearby.

A water sample analysis usually will cost between $100 and $200 depending upon the tests performed. Even if you've had your water tested before, it's a good idea to have the nitrate and bacterial tests repeated yearly. The water for the sample should be the first water drawn from the tap in the morning. If any contaminates or metals are leaching from the pipes, they will be more concentrated in the morning after the water has been sitting in the pipes all night.

The presence of a pesticide or any contaminate in your drinking water does not mean that the water is unsafe. It is important to consider the level of concentration. Minute quantities of some chemicals may not pose any health hazard. The EPA publishes Health Advisory Summaries that offer guidance on the possible health effects of various substances and the levels that may be tolerated.

The number of chemicals or contaminates in the water also should be considered. Exposure to a few contaminates often can multiply or exacerbate the effects of a single substance. In addition, the age and health status of each individual is another factor to take into consideration. Water that is relatively safe for healthy adults still may pose some risks for children, older people, pregnant women, and people with health problems. ⊕

Water Treatment

If you have had your water tested, and the results show that it is tainted, what are your alternatives? You really have only two; you can switch to bottled water, or you can filter the household water.

For a small family, drinking bottled water can be a viable option, but larger families may find that it can be expensive. Most people are under the impression that all bottled water comes from pristine mountain lakes and streams or natural wells. While most bottled water does indeed come from natural sources, at least 25 percent is simply tap water that has been filtered for taste. Remember that if you switch to bottled water, it should be used for cooking, which may kill harmful bacteria but it will not remove mineral or metal deposits, and for making ice cubes as well as for drinking.

Filtering the household water can be an effective way to treat tainted water. Unfortunately, no one filter will eliminate all contaminates. It's important to read the specifications on each product to be sure that it can solve your particular problem. In extreme cases in may be necessary to hook up two different filters in tandem to clear the water.

Five types of water-treatment units are available: physical filters, activated carbon filters, reverse osmosis (RO) filters, distillation units, and ultraviolet (UV) disinfection units. Physical filters are essentially fine-mesh screens that are designed to remove particles from the water. The screens may be made of ceramic, fiber, metal, or fabric. They are good for filtering out dirt, rust, and other sediments from the water. Some extrafine filters can be effective in removing some bacteria and even asbestos fibers. Physical filters cannot, however, remove all microorganisms and should not be used to treat biologically contaminated water.

TOOL BOX

■ **PLUMBING TOOLS
(SPECIFIC TOOLS WILL VARY
DEPENDING UPON THE PLUMBING
SYSTEM IN EACH HOUSE)**

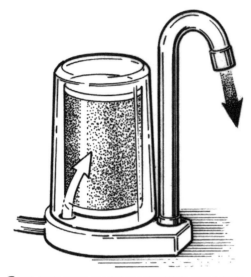

COUNTER-TOP CARBON FILTERS COLLECT IMPURITIES THROUGH ABSORPTION. FAUCET VERSIONS AND IN-LINE MODELS ARE ALSO AVAILABLE.

ACTIVATED CARBON FILTERS: Activated carbon filters are the most popular form of water treatment device because they can be utilized to deal with many water contaminates. They can be used to remove organic compounds, such as benzene, carbon tetrachloride, and pesticides, and to remove residual chlorine. Some specially prepared carbon filters are effective in lead removal. They should not, however, be used exclusively to treat water that contains harmful microorganisms. It's difficult to tell when carbon filters become saturated with the impurities that they are designed to remove, so it's important to replace the filter element periodically to prevent the contaminates from leaching back into the water.

REVERSE-OSMOSIS UNITS: Reverse-osmosis (RO) units filter water by forcing it through a semipermeable membrane. They can remove a substantial amount of inorganic chemicals, such as dissolved salts, nitrates, most metals — including lead — and some organic contaminates. RO units do not remove bacteria or other microorganisms. The membranes on those units decay over time and must be replaced periodically. The major disadvantage to RO units is that they waste a lot of water; for every gallon of filtered water, 3 to 5 gallons are flushed away.

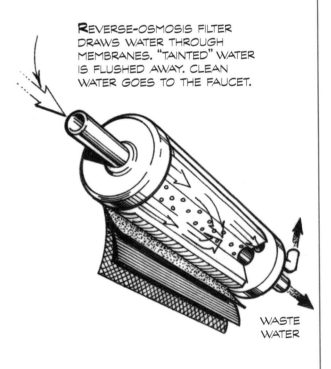

REVERSE-OSMOSIS FILTER DRAWS WATER THROUGH MEMBRANES. "TAINTED" WATER IS FLUSHED AWAY. CLEAN WATER GOES TO THE FAUCET.

WASTE WATER

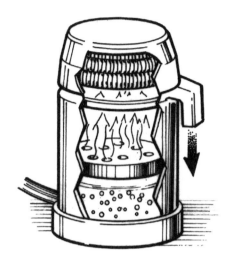

A DISTILLATION UNIT IS BASICALLY A COUNTER-TOP STILL THAT BOILS WATER INTO STEAM, THEN TRAPS THE VAPOR BACK TO A LIQUID IN THE COOLING CHAMBER.

DISTILLATION UNITS: Unlike the filtration units that work by removing the impurities from the water, distillation units heat and vaporize the water and leave the impurities behind. In effect, they remove the water from the contaminates. The water vapor is trapped, cooled, and condensed back to a liquid. That process will remove most of the dissolved solids and metals but not all organic compounds — benzene, chlorine, and some bacteria. There are no filters to replace, but the boiler unit collects sediment, so periodic cleaning is a must. One problem with distillation units is that the heating elements may cause an increase in energy bills.

Another is that the water produced is often flat and tasteless because the mineral content has been removed.

ULTRAVIOLET DISINFECTION UNITS: Ultraviolet (UV) disinfection units operate by exposing the water to ultraviolet light. That will destroy most bacteria and inactivate viruses, but the process does not remove metals, salts, fibers, or minerals. Some manufacturers claim that their UV units also will destroy spores and cysts, but the EPA feels that not enough evidence is available to support those claims. Periodic maintenance consists of cleaning the UV lamp and lenses to make sure that the water is exposed properly to the light.

FILTERING OPTIONS: A number of other factors must be considered besides the type of unit required. Cost is obviously a factor, as is the amount of routine maintenance required to keep the unit functioning properly. Also consider how difficult it will be to install the unit.

Some filtration devices require no installation at all. They are pour-through carafes that resemble a large water pitcher. All you have to do is pour water through the top and allow gravity to carry it through the filter. Unfortunately, they produce only about a gallon of clean water at a time; that can be a

POUR-THROUGH CARAFE RESEMBLES A LARGE WATER PITCHER. IT NEEDS NO INSTALLATION. REPLACE THE FILTER AFTER PROCESSING ABOUT 35 GALLONS OF WATER.

disadvantage for a large family. The filter in the carafe should be replaced after processing 35 gallons of water.

If you can screw an ordinary light bulb into a socket you probably can install a faucet filter. Smaller faucet filters screw directly onto the faucet spout. Larger units, about the size of an electric coffee grinder, rest on the counter but have a hose that runs from the filter to the faucet spout. Water flows from the faucet, through the hose, and into the filter, where it can be drained through a spigot.

More difficult to install are in-line filters, which usually include reverse osmosis units and some activated carbon filters. To install an in-line filter, you'll have to cut into the incoming water line and attach the filter with special fittings. That, however, is not especially difficult if you have some plumbing experience and the right tools. ⊕

HOUSEHOLD HELPS • WORK SMART

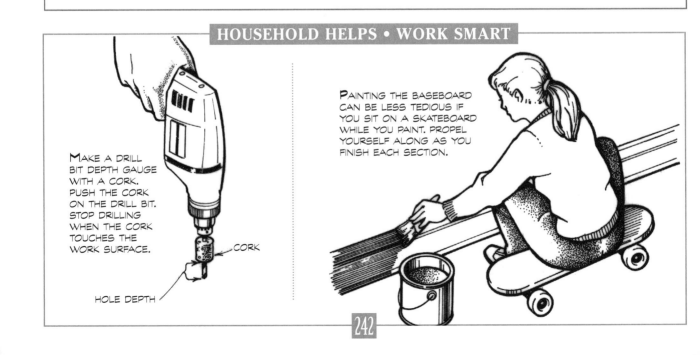

MAKE A DRILL BIT DEPTH GAUGE WITH A CORK. PUSH THE CORK ON THE DRILL BIT. STOP DRILLING WHEN THE CORK TOUCHES THE WORK SURFACE.

CORK

HOLE DEPTH

PAINTING THE BASEBOARD CAN BE LESS TEDIOUS IF YOU SIT ON A SKATEBOARD WHILE YOU PAINT. PROPEL YOURSELF ALONG AS YOU FINISH EACH SECTION.

Wallboard Repairs

Almost all homes built today have their interior walls finished with wallboard, not plaster. Wallboard is essentially a layer of gypsum or plaster sandwiched between two sheets of manila paper. It is also called drywall, gypsum board, or plasterboard. Sheetrock is a trade name for the product. Unlike plaster, which must be mixed and applied wet to a lath base, wallboard is nailed in a dry state directly to the studs. The seams between sheets of wallboard are covered with joint compound and paper tape.

Wallboard is less likely to crack than plaster, but it is easier to dent or puncture, and in some cases the nails or tape can work loose. Fortunately, wallboard damage is easy to repair. The tools required are simple and inexpensive: a 6-inch taping or putty knife, an 8-inch joint knife, a utility knife, a compass or a wallboard saw, a metal straight edge, sandpaper, and a dust mask.

You'll also need some compound for sealing cracks and patching dents. The variety and nomenclature of those compounds may be a little confusing at first.

- **TAPING KNIFE**
- **8-INCH JOINT KNIFE**
- **UTILITY KNIFE**
- **COMPASS- OR WALLBOARD-SAW**
- **METAL STRAIGHT EDGE**
- **SANDPAPER**
- **DUST MASK**
- **HAMMER AND WALLBOARD NAILS**

There's patching plaster, spackling compound, joint taping compound, joint topping compound, and all-purpose joint compound. Patching plaster dries quickly but is difficult to sand. It also requires mixing. It's not a good choice for general repair. Spackling compound is designed to fill cracks and dents in wallboard. It dries faster, with less shrinkage, than joint compound but is harder to sand smooth. Taping compounds are used to fill in joints and apply tape. Topping compounds are used for second and third layers over the tape. All-purpose joint compound combines the advantages of taping and topping compounds. It takes longer to dry than spackling compound but is easier to sand. If you have the time and patience to make the repair, then all-purpose joint compound is best.

In newly constructed houses the studs sometimes can warp or shrink, which causes the nails to loosen and pop out. If possible, pull the nail out and drive a new nail an inch away from the original one. Hammer the new nail slightly below the surface of the wall-board, creating a dimple; but do not tear the paper surface of the panel. Use the 6-inch taping knife to fill the dimple with patching compound. Let it dry and then apply a second coat. When it dries, sand it smooth, wearing the dust mask, and then prime and paint.

TAPING JOINTS: Sometimes the paper tape covering the panel joints can work loose and lift up. When that happens cut the tape at the top and bottom of the section; then peel off the loose tape. Next, apply a generous coat of joint compound over the area. Cut a strip of paper tape to the length of the old piece and embed it in the compound. Using the taping knife, make a pass over the tape. That should smooth the joint and remove excess compound. Allow it to dry, and then apply a second thin coat covering the

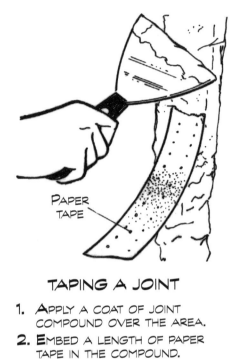

PAPER TAPE

TAPING A JOINT

1. APPLY A COAT OF JOINT COMPOUND OVER THE AREA.
2. EMBED A LENGTH OF PAPER TAPE IN THE COMPOUND.
3. APPLY ADDITIONAL COATS OF COMPOUND OVER THE TAPE.

tape. Let that dry and apply a third coat with the 8-inch joint knife, drawing the compound smooth and feathering the edges so that they blend into the surrounding wall.

Filling a small dent in wallboard is essentially the same as filling a nail dimple. Fill the dent with patching compound; then smooth the area with the taping knife. When the area is dry, apply a second coat by drawing the knife across the patch at right angles to the first pass. That crisscrossed technique will ensure that the final coat is smooth.

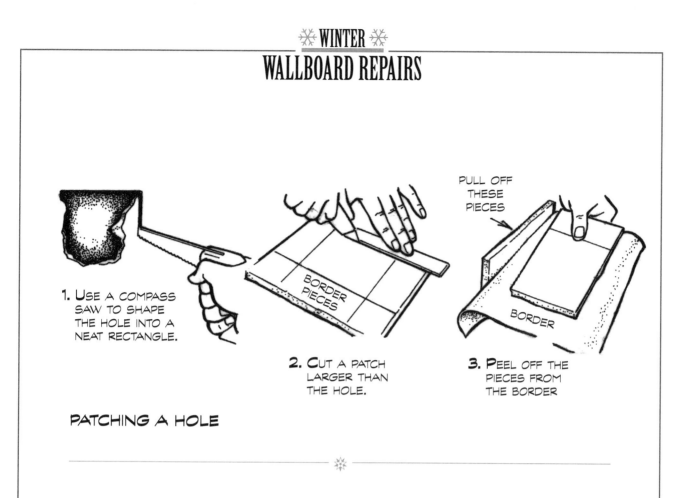

1. USE A COMPASS SAW TO SHAPE THE HOLE INTO A NEAT RECTANGLE.

BORDER PIECES

PULL OFF THESE PIECES

BORDER

2. CUT A PATCH LARGER THAN THE HOLE.

3. PEEL OFF THE PIECES FROM THE BORDER

PATCHING A HOLE

REPAIRING HOLES: You can use the same dent-filling technique to repair small holes, but holes larger than 2 inches require a more substantial patch. First, use a compass or wallboard saw to shape the hole into a neat rectangle. Before making those cuts, check to make sure that there are no pipes or wires behind the wall.

Cut a wallboard patch about 2 inches larger than the hole on each side. If the hole is 2 inches by 2 inches, the patch will be 6 inches by 6 inches. Place the patch face down on a table and with a utility knife cut through the paper backing into the plaster core. Do not cut completely through the plaster or

the paper on the face side. Snap and peel off the plaster pieces from the borders. Leave the center rectangle attached to the face paper. You then will have a solid rectangular core of plaster surrounded by a 2-inch-wide paper border.

Smear a generous amount of joint compound on the paper border and also around the edges of the hole in the wall. Position the patch so that the center block fits into the opening of the damaged area. The border flaps will then overlap the surrounding wall. Go over the patch with the 6-inch taping knife and squeeze the excess joint compound from around the edges. Allow

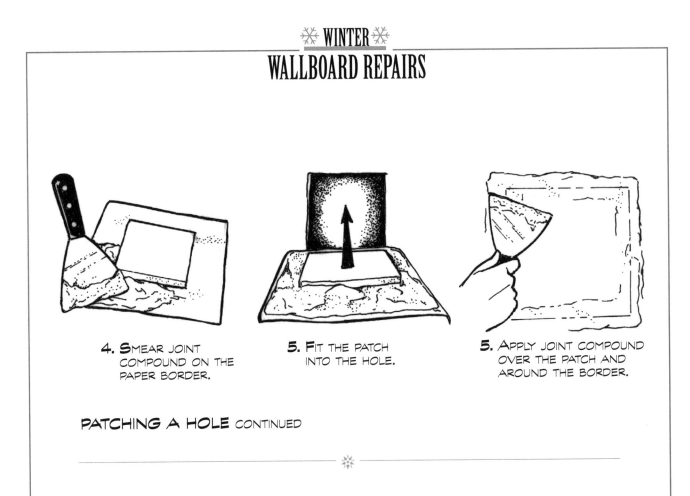

4. SMEAR JOINT COMPOUND ON THE PAPER BORDER.

5. FIT THE PATCH INTO THE HOLE.

5. APPLY JOINT COMPOUND OVER THE PATCH AND AROUND THE BORDER.

PATCHING A HOLE CONTINUED

❄

the patch to dry for 24 hours before applying a second coat of compound. Apply the second coat on top of the patch and around the border flaps. Feather that coat so that it blends in smoothly with the surrounding walls. Apply a final thin coat when the second coat is dry, sand it smooth, and then prime and paint.

For large holes and damaged areas, it's necessary to enlarge the hole by cutting it back to the center of the near-est studs. Since the studs are usually 16 inches apart from center to center, the patch will be 16 inches wide. Trim the damaged area with a utility knife to make a rectangular opening. Cut a patch from the wallboard to fit the opening; then nail it to the studs. Tape the joints; then spread a thin layer of compound over the repaired area, feathering the edges. When the patch is dry, sand the patch smooth; then prime and paint. ⊕

Door Problems

Doors that bind or won't close properly are common problems occurring with hinged doors. Usually, the average do-it-yourselfer attempts to solve those problems by shaving off the edge of the door with a hand plane. Sometimes that can remedy the snag, but frequently the solution lies on the other side, the hinge side, of the door.

Often a hinge can work loose, causing the door to bind against the frame. Before attempting to trim the door, open it and examine the hinges. Test each screw by tightening it with a screwdriver. This may be difficult on older doors that have been painted, because accumulated layers of paint can obscure the screw slots. To clear them, apply a small amount of paint remover with a small brush; allow a few minutes for the remover to loosen the paint; then scrape the slots with a knife or a paper clip.

TIGHTENING LOOSE HINGE SCREWS: Sometimes the screws cannot be tightened because the wood is worn and the screw holes are enlarged. In that case plug the holes with short lengths of

wooden dowel dipped in carpenter's glue. First, remove the screws; then swing the hinge leaves out of the way. You'll probably be able to make the repair without removing the door, but before unscrewing the hinge, swing the door open and prop it up by wedging a magazine under the outside corner. That will support the door when the hinge is released from the frame.

Cut the dowel to length, about 1 to 1 1/2 inches long, before tapping it in place. You also can fill the holes with wooden toothpicks or even a golf tee; with these materials it's best to trim them with a utility knife after they have

TOOL BOX

- HAND PLANE
- SCREWDRIVER
- KNIFE
- DRILL AND BITS
- HAMMER AND 8d NAIL
- CHISEL
- SANDPAPER

HINGE SCREWS WON'T TIGHTEN

APPLY GLUE BEFORE INSERTING THE DOWEL.

PLUG "STRIPPED" SCREW HOLES WITH A DOWEL. APPLY GLUE FIRST. LET IT DRY, THEN DRILL PILOT HOLES.

been glued in place. Let the glue dry, drill pilot holes, and then replace the screws.

REPAIRING BINDING & SAGGING DOORS: If the door binds and the hinges are secure, the problem may be with the way the hinges are mounted. Open and close the door to see exactly where the hang-up occurs. Look for signs of abrasion on the edge of the door and also for uneven gaps between the jamb and the door. If the door binds on the hinge side of the door, the hinges may be too deep. If the door binds on the knob side of the door, the hinges are too shallow. These problems can be corrected by resetting the hinges.

Hinges that are too deep can be corrected by inserting cardboard shims between the hinge leaf and the mortise, the recess cut into the wood to accept the hinge leaf. Shimming can close gaps between the door and the frame; it also can realign a sagging door. If a door sticks at one point like the top corner,

BINDING AND SAGGING

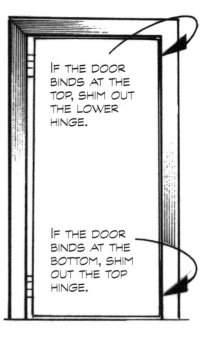

IF THE DOOR BINDS AT THE TOP, SHIM OUT THE LOWER HINGE.

IF THE DOOR BINDS AT THE BOTTOM, SHIM OUT THE TOP HINGE.

LOOSE OR IMPROPERLY MOUNTED HINGES MAY CAUSE A DOOR TO BIND. TIGHTEN LOOSE HINGES AND SHIM OUT DEEP-SET ONES.

the problem may be caused by a lower hinge that is set too deep. The bottom of the door is pulled inward when it closes. That can be corrected by inserting a shim in the lower hinge.

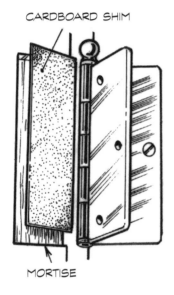

CARDBOARD SHIM

MORTISE

Shimming is not practical when there is not enough clearance between the knob edge of the door and the jamb. Here it's better to set the hinge deeper by cutting into the mortise. You'll have to remove the door to work on the mortises.

Close the door and wedge it to keep it stable as you work. Next remove the hinge pins from the hinges. Most modern hinges have a hole on the underside. You can insert an 8d nail in the hole and tap the pin out with a hammer.

On hinges without a bottom opening, position a screwdriver under the head of the pin and push it upward. Loosen the bottom hinge first, then the top one. Before replacing the hinge pins, clean them with steel wool and coat them with light oil.

The only tool you'll need to deepen an existing mortise is a sharp chisel. Start by holding it perpendicular to the surface and tapping around the perimeter of the mortise. With the chisel still in the vertical position, tap a series of light cuts across the surface of the mortise. Now lower the chisel to a horizontal position and remove the surplus wood by pushing the chisel across the grain. Resist the temptation to use a hammer with the chisel; it may result in removing too much wood.

FIXING DOORS THAT STICK: Sometimes the hinges are fine, yet the door still sticks. Here the door may have expanded or warped, and it should be sanded or planed. It may be possible to do so without removing the door if the distortion is slight. If you have to plane the entire length of the door, then it will be necessary to take it down. When planing the entire door, it's best to work on the hinge side. If you plane the lock side, you'll have to remove and reposition the lock — a difficult job at best. After planing, seal the raw edges with

TRIMMING A DOOR

MARK THE CUTTING LINE THEN SCORE THE VENEER WITH A SHARP UTILITY KNIFE.

CLAMP A PIECE OF WOOD ON THE DOOR AS A SAW GUIDE. AFTER TRIMMING THE DOOR SEAL THE BOTTOM.

paint or varnish. That will keep the exposed wood from absorbing moisture and warping.

There may be those times when you'll have to shorten the door to allow clearance for a newly laid carpet. Measure the thickness of the carpet so you'll know how much to cut from the door. Remove the door but first mark the bottom so that you won't cut from the wrong end. Lay the door on a table or saw horses; then mark the cutting line. If the door has a veneer surface, score the cutting line with a sharp utility knife. That will minimize splintering when you saw through the veneer. If you use a circular saw, clamp a board on the door to act as a cutting guide. After cutting, smooth the edges with fine sandpaper, seal the bottom of the door, then rehang it. ⊕

HOUSEHOLD HELPS • MEASURING

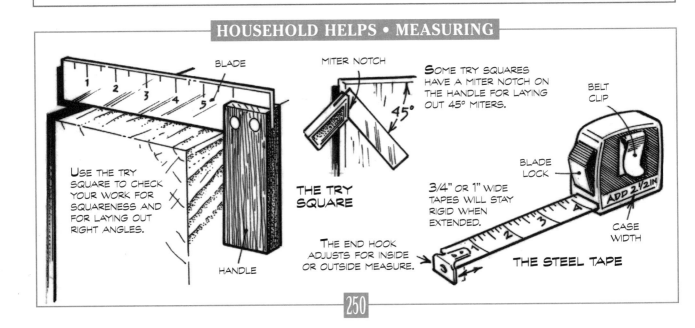

BLADE

USE THE TRY SQUARE TO CHECK YOUR WORK FOR SQUARENESS AND FOR LAYING OUT RIGHT ANGLES.

HANDLE

MITER NOTCH

45°

THE TRY SQUARE

SOME TRY SQUARES HAVE A MITER NOTCH ON THE HANDLE FOR LAYING OUT 45° MITERS.

3/4" OR 1" WIDE TAPES WILL STAY RIGID WHEN EXTENDED.

THE END HOOK ADJUSTS FOR INSIDE OR OUTSIDE MEASURE.

BELT CLIP

BLADE LOCK

ADD 2 1/2 IN

CASE WIDTH

THE STEEL TAPE

Wood Floor Care

A wood floor is a thing of beauty, but wood floors take abuse and require proper care to keep them looking good.

To preserve the finish of a wood floor it is essential to keep it clean. Dirt and dust are natural abrasives that shorten the life of the finish and stain the wood. One way to minimize dirt is to keep doormats at all entrances.

That will help, of course, but it's still important to dust and vacuum often. Do not sweep the floor with a broom, because the bristles scratch the floor's finish. Instead use a dust mop or a vacuum. Buy a dust mop with wool or synthetic fibers: They create a static charge that attracts dust particles. Dust heavily trafficked areas every day and less-used floors once a week.

If dusting and vacuuming do not clean the floor, try a commercial self-cleaning polish. Such preparations dissolve the old wax and remove dirt while applying a new coat of wax. Read the label carefully to make sure that the cleaner is solvent based, not water based. Change the applicator pad or cloth frequently.

If the floor still seems dull, it may be necessary to strip off all the old wax completely, and then apply a new coat. Use a solvent-based wax remover and read all directions carefully.

FREQUENT VACUUMING AND DUSTING WILL REMOVE ABRASIVE DUST PARTICLES THAT CAN MAR THE FINISH.

WOOD FLOOR CARE

Apply the dewaxer with clean cloths or No. 2 grade steel wool. After removing the old wax, apply a new coat. Paste wax is more durable than liquid wax, but it's also harder to apply. First, apply the wax with a damp cloth and then buff to a smooth shine. A power buffer fitted with a lambs' wool pad, which can be rented, makes the job easier and produces a better finish.

Do not overwax a floor; that invites dirt build up and can make the floor slippery. Usually, a light coat of wax applied once or twice a year is all that's necessary to keep the floor looking new.

Wax will give the floor luster and offer some protection, but mishaps will occur that require more care.

Black scuff marks are a common problem. You sometimes can remove them by rubbing them with a rag dipped in solid vegetable shortening, like Crisco. If that fails, rub the marks with fine steel wool and mineral spirits.

Some heel marks can be more damaging to floors. Heel marks are the dents caused by high-heeled shoes. The only way to remove them is to resand the floor. It's best to try and prevent them by treading lightly or removing all high-heeled shoes. If that is not possible, then protect the floor with area rugs.

Spilled liquids present other problems. Once they penetrate into the floor, they can warp the boards and

TOOL BOX

- ■ **DUST MOP**
- ■ **VACUUM**
- ■ **WAX APPLICATOR**
- ■ **STEEL WOOL**
- ■ **VEGETABLE SHORTENING**
- ■ **MINERAL SPIRITS**
- ■ **OXALIC ACID**
- ■ **RUBBER GLOVES**
- ■ **PUTTY KNIFE**
- ■ **WAX TOUCH-UP CRAYON**
- ■ **WOOD FILLER**
- ■ **SANDPAPER**

stain the wood. Wipe up all liquid spills before they penetrate.

Deep stains usually can be removed. A light-colored stain indicates that only the wax is affected, and the wood underneath is untouched. Remove the wax and the stain by lightly rubbing the area with fine steel wool dipped in mineral spirits, and then apply a new coat of wax.

A dark stain indicates that the liquid has penetrated into the wood floor. First, remove the wax with steel wool and mineral spirits; then lay a clean cloth over the area and saturate it with white distilled vinegar. It should bleach the stain. If there is no change after 10 minutes, you will need something stronger than vinegar.

You can make an effective wood bleach solution by dissolving oxalic acid crystals, which are available in hardware stores, in very hot water. Wear rubber gloves and mix the crystals and hot water together in a glass or enamel pan. Soak a cloth in the solution and apply it to the stain. Let it stand for an hour; then wash the area with water and let it dry. Then apply wax.

Chewing gum can be a difficult substance to remove, but applying ice will help. Place an ice cube, wrapped in plastic, on the blob until it hardens and becomes brittle enough to scrape up with a putty knife. You also can apply mineral spirits around the perimeter of the gum with an eyedropper or a spoon. Let the solvent penetrate under the blob. You should then be able to dislodge it with a knife.

FIXING A SCRATCH: Scratches on a wood floor are noticeable because they are a lighter color than the surrounding floor. You can fix them by coloring them with a special felt-tipped furniture marker or a wax touch-up crayon. They are available at most home centers. You can color the scratch with oil-based wood stain. Use a small sable brush to touch up the scratch.

FIXING a SCRATCH

1. FURNITURE TOUCH-UP MARKER

2. APPLY POLYURETHANE

Let the color dry and then brush on polyurethane varnish. Build up the polyurethane with successive coats until the patch matches the surrounding floor.

FILLING A GOUGE: Gouges in the wood require fillers as well as stain. Use commercial colored-wood putty or color your own wood filler by mixing stain with neutral-colored putty. Pack the filler firmly into the gouge, allowing it to bulge slightly above the surface to allow for shrinkage. Once the filler has hardened, sand it, starting with a medium and going to a fine-grit sand paper. Then apply polyurethane.

It is important to treat scratches and gouges when they occur because they can collect dirt and discolor the wood.

Wood floors are affected by humidity. In the winter the air is dry; in the summer it's humid. A wood floor expands or contracts with those fluctuations in humidity and creates warps or cracks. The best way to avoid such problems is by controlling the humidity in your home. Install vapor barriers in crawl spaces to keep moisture from rising into the floor above. In damp areas run a dehumidifier; in very dry areas, such as a room directly over the furnace, run a humidifier. ⊕

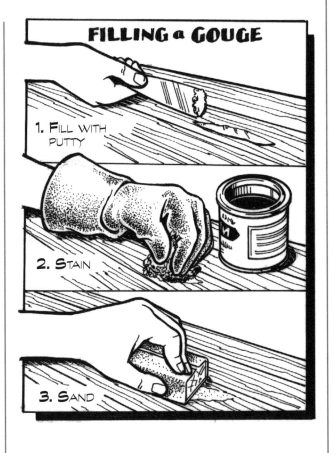

FILLING a GOUGE

1. FILL WITH PUTTY

2. STAIN

3. SAND

HOUSEHOLD HELPS • FIXING FLOOR SQUEAKS

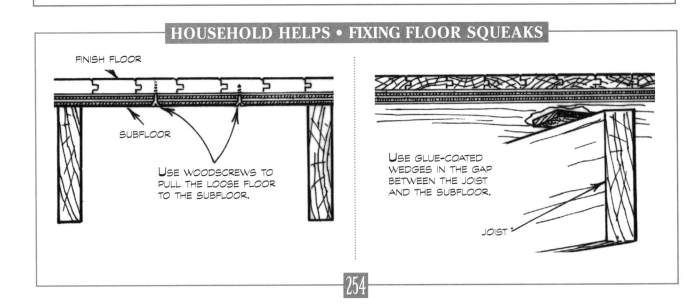

FINISH FLOOR

SUBFLOOR

USE WOODSCREWS TO PULL THE LOOSE FLOOR TO THE SUBFLOOR.

USE GLUE-COATED WEDGES IN THE GAP BETWEEN THE JOIST AND THE SUBFLOOR.

JOIST

Furniture Repair

Time can take its toll on furniture, and even well-made pieces need maintenance and repair occasionally. The average do-it-yourselfer easily can tackle the simple repairs, while more complex tasks, such as replicating intricate parts, veneering, or reupholstering, usually require professional help. Obviously, repairs to valuable heirlooms or prized antiques should be left to seasoned professionals.

IDENTIFYING THE DAMAGE: Before attempting any repairs, make a thorough examination of the piece to determine the extent of damage. Look for structural damage, such as wood rot, worm holes, loose joints, missing, or broken pieces, before attempting to correct surface defects, such as dents, scratches, burn marks, and blistered veneer.

Wood rot is not a common furniture problem, but it is often present in pieces that have been stored in damp basements, garages, or barns. Probe the wood with a large needle or ice pick to find out how much has been damaged. Small areas can be treated by

TOOL BOX

- ICE PICK OR AWL
- WOOD FILLER
- WAX CRAYON
- RUBBER MALLET
- SANDPAPER
- KNIFE
- CLAMPS AND CORD
- GLUE

applying a consolidant and a filler, both of which are available in a single package at home centers and lumber yards. The filler, which replaces the decayed wood, will be invisible if painted but obvious when finished with varnish or shellac. Structural members, chair legs, for example, with parts that have extensive damage should be replaced.

Woodworm is a small parasitic insect that eats its way into furniture. The obvious signs of infestation are small holes on the surface of the wood. In treating woodworm, you must kill the parasite and then evaluate the damage.

You usually can kill the worm by injecting insecticide into the holes with an eyedropper or an oiling can. Next, probe the wood with a needle or an ice pick. If the damage is minor, you can fill the holes with wood filler.

Not everyone agrees that worm holes should be filled. Some individuals feel that the holes give furniture an aura of antiquity. A few dealers may even go so far as to fake the holes with a drill or finishing nail. One even hears tales of people blasting away at chairs or tables with a shotgun loaded with bird shot. But those stories are more imaginative than true: The shot would never penetrate deep enough into wood to disappear.

FIXING LOOSE JOINTS: Once you're sure that the wood is sound, you can proceed to check the piece for loose joints, a common problem with used furniture. Furniture joints release when the wood ages and shrinks or when the glue securing the joint dries out. To repair a loose joint, you'll first have to separate the pieces, and then scrape away the old, brittle glue to expose the bare wood. Do not attempt to secure loose joints with nails, screws, or metal angles or plates. Metal fasteners are not so strong as a good glue joint, and frequently such make-shift repair measures cause more damage.

It's possible that only one joint is loose, but frequently all the joints will need to be reglued. If that's the case, you'll have to disassemble the entire piece. Before attempting this, study the construction of the piece carefully so that you understand exactly how it is put together. Then mark all the joints with a wax crayon or with a felt-tipped marker on pieces of masking tape to guide you in reassembly.

You may be able to pull a few joints apart with muscle power, but for most you'll have to tap them apart gently with a rubber mallet. If you don't have a rubber mallet, you can improvise by wrapping an ordinary hammer with

USE A SOFT RUBBER MALLET TO KNOCK LOOSE JOINTS APART.

STEP 1.
PADDING

SPLAT JOINT A

LABEL ALL JOINTS BEFORE DISASSEMBLY.

STEP 2.

DO-IT-YOURSELF SOFT-FACE HAMMER

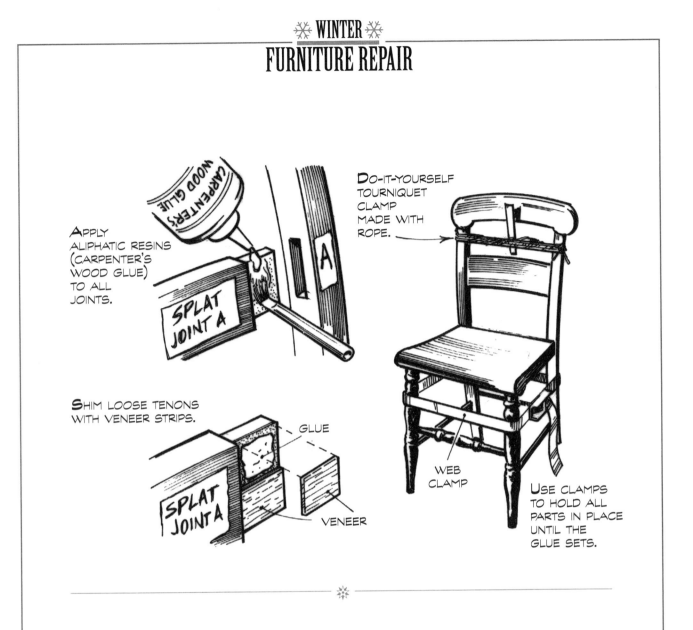

APPLY ALIPHATIC RESINS (CARPENTER'S WOOD GLUE) TO ALL JOINTS.

SPLAT JOINT A

A

DO-IT-YOURSELF TOURNIQUET CLAMP MADE WITH ROPE.

SHIM LOOSE TENONS WITH VENEER STRIPS.

GLUE

SPLAT JOINT A

VENEER

WEB CLAMP

USE CLAMPS TO HOLD ALL PARTS IN PLACE UNTIL THE GLUE SETS.

generous layers of rags. It's important to use a soft mallet or hammer to avoid denting the wood or damaging the surface of the work. If an individual joint is loose but will not yield to the mallet, you sometimes can soften the old glue by injecting a few drops of hot water into the joint seam. As you dismantle the piece, carefully lay out all the parts in systematic order so that they you'll be able to reconstruct it later.

Once the parts are separated, you can turn your attention to cleaning them. Use medium-grit sandpaper or a sharp knife to scrape away any dirt and all traces of the old glue, but be careful not to remove any wood. When the pieces are cleaned, try reassembling the individual joints without glue to see how they fit. Some joints may be loose. You cannot depend upon the glue alone to hold them in place. ⊕

Clothes Dryers

The clothes dryer was introduced in the 1920s. These appliances were simply large cabinets filled with hot air. The wet clothes were hung on racks and left to dry in the hot air, but the large size of the units made them impractical for home use.

The spin dryer was a German invention, but American manufacturers were quick to adopt the technology and sell American-made dryer units. After World War II, manufacturers introduced the combination automatic washer and dryer. The clothes were washed and then dried in the same unit. Unfortunately, the appliances were plagued with so many service problems that consumers refused to buy them. Manufacturers found it easier to make and sell separate washers and dryers. Today most homes have a separate washing machine and dryer.

The clothes dryer is a durable and reliable appliance that has a life expectancy of about 13 years. It is an uncomplicated device that dries clothes by tumbling them in a steady flow of hot air. The wet clothes are tumbled in a drum rotated by an electric motor. The motor also powers a blower fan that pulls room air in through the dryers' intake vent and circulates it past a heating unit, either electric or gas, then into the rotating drum. The hot air absorbs the moisture from the wet clothes and is then forced through a lint filter and vented to the outside air.

TOOL BOX

- DUCT TAPE
- VACUUM AND BRUSHES
- WRENCH
- SCREWDRIVER
- LIGHT-WEIGHT MACHINE OIL
- PUTTY KNIFE
- WOOD BLOCK

In order for the dryer to function satisfactorily, it must be level and properly vented. Usually that is done when the dryer is installed. However, it is not uncommon for machine vibrations to disturb the machine's equilibrium and

upset the level; and if the unit has been moved for any reason, it may need to be releveled. You easily can check the plumb and level of your machine with a carpenter's level. If the dryer is unlevel, you can adjust it by turning either or both of the leveling legs under the front corners of the dryer cabinet.

INSPECTING DRYER VENTS: How can you be sure that your dryer is vented properly? Here are a few guidelines. The vent ducts and elbows should be at least 4 inches in diameter and of rigid tubing.

The dryer should have a minimum of flexible foil or plastic ducting because that material traps lint that can clog the vent. The duct should be as straight and as short as possible. Most manufacturers recommend a maximum length of 16 feet. All joints should be sealed with duct tape or clamps, not sheet-metal screws. The bottom of the exhaust vent should be at least 12 inches from the ground. If your dryer is located in a small utility room, it's a good idea to install a vent in the door to allow fresh air to circulate into the room.

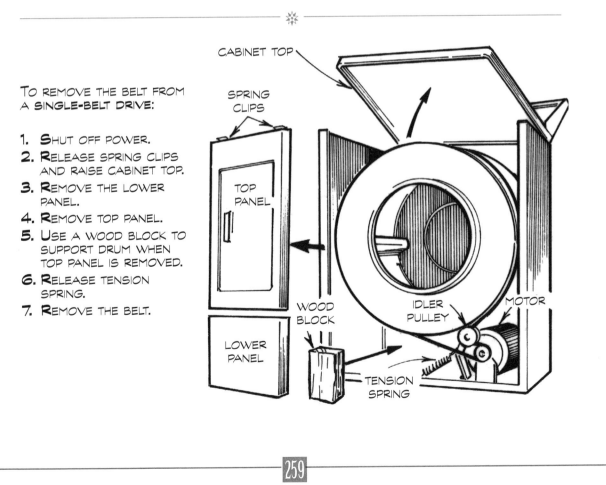

TO REMOVE THE BELT FROM A SINGLE-BELT DRIVE:

1. SHUT OFF POWER.
2. RELEASE SPRING CLIPS AND RAISE CABINET TOP.
3. REMOVE THE LOWER PANEL.
4. REMOVE TOP PANEL.
5. USE A WOOD BLOCK TO SUPPORT DRUM WHEN TOP PANEL IS REMOVED.
6. RELEASE TENSION SPRING.
7. REMOVE THE BELT.

CABINET TOP

SPRING CLIPS

TOP PANEL

LOWER PANEL

WOOD BLOCK

IDLER PULLEY

MOTOR

TENSION SPRING

You should disassemble the ducts yearly to remove any accumulated lint. Lint buildup can stop dryer airflow, reduce the dryer's efficiency, and create a fire hazard. In addition to cleaning the vent ducts, remember to remove and clean the lint filter in the dryer every time you dry a new load.

REPLACING WORN BELTS: The motor in the dryer rotates the drum by a drive belt. A worn belt will slip frequently, causing intermittent drum rotation. If the belt breaks, the drum will not turn at all. In either case the belt should be replaced. Remember to switch off the main power to the dryer before performing any maintenance.

Clothes dryers have two basic belt configurations. The most common set-up uses a single belt that wraps around the drum and the motor pulley. The belt also winds around a spring-mounted idler-wheel assembly. The idler wheel maintains the proper belt tension between the motor and the drum. To change the drive belt, you'll have to remove the front panels from the appliance.

The second configuration uses two drive belts. One belt passes around the

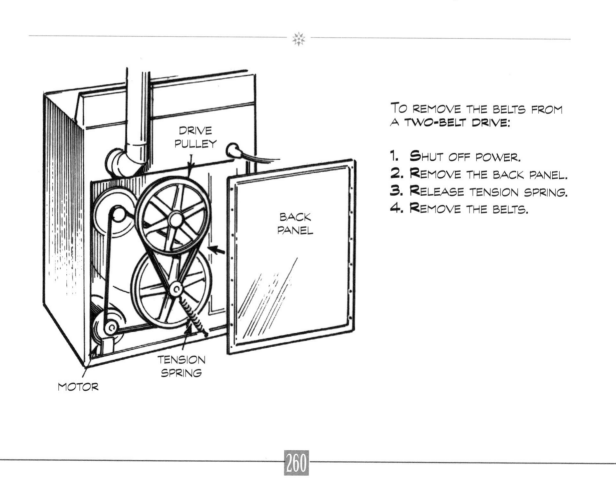

DRIVE PULLEY

BACK PANEL

MOTOR

TENSION SPRING

TO REMOVE THE BELTS FROM A TWO-BELT DRIVE:

1. SHUT OFF POWER.
2. REMOVE THE BACK PANEL.
3. RELEASE TENSION SPRING.
4. REMOVE THE BELTS.

motor pulley, which drives a blower and an idler pulley. The second drive belt connects the idler pulley to the drum. To service the system, you'll have to remove the rear access panel; it's held in place with retaining screws.

If you have a dryer with a two-belt drive system, you should open the rear access panel yearly and lubricate the blower bearings with nondetergent SAE 30 motor oil. Most dryers have a lubrication wick that can be saturated with the oil. That will keep the bearings lubricated for at least a year.

If you're not sure which belt configuration your machine has, you can check by removing the rear access panel. That is easier than removing the front panels. If there are no drive belts in the rear of the dryer, you'll have to remove the front panels to get at the drive system.

Lift the cabinet top up to free the front panel. The top may be secured with retaining screws at the rear corners or near the lint trap. In addition, the top will be secured with spring clips at the front corners. To release the clips, insert a stiff putty knife under the cabinet top and push against the clips.

Remove the lower access panel next. Pry the panel away from the cabinet by inserting a screwdriver behind the panel and twisting the blade slightly. The main panel usually is held in place with retaining screws and two springs located at the bottom corners. Unhook the springs before removing the screws. On many dryers the front panel supports the drum. So have a block of wood handy to prop up the drum when you remove the panel.

You now can remove the old belt and fit an identical replacement around the drum, motor and idler pulleys. Vacuum the inside of the cabinet to remove lint and dust, then replace the front panels and restore the power. ⊕

Refrigerators

Early American homeowners kept their food cold by storing it in cellars. The first cellars were not located under the house but usually were situated a few feet away. Some cellars had a horizontal underground shaft that connected them to the nearby well. The shaft allowed the cool air in the well to circulate in the cellar to provide additional chilling. During the winter homeowners who lived near a lake or a pond collected ice from the frozen water and stored it in their cellars for the spring and summer months.

The 19th century saw the introduction of the icebox. Essentially, it was an insulated wooden cabinet with a metal lining. The insulation was either sawdust, ground cork, or charcoal. A block of ice kept the food from spoiling.

By the end of the 19th century many urban homes had electricity and wealthy families could afford to install refrigeration units, but they were large and noisy. The cooling coils were housed in the icebox in the kitchen, but the compressor, condenser coils and motor had to be situated in a separate room.

Manufacturers eventually were able to make smaller motors, compressors, and coils that could fit in self-contained units. In 1926 General Electric introduced its now-famous Monitor Top refrigerator, which had the motor, compressor, and condenser housed in a drum-like container on top of the cabinet.

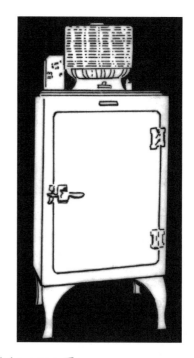

THE MONITOR TOP REFRIGERATOR HAD THE MOTOR, COILS AND COMPRESSOR IN A DRUM-LIKE CONTAINER ON TOP.

Those early refrigerators stood on high legs and were designed to look like individual pieces of furniture. By the 1930s the concept of appliance design changed, and the "built-in" look became the standard. Working components were housed within the cabinet, legs were eliminated, handles and hinges became streamlined and less cabinet-like; the refrigerator became an integral part of the kitchen decor.

Even though today's refrigerators have features, such as ice-makers, cycle defrost systems, and frost-free systems, that were unavailable on the early models, the basic refrigerating principle is essentially the same. Liquid refrigerant enters a low-pressure area, called the evaporator, and expands into a gas. The expanding gas absorbs heat from the adjacent area, cooling it. The heat-laden gas then is compressed and pumped into condenser coils, where it condenses into a liquid. As the liquid compresses it releases the captured heat to the surrounding air. Early refrigerators used toxic sulfur dioxide as a refrigerant, but modern units use safer refrigerants.

Most refrigerators are well designed and durable. Even so, with a little routine maintenance your refrigerator will run longer with improved efficiency and less cost. Before working on your refrigerator, it's a good idea to pull the

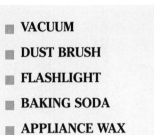

- **VACUUM**
- **DUST BRUSH**
- **FLASHLIGHT**
- **BAKING SODA**
- **APPLIANCE WAX**

plug. With the electricity off, you won't have to worry about contacting any live circuits or getting caught in the spinning blades of the compressor fan. To get at the plug, you probably will have to move the refrigerator away from the wall. Before doing that, take anything off the top of the appliance and remove anything inside that might tip over and spill.

CLEANING THE COILS: Once the refrigerator is unplugged, check to see if you have a natural- or forced-draft condenser. If you have a natural-draft, also called static-draft, the condenser coils will be mounted on the back of the unit. Dust and dirt collect on the coils and prevent the refrigerant from discharging collected heat into the surrounding air. Clean the coils carefully with a dust brush and vacuum. Be careful not to bend or nick the coils.

If you have a forced-draft model the condenser coils are housed under the

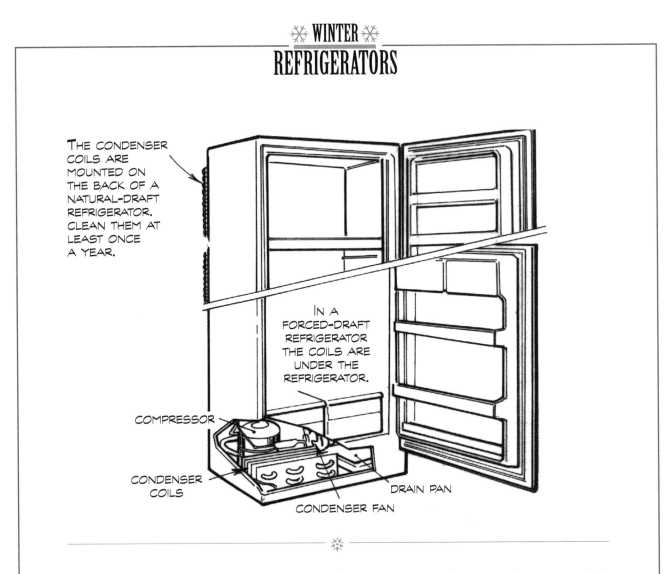

THE CONDENSER COILS ARE MOUNTED ON THE BACK OF A NATURAL-DRAFT REFRIGERATOR. CLEAN THEM AT LEAST ONCE A YEAR.

IN A FORCED-DRAFT REFRIGERATOR THE COILS ARE UNDER THE REFRIGERATOR.

COMPRESSOR

CONDENSER COILS

CONDENSER FAN

DRAIN PAN

refrigerator. A small fan in the same compartment blows air across the coils to dissipate the heat from the condensed coolant. Removing the front grill will give you access to the coils. Use a flashlight and a vacuum cleaner with a narrow nozzle to remove dust and grime. Again be careful not to damage the coils.

Clean the back coils on natural-draft refrigerators at least once a year. Forced-draft units push more air around, so they should be cleaned every month or so. Conditions vary in different homes; if

you own a pet, for example, it is possible that airborne hair might necessitate more frequent cleaning.

Next, remove the rear cover from the refrigerator. That will expose the compressor, sealed in a metal canister, and the compressor fan. Vacuum around them, but be careful not to damage or bend the fan blades. Warped fan blades will wobble and wear out the fan bearings. After cleaning this area, replace the back cover.

If you have a frost-free refrigerator, you probably have an evaporation pan

under the unit. The pan should be cleaned every three to six months. Be careful to replace it properly in its cradle, because it does more than collect water. It also acts as a baffle to control air circulation around the coils.

CHILLER TRAY BAFFLE

THE NORMAL POSITION FOR THE CHILLER TRAY BAFFLE IS OUT.

FOR COLDER FRESH FOOD COMPARTMENT TEMPERATURE DURING HOT WEATHER, PLACE THE CHILLER BAFFLE IN THE IN POSITION.

CHILLER TRAY BAFFLES: Now look inside the refrigerator compartment. Your unit may have a drip tray under the freezer compartment. Most people assume that the tray is designed just to catch water when defrosting the freezer. That is one purpose, but it also helps to control air currents inside the refrigerator. Many trays have a baffle or flap that must be positioned correctly for maximum efficiency. The normal position for the baffle should be out, but during the hot summer months it should be turned in.

GENERAL CLEANING: The inside of the refrigerator should be cleaned at least once a year. Use warm water and a baking soda solution, about one tablespoon of baking soda to a quart of water. Use that solution to clean the door gaskets also. Do not use cleansing powders or abrasive cleaners.

Clean the outside of the refrigerator with mild liquid detergent. Do not wipe the surface with a soiled dishwashing cloth or towel. They may leave a residue that can erode the finish. You also should apply a coat of kitchen/appliance wax, available at appliance parts dealers, at least twice a year. ⊕

Condensation

During the fall homeowners often awake to find their windows fogged over. In the winter the windows may be covered with a thin layer of frost. Both the fog and the frost are examples of condensation. It occurs when the moisture, in the form of invisible vapor, in the warm interior air meets with the cold surface of the window pane.

Moderate condensation is not a cause for concern as long as it evaporates when the windows warm up, but in extreme cases it may not dry up. Then it will collect and run down to soak the window sash and sill. Heavy persistent condensation will flow past the sill to saturate the wall. Damp walls will encourage mold and mildew growth. Eventually, the moisture will penetrate through the walls and rot the framing.

Unfortunately, condensation is not always so obvious as foggy or frosted windows. Sometimes the warm moist air penetrates through the wallboard into the wall cavities. Here it meets with cold air and condenses as water droplets on the wall insulation. That moisture eventually may dry out during the spring and summer months, or it may remain and eventually deteriorate the insulation quality.

- **INCENSE STICK**
- **MOISTURE SEALER AND BRUSH**

Condensation is rarely a problem in the spring or the summer because the outside air never gets cold enough to cool and condense the vapor in the warm indoor air. In the fall all homes will have some condensation because a certain amount of residual moisture is left in the air from the hot, humid days of summer. In time, with adequate ventilation, that will dissipate, and the condensation should cease. In winter months condensation may become an annoying problem because there is not enough ventilation to remove the moist air. The problem may be exacerbated when a variety of indoor sources add to the humidity in the air.

One way to prevent condensation is by lowering the humidity. This task is not so easy as it sounds because ordinary activities, such as cooking and showering, add significant amounts of moisture to the air. Opening a window for five minutes after cooking or showering may be enough to flush out the moist air. A better solution, however, would be to install exhaust fans over the stove and in the bathroom. Fans would pull the moisture out without introducing cold air into the room.

Exhaust fans are effective in pulling out the damp air, but they could cause backdrafting in some home environments. The air is that pulled out by exhaust fans must be replaced. Backdrafting occurs when the replacement air is sucked in through the chimney or furnace flue. It is not a significant problem in older homes because replacement air usually comes through gaps and cracks around the windows and doors. Newer homes are constructed tightly so they have far less gaps.

You can test for backdrafting by holding a smoking incense stick below the chimney flue. If the smoke from the stick is drawn into the house, you have

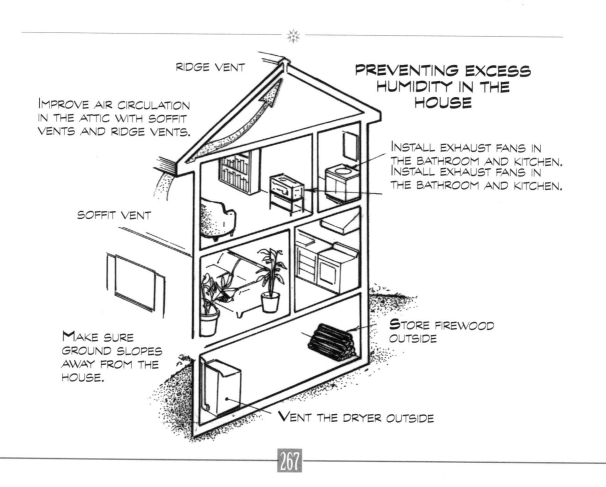

RIDGE VENT

IMPROVE AIR CIRCULATION IN THE ATTIC WITH SOFFIT VENTS AND RIDGE VENTS.

SOFFIT VENT

MAKE SURE GROUND SLOPES AWAY FROM THE HOUSE.

PREVENTING EXCESS HUMIDITY IN THE HOUSE

INSTALL EXHAUST FANS IN THE BATHROOM AND KITCHEN. INSTALL EXHAUST FANS IN THE BATHROOM AND KITCHEN.

STORE FIREWOOD OUTSIDE

VENT THE DRYER OUTSIDE

CONDENSATION AT THE WINDOWS

INSIDE
WINDOW

IF WARM INTERIOR AIR
LEAKS PAST THE INSIDE
WINDOW, CONDENSATION
WILL FORM ON THE STORM
WINDOW. (LEFT)

STORM
WINDOW

(RIGHT) IF COLD AIR
LEAKS PAST THE STORM
WINDOW CONDENSATION
WILL FORM ON THE
INSIDE WINDOW.

a backdrafting problem. Opening a window will alleviate it, but that is only a short-term solution. The best way to solve the problem is to consult with a heating professional about installing ductwork to provide fresh air directly to the furnace.

Another potential source of indoor moisture is the clothes dryer. Make sure it is properly vented to the outside; otherwise, all the moisture from the freshly washed clothes will be discharged into the inside environment.

Houseplants also can throw off a lot of moisture. If possible, limit the number of plants in your home or place most of the plants in a separate room and run a dehumidifier periodically. Operating a dehumidifier may seem like the best way to remove moisture from the air, but beware; it can drive electric bills up.

Ground moisture seeping up from the soil in a crawlspace or through a concrete floor also can add considerable amounts of moisture to the air. In the crawlspace lay down sheets of 6 mil polyethylene over the ground. Seal concrete floors and walls with a moisture sealer. In addition, check the ground slope around your home. It should slope away from the house so that all rainwater drains away.

Other sources of indoor moisture may surprise you. Storing large amounts of green firewood in the basement may increase the relative humidity by as much as 15 percent. The obvious solution is to store most of the wood outdoors or in the garage. A large aquarium can add to the humidity as the water in the tank evaporates. Placing a cover across the top of the tank will contain most of that moisture.

Remember that reducing indoor humidity is important if condensation is a problem. If not, then making the air too dry — less than 40-percent humidity — can create respiratory and allergy problems. ⊕

Heat-Saving Tips

Energy experts estimate that 75 percent of the heat in an uninsulated home is lost to the outside environment. Adding insulation to the walls, floors, and roof can reduce that figure to 20 percent. That's certainly an improvement, but that still means that 20 percent of your heat escapes to the cold air outside. You can do several things to save some of that heat.

Start by eliminating drafts. No room can be entirely warm as long as little currents and eddies of cold air are swirling about. They occur wherever gaps or cracks allow cold air to mix with the warm. The obvious solution is to plug up the gaps. First, however, you have to find them. You can do that by conducting a "candle search." Wait for a windy day; then walk around the house with a lighted candle. Watch the flame for flickering. When the flame flickers, it probably means that a draft is coming in from somewhere. Move the candle about to locate the source. Check around windows and doors. Investigate around moldings and also probe any hole that has been cut into a wall, floor or ceiling. That includes holes for elec-

- ■ **CANDLE**
- ■ **CAULK AND CAULKING GUN**
- ■ **WEATHERSTRIPPING**
- ■ **INTERIOR STORM WINDOW KIT**

trical fixtures, switches and sockets and holes cut to accommodate plumbing or heating fixtures.

CAULKING & WEATHERSTRIPPING: To fill cracks, use latex caulk, which can be painted. Stuff insulation into holes around plumbing fixtures or else use polyurethane foam. Polyurethane foam

FOAM PADS PLACED IN OUTLETS STOP DRAFTS.

is sticky stuff, so be sure to wear gloves when you are working with it. Stop drafts that emanate from wall switches and outlets by placing foam pads behind the face plates. The pads are available at hardware stores and home centers.

It's easy to caulk gaps in a fixed surface, but what about the cracks around doors and windows? You can't really plug up a door, but you can attach weatherstripping around the edges. Six types of weatherstripping are available. Felt is the cheapest but also the least durable. Adhesive-backed foam strips are good for sealing gaps that vary in width. Wood strips that are edged with felt, foam, or vinyl tubing are more durable than either felt or foam, but the wood must be painted. Molded vinyl tubing is a good choice; the tubing with a metal backing is usually easier to install. Spring metal is extremely durable, but it cannot seal gaps that vary in width. V or J strips are interlocking strips of metal for doors only; do-it-yourselfers with minimal skills find them difficult to install.

Even the best weatherstripping cannot stop cold air from entering the house when someone opens the door. A storm door can be helpful in keeping the heat inside, but it is of little use when the door has to be opened. The ideal solution is to install an air lock. An

WEATHERSTRIPPING

FELT

ADHESIVE-BACKED FOAM

WOOD & FOAM

VINYL TUBING

SPRING METAL

"V" STRIPS

air lock is essentially a small chamber that a person enters, closing the storm door behind him, before opening the door to the house. While that may seem like a space-age invention, it is, in fact, quite old. Rural houses in the last century often had "mud rooms." Their purpose was ostensibly to allow a person to remove muddy boots before entering the house, but the mud room also served as an efficient air lock. Urban townhouses often had foyers that functioned in the same manner. Curiously, modern houses have eliminated that feature.

If you cannot build an airlock, you can blunt the power of the cold wind by planting trees or shrubs near the door or by erecting a decorative wall.

WINDOW INSULATION: No one would want to live in a home without windows. They allow sunlight and solar radiation to enter. Unfortunately, they also allow 10 percent of the heat to escape. That's because glass is a poor insulator. Storm windows help to conserve heat because they trap a pocket of air, which is a good insulator, between the two windows. You can make your own indoor storm window with a kit sold in most hardware stores and home centers. The kit consists of double stick tape, which is applied around the window molding. A sheet of

clear vinyl is positioned over the tape. You can then shrink away wrinkles by blowing hot air from a hair dryer across the surface of the film.

Even with storm windows a great deal of heat passes through the glass when the sun goes down at night. Early American homeowners usually conserved heat by closing the shutters at night. Contemporary homeowners try to conserve heat by hanging heavy drapes across the windows. Drapes, however, have limited value if they are hung conventionally. That's because

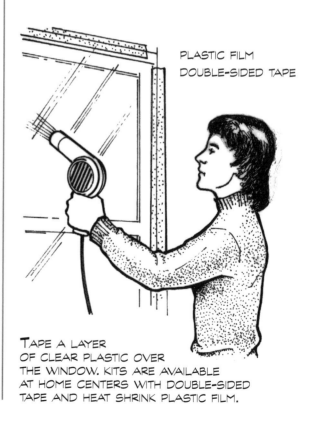

PLASTIC FILM
DOUBLE-SIDED TAPE

TAPE A LAYER
OF CLEAR PLASTIC OVER
THE WINDOW. KITS ARE AVAILABLE
AT HOME CENTERS WITH DOUBLE-SIDED
TAPE AND HEAT SHRINK PLASTIC FILM.

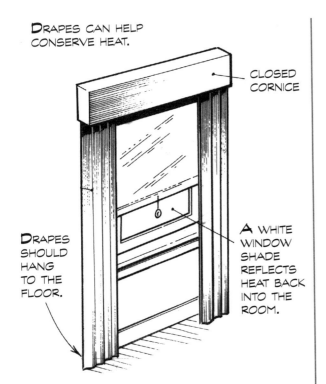

DRAPES CAN HELP CONSERVE HEAT.

CLOSED CORNICE

DRAPES SHOULD HANG TO THE FLOOR.

A WHITE WINDOW SHADE REFLECTS HEAT BACK INTO THE ROOM.

there is a column of air between the drape and the window. Once that air becomes cooled at the window, it drops to floor level pulling more warm air from the room. To be effective, drapes should come down to the floor and have a closed cornice or valance at the top. Those additions will trap the air and prevent it from circulating.

Window shades also can help to conserve heat. The shade should be white to reflect heat back into the room, and it should be mounted inside the window frame close to the glass. Hang drapes and window shades on all northern windows, where there is less sunlight, and western windows, where the cold wind is more intense.

When making physical improvements to conserve heat, don't ignore the psychological factors. While the human brain cannot heat a room, it can help to make a person feel warm. Research studies at Kansas State University show that subjects in carpeted rooms decorated with bright colors felt warm and comfortable at lower temperatures than subjects in sparsely furnished, light-colored rooms. The lesson is obvious: Use bright colors in your decorating scheme, put carpets on the floor, and furnish the room with chairs and sofas upholstered in textured fabrics. ⊕

Cold Rooms

Some homeowners are disturbed to find that even though they have a new furnace with a state-of-the-art heating system, one room in the house is always cold. Turning up the thermostat will warm the room, but it may also make the rest of the house too hot, and it can create higher heating bills.

What then is the best way to bring heat into that cold room? Unfortunately, that question has no easy answer because the chill may come from a number of causes. First, it's important to examine the heating system to make sure that heat indeed is being delivered to the room. In extreme cases it may be necessary to consult a heating specialist who can evaluate your home heating system to determine if it is working efficiently.

Before doing that, however, it's a good idea to inspect the system yourself to see if it has any obvious malfunctions. With a few simple adjustments you may be able to correct the problem and save yourself a consultation fee.

If you have a forced-air system, look first at the air filter. A dirty air filter can

- ■ **AIR FILTER**
- ■ **FLASHLIGHT**
- ■ **LEVEL**
- ■ **SCREWDRIVER OR RADIATOR KEY**

restrict the flow of hot air from the furnace to the delivery ducts. As obvious as that sounds, many homeowners neglect to change air filters at the beginning of the season. As a result, the system cannot deliver heat efficiently.

With a new filter in place, inspect the register in the cold room. The register is the heat outlet. It is usually in the floor near a wall. Feel to make sure that heat is coming out. If not, it could be blocked. Unscrew the register cover and look down with a flashlight. Remove any obstructions that may be blocking the opening.

If no blockage exists, examine the ducts that feed air into the room; they usually have dampers that control the flow of air through the duct. Make cer-

BLEED THE RADIATORS. POSITION A PAN OR CUP UNDER THE BLEED VALVE. OPEN THE VALVE WITH A SCREWDRIVER (WITH SOME VALVES A RADIATOR KEY MAY BE NECESSARY). ALLOW THE AIR TO ESCAPE. CLOSE THE VALVE WHEN WATER STARTS TO FLOW.

tain that they are in the open position. If those measures do not restore the proper airflow, the problem could be more serious, like faulty duct design. It's best to consult with a heating specialist to see if that is the case.

If hot air is coming out of the register, it's likely that it is not flowing toward the center of the room. That can happen if a piece of furniture is positioned over the register. The obvious solution is to move the furniture around. Another way to redirect the air flowing from a register is by installing

plastic deflectors. Those deflectors are available in a variety of shapes that allow you to control the airflow patterns in a room.

If you have a steam-heating system with radiators, inspect the room radiators to see if they are hot. Cold radiators may not be leveled properly. A radiator that is perfectly level or pitched away from the intake valve will trap water so that steam cannot enter. Raise one end with small wood blocks so that the radiator slopes toward the valve.

Another cause of cold radiators is a blocked air vent. The air vent is the small, chrome-plated cylinder mounted on one end of the radiator. It allows air to escape from the radiator so that steam can enter. If the vent is blocked, the radiator never will heat up. Sometimes you can open a blocked vent port with a thin wire, but it's best to install a new vent.

It's possible to buy variable adjustment vents that allow you to regulate the amount of air released and consequently the amount of steam entering the radiator. If the radiator doesn't heat up, simply turn the adjustment control on top of the vent to allow more air to escape.

Modern hot-water radiators are less problematic because they are part of a closed system. Still air can collect in the radiators, and that will keep the hot water out. Those units have a purge valve that allow you to release the tapped air. Purging the air from a hot-water radiator is not difficult. Hold a metal container under the valve port and open the vent with a screwdriver. Keep the vent open until all the air is released, and water begins to flow; then close the vent.

Even the most efficient heating system will fail to keep a room warm if cold air is allowed to enter through the gaps and cracks in an old window. The best way to remedy that problem is by replacing the old windows with new, energy-efficient ones. That costs money, and such an installation may not be possible in the middle of the winter. As a temporary seasonal fix, you can install plastic indoor "storm" windows. They are available as kits at most

MAKE YOUR OWN INDOOR STORM WINDOW WITH A KIT.

VINYL SHEET

A HAIR DRYER SHRINKS THE VINYL SHEET.

DOUBLE-STICK TAPE

home centers. Tape the plastic sheet over the window and heat it with a hair dryer to make it taut. ⊕

Frozen Pipes

Winter is upon us. The cold weather brings subfreezing temperatures that can cause water in plumbing to freeze and burst the pipes. That is most likely to happen to those pipes that run in unheated portions of the house, such as attics, crawlspaces, or uninsulated outside walls.

The surest way to prevent pipes from freezing up is to drain them. That should be done in vacation homes or in your home should a major winter power failure occur. You should close and drain those parts of your plumbing system, such as pipes supplying water to outside faucets, that are vulnerable to the cold.

Plumbing inside the house should have adequate insulation to shield it from freezing winds. Pipes running in outside walls should have insulation between

TOOL BOX

- **INSULATION**
- **FLEXIBLE HEATING CABLE**
- **HANDSAW**
- **HEAT GUN OR HEAT LAMPS**

them and the outside sheathing, and the walls should be caulked to keep outside air away from the plumbing.

PREVENTING FROZEN PIPES: Bear in mind that insulation does not heat the pipes; it only conserves the heat already in them. In some cases that may not be enough. You may have to supply additional heat to ward off the cold. The best way to do that is to wrap the pipes in flexible heating cable, available at home centers and hardware stores. Wrap the pipe with the cable — making one turn every foot — and then cover it with foam-sleeve insulation. The insulation has a slit up one side that makes it easy to slip over the pipe. Once the insulation is in place, cover the slit with aluminum duct tape.

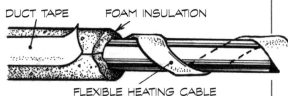

DUCT TAPE   FOAM INSULATION

FLEXIBLE HEATING CABLE

WRAP PIPES WITH FLEXIBLE HEATING CABLE AND FOAM INSULATION TO KEEP THEM FROM FREEZING.

Install a louvered vent at the base of a wall to allow warm air to circulate around the pipes.

WARM AIR

Another way to keep pipes from freezing is to allow warm air from a heated room to circulate around them. To do that, cut a small, rectangular opening at the base of the wall and install a louvered vent, which is available at home centers or at heating supply stores. On very cold days you can open the vent to allow the warm air into the wall cavity. Keep the vent closed on other days to minimize heat loss from the room.

It's obvious that some of those measures may necessitate opening a wall to expose the pipes. This takes time and effort, and it's possible that you can't get around to doing it before the cold weather sets in. You still can prevent a freeze-up by allowing the water to run in a slow trickle or fast drip. Moving water doesn't freeze, and leaving a faucet open slightly is enough to keep ice from forming.

In spite of your efforts, it is possible that a pipe still may freeze, and you'll have to thaw it out. That should be done carefully: Too much heat will turn the ice into steam that can expand and burst the pipes.

If the pipes are enclosed within a wall, you'll have to open the wall. Often opening the wall allows the warm air from the room to contact the pipes, and that may be enough to thaw them. If not, you'll need to apply heat.

Start from the valve end of the pipe. Open the valve. If it is frozen, apply heat to defrost it. You can use a heat gun, a hair dryer, or an infrared lamp to apply heat. Keep the heat unit moving to avoid overheating any one area. Once the valve is fully open, work your way from the valve down the pipe. Occasionally touch the pipe with your bare hand. The pipe never should get hotter than your hand can stand.

FROZEN PIPES

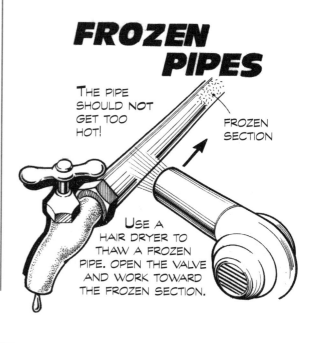

The pipe should not get too hot!

FROZEN SECTION

Use a hair dryer to thaw a frozen pipe. Open the valve and work toward the frozen section.

If you don't have a heat gun you can thaw frozen pipes by wrapping them with a thick layer or rags, and then pouring boiling water on the wrapping. The pipes also can be thawed by wrapping them with heating cable. That takes a little longer, but the cable melts the ice uniformly and lessens the danger of steam buildup.

Those measures are effective while you're in your home, but people who travel frequently have to leave their homes to the mercy of the elements. What can the traveling homeowner do to prevent damage should the heat suddenly go off? Fortunately, modern technology has a few solutions.

One is a device called Scul-tel. It is a computer-linked system that monitors room temperatures and furnace operation. The system has a battery-powered transmitter, about the size of a smoke detector, and three small sensors. The sensors are placed in strategic areas about the house. Should the temperature drop, they signal the transmitter, which transmits a message over the phone line to your local fuel distributor. The distributor then dispatches a troubleshooting crew to your home. This system is sold to fuel distributors who, in turn, lease it to their customers.

BEEP! HAPPY NEW YEAR! THE HEAT IS OFF AT HOME. BEEP!

WHILE YOU ARE AWAY YOU CAN CHECK YOUR HOME FOR POWER FAILURE WITH A REMOTE SENSOR.

Customers pay about $175 for the system and a leasing fee of about $75. Scul-tel is available only to homeowners with oil heat and only through distributors with a Scul-tel computer monitoring system.

Another device that monitors room temperatures is called Winter Watchman. It works like an automatic light timer. Plug a lamp into Winter Watchman and place the lamp in a window. Should the room temperature drop to unacceptable levels the device will light the lamp. That will alert a trusted neighbor to call your local heating company. Winter Watchman is available at most home centers and sells for about $25.

Even if you're away, you can monitor the temperature of your home with Sensaphone. This device plugs into a phone jack and an electrical outlet. Should the temperature drop below a preset level, Sensaphone automatically will dial four programmed phone numbers until someone answers. You can check the condition of your home by dialing your home phone. If there's a temperature problem, Sensaphone will transmit a busy signal. The unit sells for about $375 and is available from The Phonetics Co. in Aston, Pa ⊕

Winter Power Failure

Most people assume that the worst power failures occur in the late summer when violent thunderstorms and hurricanes assault the power lines with savage winds and harsh rainstorms. Power companies, however, point out that power failures are more likely during the cold winter months when snowstorms knock out the power lines with heavy ice deposits.

Long winter power outages can be dangerous because, in additional to the lights, the home heating system also is disabled. If the bone-chilling weather continues, the temperatures inside the house may drop below freezing.

Many homeowners simply pack up a few belongings and move to a motel or a friend's house that still has power. Unfortunately when they return home after the power has been restored, they find extensive water damage from burst pipes frozen during the power outage.

In the event of a power outage, you can take a number of steps to protect yourself and property. First, call the power company to get their assessment of the damage and estimated time for

TOOL BOX

- **PLASTIC SHEETING AND TAPE**
- **PLUMBERS ANTI-FREEZE**
- **FLASHLIGHTS AND CANDLES**

restoration of power. A lengthy downtime will require some action on your part.

Next, call your municipal water supply facility to find out how long it can continue to supply water after the power dies. The majority of water suppliers use electric power to pump water. In the event of a power failure most companies have standby diesel generators to power the pumps. Other water suppliers depend on storage tanks as a backup system. Their ability to supply water will depend upon the size of their storage facilities and the demands of the community.

If you suspect that the faucets will run dry before power is restored, start filling household containers. You also may want to purchase bottled water at the local supermarket. If you cannot lay

WINTER POWER FAILURE

in a supply of water and expect an extended power outage, it's probably best to leave your house.

A power failure will shut down the furnace, and the house will gradually get colder. You can do a number of things to conserve heat. First, restrict entry and egress to a single door; choose one that has a storm door and an airlock if possible. Keep drafts from penetrating around the other doors by sealing up the cracks around the edges with tape; place a rolled-up towel against the bottom crack.

Make sure that all the windows, including the storm windows, are tightly closed. If possible, tape a layer of clear plastic over the inside of the window. Raise the shade and open the drapes to allow the sunlight to enter. At dusk close the drapes and shades to keep the heat in.

Of course, you also will want to try and generate heat. A fireplace can certainly help, but beware: The flue draft can suck the heated air from the entire house. So before starting a fire, close off the room with the fireplace from the rest of the house. Build the fire near the back wall of the fireplace and avoid making a large, roaring fire. Large fires pull heated air up the flue.

If you have a gas oven, you may be tempted to use it as a heat source. It can be used, but do not leave the door open with the burners on. That could warp the heating elements, causing them to malfunction and emit carbon monoxide gas. To use the oven for heating, start the oven, and then turn the dial to 350 degrees. Leave the door closed and allow the oven to heat the kitchen slowly.

If you still have running water, open all the faucets to allow a fast drip. That will keep the water in the pipes moving and prevent a freeze-up. Every four hours open the faucets up to flush the water in the drain traps, which will keep them from freezing. Should the water supply shut down, close the main supply valve and drain the water lines. Pour antifreeze in the traps, including the toilet trap, also. Ordinary automo-

WHEN THE TEMPERATURE DROPS BELOW 32° POUR ANTI-FREEZE INTO THE TOILET TRAPS AND SINK TRAPS. BE SURE TO DRAIN THE TOILET TANK.

TOILET CROSS-SECTION

WINTER POWER FAILURE

tive antifreeze is poisonous, so be careful to seal all drains and lock the toilet lid so pets do not try to drink. You also can go to a plumbing supply store and buy a special nontoxic antifreeze for this purpose. Your automatic dishwasher has drain lines with standing water. To keep those lines from freezing up, pour some antifreeze directly into the bottom of the washer.

DRAIN THE RADIATORS AND FURNACE WHEN THE TEMPERATURE DROPS BELOW 32°. OPEN THE VALVES AND THE BOILER DRAIN.

If you have a hot-water heating system and anticipate the power outage to last more than 36 hours, consider draining the system. Since there is no effective way to keep the water circulating, the pipes are likely to freeze up.

To drain the water from a hot-water system, first shut off the switch to the circulating pump. Then close the fuel supply valve and the water supply valve. Open the boiler drain cock and allow the water to drain. It will be easier if you can run a garden hose from the drain cock to a nearby drain. If not, you'll have to carry buckets of water to the drain.

Lighting is another problem you'll have to contend with. Ideally, a flashlight should already be in every bedroom. It is handy should the power failure occur at night. Remember, too, to keep an adequate supply of batteries on hand.

In addition to the flashlights, you should have a 6-volt, battery-powered lantern that can be used for illuminating a room. Candles are useful as an emergency light source, but they are also a fire hazard, so never leave a candle burning in an unoccupied room. Kerosene lamps and lanterns have protected flames and are a better substitute for candles.

If you have pets, consider their health as well. Mammalian animals, such as dogs and cats probably will be able to stand a cold house along with the human occupants. But other pets, such as reptiles, tropical birds, and fish, are more sensitive to cold conditions and should be relocated to a warmer house. ⊕

Ice Dams

Many homeowners add caulking, insulation, and efficient heating systems to their home in an effort to provide greater comfort. But while they may add comfort and decrease fuel bills, those improvements also may create an unexpected problem: the formation of ice dams on the roof.

Ice dams can occur when snow collects on the roof. Inside, inadequate ceiling insulation and poor attic ventilation allow the heat from the living space to rise through the ceiling and collect in the attic. As the hot air continues to rise, it concentrates in the peak and heats the roof ridge line. If the peak gets

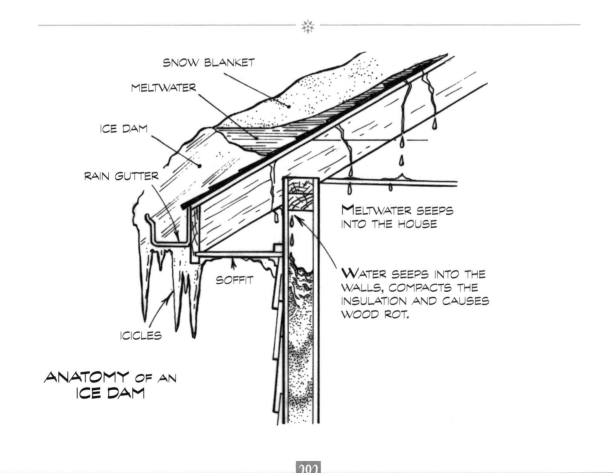

SNOW BLANKET

MELTWATER

ICE DAM

RAIN GUTTER

MELTWATER SEEPS INTO THE HOUSE

WATER SEEPS INTO THE WALLS, COMPACTS THE INSULATION AND CAUSES WOOD ROT.

SOFFIT

ICICLES

ANATOMY OF AN ICE DAM

warm enough, it will melt the snow on the roof; the water will run down the roof toward the eaves.

This would be fine if the water continued to flow off the roof, but the eaves, being lower than the ridge line, are usually cold. When the meltwater reaches the cold eaves, it freezes into ice. As the melting-and-freezing cycle continues, an ice barrier is created, which grows upward toward the roof peak. At a certain level the barrier meets the warm roof area. The ice can go no farther, but it remains as an impenetrable barrier to additional meltwater. The water does not freeze because it remains on the warm roof; instead, it collects behind the ice.

If the ice dam and water pool are large enough, the combined weight can become a strain on the roof supports. Even small pools of meltwater can create major headaches, however. The water gradually backs up and seeps under the shingles, where it penetrates through the sheathing into the attic. Here it can cause wood rot and compact the insulation. Eventually, it will seep into the ceiling below the attic and cause further damage.

How can you tell if ice dams are forming on your roof? Begin with a visual inspection from outside. Do not attempt to climb on the roof; that can be dangerous. It's safer to examine the

TOOL BOX

- **FIELD GLASSES**
- **LONG-HANDLED SCRAPER**
- **HEATING CABLE**

roof, eaves, and soffits from the ground with a pair of field glasses. Sometimes the collected water and ice are obvious, but usually they are hidden under a blanket of snow. However, a roof with a bare ridge area and snow-covered eaves is certainly suspect. Icicles hanging from the soffits, water stains running down the walls, and damaged shingles near the eaves are additional clues.

Continue your inspection in the attic. Here matted insulation, water stains, and wood rot suggest a leaking roof caused by ice dams.

If you suspect the presence of ice dams on the roof, what can you do about it? First, you must remove the snow and ice from the roof. It's perilous to climb onto a snow-covered roof, but it may be possible to clear it from the ground, depending on the size and height of your roof. Some home centers sell long-handled scrapers that can be effective on low-rise houses. If you use a scraper, however, you must remove all the snow from the roof, not just accumulations around the eaves. Be careful to avoid power lines with the scraper.

Another solution is to contact a local roofing company. Some roofers offer a steam-cleaning service to remove the snow and ice from roofs. The service is effective, but it can be expensive — $200 or more per treatment.

PREVENTING ICE DAMS: The newly cleared roof eliminates the ice-dam problem until the next snowstorm. Then you'll have to contend with the problem again. You can prevent the problem from recurring in a number of ways.

On some houses it is possible to attach panels of galvanized sheet metal to the cold portion of the roof. The metal would extend from the eaves onto the roof by 2 to 4 feet. Theoretically, the metal would prevent the formation of ice dams in two ways. First, the metal, being a good conductor of heat, would warm up under the sun and keep the lower roof hot. Second, snow would not collect on the slippery metal surface but would fall onto the ground.

That solution is not always effective. On cold cloudy days the metal may not heat up enough to melt any snow. In

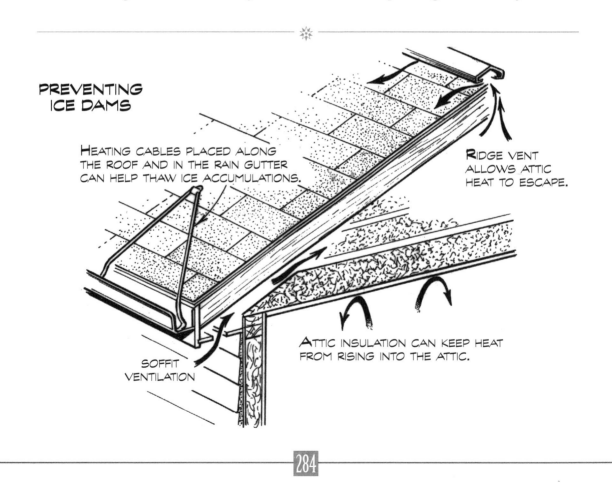

PREVENTING ICE DAMS

HEATING CABLES PLACED ALONG THE ROOF AND IN THE RAIN GUTTER CAN HELP THAW ICE ACCUMULATIONS.

RIDGE VENT ALLOWS ATTIC HEAT TO ESCAPE.

ATTIC INSULATION CAN KEEP HEAT FROM RISING INTO THE ATTIC.

SOFFIT VENTILATION

addition, snow will not slide off the metal surface unless the roof has a steep pitch. Finally, the addition of a bright, shiny metallic band to the roof line can become an eyesore on some homes.

Another way to heat up the cold roof is by laying electric heating cables in a zigzag pattern across the eaves. The cables also should run through the rain gutters and downspouts. Heating cables are available at most home centers and will cost about three dollars a foot to cover the eaves. However, there are two major pitfalls to consider if you use heating cables: If the cables do not extend onto the heated portion of the roof, the ice dams can form above them; and some roofing material can deteriorate with overuse of the cables. Furthermore, keep in mind that leaving the cable plugged in during a snow

storm presents an additional cost. Some building codes prohibit roof heating cables, so check with local authorities before proceeding.

Perhaps the best solution is not to add heat but to remove it. You can prevent the buildup of attic heat by adding additional insulation along the attic floor to prevent heat from rising from the living space. In addition, it is necessary to add attic ventilators, which will allow any hot air to escape and equalize the roof temperature.

It's difficult to make major modifications to your attic in the winter. You can, however, study your roof and attic during the cold months and decide if you have an ice problem. If so, you can consult with professional contractors to determine the best solution. Then in the warmer months ahead you can rectify the situation. ⊕

Snow Blowers

It's a good idea to pull the snow blower out of storage before the first snowfall. You can check out your snow blower and avoid those breakdowns and malfunctions that are apt to occur on cold, snowy days.

Begin by rereading your owner's manual. It lists all the specifications you need to check belt or chain tolerances, spark plug clearances, and other technical data. Use your owner's manual to adjust the drive clutch and auger clutch for proper tolerances. You'll want to lubricate the linkage and drive controls. The manual usually will recommend types of lubricants to use. Your machine may have grease fittings; if so, your manual will help you locate them and specify the proper grease to use. If you don't have a manual, you can usually buy a new one from a dealer who sells your brand. Check the yellow pages.

Since you will be working with gasoline it's best to work outdoors or in the garage. Ensure that the ventilation is adequate, and keep a fire extinguisher handy.

Before doing any maintenance, disconnect the spark plug wire and tape it out of the way so that it cannot come into contact with the spark plug. That will prevent any accidental start-ups while you're working on the engine.

MAINTENANCE: Start with the fuel system. The fuel tank should be empty. If not, drain it and wash it out with fresh gasoline. You can safely dispose of this gas by pouring it in your car's tank. That small amount will be absorbed easily by the car's system and will not harm the engine. Do not fill the tank at this time, because you may not need to

CLEAN THE AIR FILTER

CARBURETOR

FUEL TANK
CLEAN THE FUEL TANK.

operate the blower immediately. It's not a good idea to leave gasoline in the tank for more than 30 days because it evaporates quickly and leaves a gummy residue that can foul up the engine.

If your blower has a four-cycle engine, it will have a separate oil reserve system — two-cycle engines mix the oil and gasoline together. Change the oil (you can dispose of the old oil by taking it to a gas station or a specialty oil-change shop). Consult your owner's manual for recommended weight and the amount of oil to add. Using a multiple-viscosity oil will make starting easier in cold weather.

Next, check the filters. All machines have air and fuel filters, and some have oil filters, which not only keep dust out of the engine but also prevent moisture — a major problem in the winter — from entering and freezing the motor. Filters with disposable paper elements

- **WRENCHES**
- **WIRE SPARKPLUG-GAUGE**
- **TAPE**
- **STEEL WOOL**
- **AUTOMOBILE WAX**

should be replaced. Those with foam elements or screens can be cleaned with solvent and dried with compressed air.

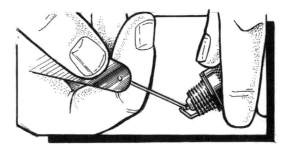

SET THE SPARK PLUG GAP TO MANUFACTURER'S SPECIFICATION. USE WIRE FEELER GAUGE.

Check the ignition system. Remove the spark plug and look at the color and condition of the electrode. If it's light tan, you probably can continue to use it. If it's black, or if you're doubtful about its condition, then it's best to buy a new one. Before replacing the plug, check the gap with a wire gauge. Inspect the plug cable and boot for cracks or excessive wear and replace them if necessary.

Next, inspect the drive belts. They transfer power from the engine to the transmission that runs the auger. Look for cracking or fraying and replace the belts if they show signs of excessive wear. It's a good idea to keep spare belts on hand, because a broken drive belt will make the blower useless.

SNOW BLOWERS

CHECK THE DRIVE BELTS

APPLY WAX TO THE CHUTE.

AUGER

AUGER

SHEAR PIN

KEEP SPARE SHEAR PINS ON HAND IN CASE YOU HIT AN OBSTRUCTION. THE AUGER WON'T TURN WITH A BROKEN PIN.

If you have a snow blower with a chain drive, lubricate the chain. Use motorcycle chain oil because it congeals and will not be thrown off when the chain spins. Make sure that you also have a spare master link on hand in case the chain breaks.

Your list of spare parts also should include shear pins, which are special bolts made of soft metal. They are mounted on the drive axle and are designed to shear off should the auger hit some obstruction. This stops the auger from rotating and prevents damage to the engine and auger. They're easy to replace if you have them.

Some blowers have rubber auger blades. They should be at least 1/16-inch thick; if not, replace them.

GENERAL UPKEEP: Now tighten all nuts and bolts. It's a good idea to do this after every use because vibrations from machine operation can cause fittings to work loose. If that is a recurring problem with your unit, you can coat bolt threads with a thread-locking compound, which is available at auto supply stores.

Check the tires for excessive wear. If you have chains on the tires, check them also for weak links and couplings.

Examine the motor and auger housing for rust and corrosion. Remove any spots with steel wool or silicon carbide paper; then prime and paint them with paints formulated for metal.

Finally, apply a generous coating of automobile wax to the auger and the inside of the discharge chute. That not only will protect the metal but also will keep snow from sticking and clogging the blower.

When the first snow falls and it's time to use your blower, take it outside and fill the gas tank. If you have a gravel driveway, set the auger blades high so that they don't pick up the stones. After each use, brush off accumulated snow. It is always possible that snow and water may freeze within the workings. Before starting the blower again, rotate the auger by hand to make certain that it turns freely. First, however, disconnect the spark plug wire to prevent accidental start-ups.

Make sure that you are thoroughly familiar with the operation of your machine. The discharge from the snow chute can be dangerous so be sure that no one is within your immediate work area. ⊕

Removing Snow

During the winter months we usually can expect at least one heavy snowstorm. Homeowners then face the task of removing the snow from their driveways and walks. Those with snow throwers are less troubled by snow removal because the machine does most of the work. Other homeowners must move the snow with a shovel and muscle power.

Snow is heavy, especially when it's wet; and excavating large amounts can be taxing and can cause personal injury. Many hospital emergency rooms report a rise in the number of heart attack cases after a heavy snowstorm — the result of trying to shovel too much heavy snow. Even people with strong constitutions frequently suffer back and shoulder injuries if they are not careful. That's why it's important to choose your tools carefully and understand the techniques and mechanics of shoveling snow.

Start with the shovel. Choose one with a light but sturdy blade. A steel blade is more durable, but a lightweight aluminum one requires less effort to lift. The shaft should be the right length for your frame. A shaft that's too short will cause you to bend over more, forcing you to lift away from your center of gravity. The result is a sore back. An extralong shaft will reduce your leverage and increase the weight at the end, which will tax your strength quickly. An ideal shaft length will provide the proper leverage and allow you to keep your back as straight as possible while shoveling.

TOOL BOX

- **SHOVEL**
- **PARAFFIN WAX OR NONSTICK COOKING SPRAY**

You can check your shovel for proper shaft length with this simple test. Grasp the handle with one hand. Position the other hand about 14 to 18 inches from the point where the shaft joins the blade. If the length is right, your hands should be a little more than shoulder width apart.

Not all shovels have straight shafts; some models have bent shafts. Manu-

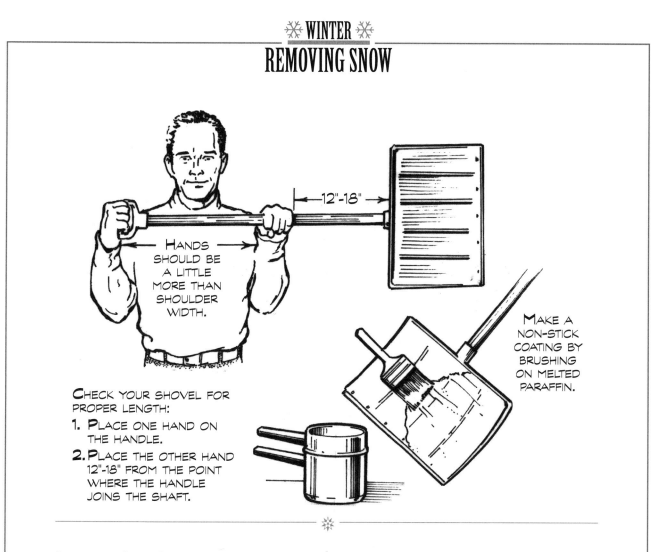

CHECK YOUR SHOVEL FOR
PROPER LENGTH:

1. PLACE ONE HAND ON
   THE HANDLE.
2. PLACE THE OTHER HAND
   12"-18" FROM THE POINT
   WHERE THE HANDLE
   JOINS THE SHAFT.

HANDS SHOULD BE A LITTLE MORE THAN SHOULDER WIDTH.

12"-18"

MAKE A NON-STICK COATING BY BRUSHING ON MELTED PARAFFIN.

facturers claim that this design requires less bending and is therefore a good choice for those with a weak back.

Many snow shovels are now available with special "no-stick" coatings on the blade, which can eliminate the annoying problem of trying to remove the snow that frequently sticks to a shovel. If your shovel doesn't have such a coating you can make one with paraffin wax. Melt the wax in a double boiler and brush it on the blade with an old paintbrush. The coating should not be too thick, or else it will crack and flake off when it freezes. Paraffin wax is available at some hardware stores and in large supermarkets.

If melting paraffin wax seems like too much trouble, you can coat the blade with "nonstick" cooking spray. That is easier to apply but is less durable than paraffin, and frequent applications may be needed.

After you've prepared your shovel, you should consider your own physical well-being. Shoveling snow is hard work, and the job is exacerbated by the low temperatures in which you must work. Medical tests reveal that cold weather can cause blood pressure to rise. Doctors theorize that this happens when the cold receptors in the skin signal the nervous system to conserve heat by constricting the blood vessels.

It's important then to avoid drinking coffee, smoking cigarettes, or taking decongestants that contain caffeine before going out to attack the snowdrifts. Those substances are stimulants, which constrict blood vessels and speed up heart rate.

In addition, health experts recommend doing at least five minutes of warm-up exercises, like jumping jacks or stretching exercises, before picking up the snow shovel. The idea of doing preliminary calisthenics may seem a little foolish to some people, but physical therapists report that a good warm-up can help to prevent pulled muscles and torn ligaments.

It's also important to dress properly. As you work, your body could overheat causing the blood vessels in your arms and legs to open up, restricting blood flow to the heart. So dress in layers and remove layers as you heat up.

You're less likely to pull or strain a muscle if you understand and apply the proper techniques when you shovel the snow. When shoveling, scoop straight by pushing the shovel directly in front

WARM-UP WITH CALISTHENICS FIRST. WEAR LAYERED CLOTHING TO AVOID BECOMING OVERHEATED.

AVOID LIFTING A HEAVY LOAD OF SNOW.

LIFT WITH YOUR LEGS.

of you into the snow. Use your legs to lift, not your back. Avoid lifting a too-heavy load of snow.

Many people in good shape injure themselves simply because they rely on brute strength rather than on sound mechanics to shovel the snow. When you are dumping the snow to one side, it's better to take small steps and turn your entire body rather than twisting from the waist. Remember to take frequent breaks to relax your muscles. Give your back a rest by straightening up and walking about.

Using a snow thrower to remove snow requires less exertion and physical effort, but those machines can cause injury to an unwary operator. Hospitals report at least 3,000 snow-thrower-related injuries each year. They usually are lacerations, broken bones, or amputations that result when operators reach into the rotor blades or discharge chute in an attempt to clear obstructions.

Now most people are aware that it's essential to shut off the power before trying to remove any obstruction. What they may not be aware of, however, is that the blocked blades still may be under tension even with the power off. Removing the blockage will release the tension. This can cause the blades to suddenly snap back or spin forward.

The best way to remove an obstruction is with a pole or a stick. Never put your hands into the rotor blades or discharge chute. In addition, you should review your owner's manual so that you are thoroughly familiar with safe operating procedures for your snow thrower.

As a homeowner, you are responsible to make your walk safe for pedestrians; so remove all ice and uncover any hidden hazards, such as tree roots. ⊕

O Christmas Tree, O Christmas Tree

This is the time of year when many people think about their Christmas tree. Some people prefer an artificial tree because it is cost effective. Others like it because they feel that it preserves the environment and saves trees. There is a wrinkle to this argument, however; artificial trees are made from petroleum products that are a nonrenewable resource. Live trees are 100-percent recyclable, and new ones are replanted to replace the cut ones.

THE CUT TREE

TEST FOR FRESHNESS BY SHAKING THE TREE AND BY RUNNING YOUR FINGER ALONG THE BRANCHES.

If you choose to purchase a live tree, you have two choices. You can purchase a cut tree — one that is either already-cut or one that you can cut yourself — or you can buy a live tree that is suitable for replanting.

First, consider where you are going to display the tree. How big should it be? Will the tree be seen from all sides, or will it be placed in a corner or against the wall? If you decide on a large tree, then it's best to buy a cut tree. A live tree has a large root base that's encased in dirt and wrapped in burlap — "balled-and-burlapped." That makes the tree extremely heavy and difficult to move. So don't buy a live tree more than 5 feet tall.

Once you have a mental picture of your tree, it's time to shop for it. If you don't have access to a car, you'll probably have to pick out a tree in a local lot or supermarket. The problem here is that those trees usually are cut early in November, and their moisture content is already low. A tree with 80-percent moisture content will remain fresh for weeks. Once the moisture content drops below 80-percent, however, it will

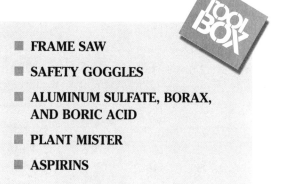

- **FRAME SAW**
- **SAFETY GOGGLES**
- **ALUMINUM SULFATE, BORAX, AND BORIC ACID**
- **PLANT MISTER**
- **ASPIRINS**

continue to dry out even though its watered daily. When the moisture content hits 20 percent the tree is dry and should be considered a fire hazard.

Of course, you can't test for moisture content without sophisticated equipment. You can be sure that your tree is fresh if you cut it yourself. There are many local cut-your-own tree farms where you can do that. Consult your local newspaper or write to the National Christmas Tree Association, 611 East Wells Street, Milwaukee, Wis. 53202-3891 for the location of a farm near you.

CUT TREES: Some farms cut a few trees fresh each day, which saves you the exertion of cutting your own. Before purchasing any ready-cut tree, run your finger up and down the branches. The needles should adhere to the tree. Try shaking the tree to see if the needles stay attached. If they do, the tree is probably fresh. You usually have the option of walking around, choosing, and cutting your own. Most tree farms provide saws, but they are usually dull from frequent use, so if possible, bring your own saw. The best saw to use is a frame saw, which has a light-weight aluminum frame that holds a coarse-toothed steel blade under tension. Cut the tree close to the ground. It's also a good idea to wear safety goggles to protect your eyes from the sharp needles.

When you get the tree home, saw off the bottom of the trunk. Make a diagonal cut about an inch above your original cut. A diagonal yields more surface area and absorbs more water. Stand the tree in a bucket and add warm water and a couple of aspirins. Warm water will dissolve the sap and tree resins and will be more readily absorbed, while the aspirins will help preserve the freshness. The tree will absorb a lot of water, so check the pail daily. You also can use a plant mister and spray water on the needles; this will help the tree retain freshness. It's best if you can let the tree stand in the garage or an enclosed back porch for a few days to let the branches settle.

You may also want to spray the tree with a fire-retardant solution for added safety. You can buy commercial preparations at some Christmas tree lots, or you can make your own by mixing 1/2 cup of aluminum sulfate, 1 tablespoon

O CHRISTMAS TREE

of borax, and 1/4 cup of boric acid in a 1/2 gallon of water. Spray that on the tree and save the remainder to add to the Christmas tree stand.

When you're ready to bring the tree into the house, saw off the trunk again. This time remove the diagonal cut and square off the end. Place the tree in a stand that provides adequate support.

LIVE TREES: Buying a live, balled-and-burlapped tree requires more thought and consideration than purchasing a cut tree. Not only must you decide where the tree will stand in the house during the holidays, but you must consider its outside location. Since Christmas trees can grow to heights of 30 feet or more, you'll want to transplant the tree far enough from the house so that it doesn't block windows and so the root structure doesn't interfere with the foundation. Also, it's a good idea to check with a county extension specialist or a local nurseryman to make sure the species of tree you're considering will grow in your area.

Usually, the nursery or tree farm allows its trees to sit outside, where the temperatures can drop to below freezing. When you buy the tree, it will be in a dormant state. It is important then to

Christmas Trees

CUTTING YOUR TREE

Use a frame saw to cut your tree. Cut it close to the ground.

When you get home, saw off the bottom. Make a diagonal cut.

Let the tree stand in the garage for a few days.

Square off the trunk before you bring the tree inside.

O CHRISTMAS TREE

acclimate the tree to the warmer house temperature gradually. Place it in an enclosed, unheated area, like the garage, if possible, or else wrap the tree in a few layers of burlap to shield it from the wind. Leave it for a few days. In the meantime, you can look at the spot the tree eventually will be transplanted to. If the ground isn't frozen, you can dig the hole that the tree will rest in. The hole should only be deep enough to cover the root ball, but it should be at least 12 inches larger than its diameter. Fill the hole with mulch and then store the excavated dirt in a warm place; that will keep both from freezing.

When you're ready to bring the tree into the house, you might want to place it in a large washtub with handles. That will make handling the tree easier and also contain any loose dirt that might fall from the root ball. Do not put the tree near any heat source and try to keep the room temperature below 68 degrees F. If the room gets too warm, the tree will emerge from dormancy. Attempting to transplant it afterward may kill it. Do not keep the tree in the house for more than 10 days. Make sure the root ball is moist at all times. Wrapping it in plastic will help to contain the moisture.

After the holidays it's time to either recycle or transplant your tree. If you have a cut tree, contact a local service

THE LIVE TREE

KEEP THE ROOT BALL MOIST

PLACING THE TREE IN A LARGE TUB WILL MAKE IT EASIER TO MOVE

PLASTIC WRAP

organization, the parks and recreation department, or a local nursery to see if they have a chip-and-compost service.

If you have a live tree, move it back to the garage or shelter to allow it to adjust to outdoor conditions again. Allow it to remain there for at least 10 days. If the weather is harsh, let it stay sheltered until the weather clears. When you're ready to put the tree into the ground, remove the mulch and place the tree in the hole. Loosen the burlap and remove the twine; the burlap can remain in the hole. Fill the hole with the reserved soil, pack it down firmly, and cover it with mulch or compost; then water the tree. ⊕

Abrasive Natural or artificial materials, usually in granular form, used to grind and smooth a surface. Abrasive papers, commonly, but erroneously, called "sandpaper," are abrasives bonded to a paper or cloth backing.

Anchor bolts Bolts that hold the sill plate to the foundation wall.

Armored cable A flexible, metal-sheathed cable used for interior wiring.

Baseboard A wide molding attached at the foot of a wall, where the wall meets the floor.

Bearing wall A wall that supports a load, such as a floor or roof. Generally a bearing wall runs at right angles to the joists above.

Binder The oil or resin content of paint. The binder forms a film that protects a surface and holds the pigments.

Bleeding A condition that occurs when the pigment in an undercoat rises and colors a top coat.

Blind nailing Driving a nail so that the head is invisible from the surface. This technique is commonly used to install tongue-and-groove flooring. The nail is driven through the tongue. The nail head is hidden when a grooved board is mated to it.

Brace A piece of lumber nailed diagonally across framing members. The brace effectively forms a triangle with the vertical or horizontal frame and gives it added stability.

Buffing or polishing compound A soft abrasive blended with wax. Used to produce a smooth luster on a surface.

Caulking gun A tool used to apply caulk, sealants, or adhesives that are contained in 11-ounce cartridges.

Circuit A path of wire from the service panel to a source (such as an outlet or fixture) and back to the service panel.

Collar beam A short horizontal beam generally about 2-inches thick that connects opposite pairs of roof rafters near the ridge.

Conduit Metal tube or pipe used to enclose electrical wires.

Cripple studs Short studs that run from the sole plate to the sill plate under a window opening.

d The symbol, an abbreviation for penny, used to designate nail sizes.

Denatured alcohol A general purpose solvent made with grain alcohol. This is a poisonous and flammable solvent.

Drywall (also called wallboard) An interior wall covering, in panels, usually 4 feet by 6 feet—although longer lengths are also available—made of gypsum plaster sandwiched between construction paper. Thickness varies from 1/4- to 5/8-inch in 1/8-inch increments. Drywall is used to cover the framing to create a smooth flat wall or ceiling surface. "Sheetrock" is a trade name of the United States Gypsum Company.

Eave The lower part of the roof that extends past the wall

Feathered edge The tapered edge of a plaster or joint-compound patch. The edge gradually diminishes in thickness to blend in with the surrounding surface.

Finger-tight Tightened with the fingers, not with pliers, screwdriver, or a wrench.

Firestops Thick pieces of wood or noncombustible material strategically placed within wall or ceiling cavities. They stop the flue action within these cavities and help

keep fires from spreading throughout a burning building

Fitting A device, such as a bushing, bolt, or faucet, used to perform a mechanical function.

Footing A course of concrete, rectangular in section, placed at the bottom of a foundation or pier. It is wider than the foundation or pier and helps to support it by distributing the load into the surrounding earth.

Frost line An imaginary line in the soil that indicates the depth of frost penetration. As the soil freezes and thaws, it will expand and contract. Footings placed below the frost line will be stable because they will not be affected by the freeze-thaw cycle. The depth of the frost line is determined by the climate so it varies throughout the country.

Fuse A safety device used to interrupt an electrical circuit should the current exceed the wiring capacity.

Grade The ground level around a structure. Natural grade is the original level before construction. Finished grade is the ground level when construction is complete.

Ground The path that allows electricity to flow from the source back to the earth.

Header In window or door openings the header is a horizontal member perpendicular to the studs. It forms the lintel above the opening. A header joist is a beam placed perpendicular to the joists.

Hot wires Wires that carry electrical current. They may be any color except white or green.

Joint compound A white, plaster-like compound used to apply joint tape and to fill holes and cracks in wallboard.

Joint tape White paper, without adhesive, used to seal the joints between wallboard panels. It is available in rolls 2 1/2 inches wide.

Joists Horizontal beams that support the floor. Joists are parallel to each other and are usually spaced 16 inches apart on center. In some cases where more support is required the joists may be closer together.

Junction box A metal or plastic box used to house electrical connections, receptacles, or switches.

Knockout A circular die-cut impression in a junction box that may be punched out to provide an opening for wiring.

Live wire or circuit A wire or circuit that supplies current.

Load A weight that bears down on a structural member. Architects recognize two types of loads: dead loads, which consist of the weight of the structure, including the walls, floors, roof, etc.; and live loads, which consist of appliances, furniture, movable objects and people.

Mineral spirits A solvent used for thinning paints and varnishes, and for degreasing. Made of petroleum distillates, it is flammable and poisonous.

Naphtha A petroleum or coal-tar distillate used as a solvent for cleaning and as a thinner for paints and varnishes. It is flammable and poisonous.

Outlet A part of the electrical circuit from which current may be obtained to power lamps, or appliances. A.k.a. a plug-in receptacle.

On center (abrev. O.C.) Measurement made from the center of one member to the center of the other. Studs, joists, and rafters are usually spaced 16 inches apart on center.

Plate A horizontal structural member that runs across the top of the wall. In some framing there may be two top plates–called a double top plate–sandwiched together. The joists rest on the top plate. The sole plate runs along the bottom and forms the base for the studs. The vertical studs rise between the two plates.

Rafter The primary structural members of a gable roof. The rafters rise at an angle from the walls and joint to the ridge board at the peak. Rafters in flat roofs are often called roof joists.

Ridge The peak of a gabled roof. The horizontal beam where the rafters meet.

Sealer A finishing solution applied to a surface to control absorption.

Service panel The main panel or metal cabinet where electricity enters the house and is distributed through circuits.

Sheathing Material that covers the framing or wires. Older houses may have sheathing made up of wide boards nailed diagonally across the frame. Modern houses usually have sheathing of plywood, particle board, or outdoor drywall panels.

Shellac A finish made of natural gums dissolved in alcohol.

Sill A horizontal piece of lumber that is fastened to the top of the foundation wall with anchor bolts. It transfers the weight of the house to the foundation. The term sill may also refer to the horizontal member that forms the bottom piece of a window frame.

Soffits The underside of the eaves.

Span The distance between columns, posts, or walls.

Subfloor Boards or panels laid directly on the floor joists. The subfloor serves as the base or substrate for finished flooring.

Stain A liquid used to color wood.

Steel wool Fine strands of steel, molded into a pad. Used to smooth varnished and painted surfaces.

Studs The vertical framing members that support a wall. Studs are generally made of 2 x 4s spaced 16 inches apart on center. In northern climates where more insulation is required, the outside walls made have wider 2 x 6s for studs.

Switch A mechanical device used to interrupt the flow of electricity in a circuit.

Tack cloth A lint-free cloth used to pick up loose dust and particles prior to applying a finish.

Toenailing Driving a nail at an angle so that it penetrates through one piece into another. This technique differs from direct, or face, nailing where the nail is driven perpendicular into the surface of the top board so that it penetrates into that board behind.

Torque Twisting force around a shaft. A wrench applies torque to tighten a bolt.

Utility knife A knife with a short, sharp, replaceable blade. Used as a general-purpose knife for marking, scoring, and cutting.

Vapor barrier A moisture-proof membrane installed behind the wallboard. It serves to keep interior vapor from penetrating into the insulation in the wall cavities.

Varnish A finish made of resins dissolved in turpentine or mineral spirits.

INDEX